Better Futures

Better Futures

Tools for dealing with uncertainty

Andy Garlick

Published by:
RA Titles
79 Derbyshire lane
Stretford
Manchester
M32 8BN
United Kingdom

Cover photograph courtesy of StockSnap on Pixabay

ISBN (print): 978-1-9996645-0-3

ISBN (ebook): 978-1-9996645-1-0

In memory of my parents

Contents

Table of figures

Preface

I sometimes wonder how it is I have made a career in risk. It's not a highly regarded function. You don't hear people saying, "I've got a risk workshop tomorrow," in tones of excited anticipation, though in truth it's a chance of a few hours break from the tedium of whatever else they would be doing to sit around and shoot the breeze on such tempting topics as "great cock-ups I have known," "this is what's gonna happen," "how bad could it be," and so on. We all enjoy a touch of *schadenfreude* even when it's close to home and in the foreseeable future. We like to bathe in the vicarious (we hope) thrill of incipient disaster.

It was an accident, of course. In the early 1980s the only place I could get a job was with the UK's Atomic Energy Authority, in its safety department. One of its objectives was to put some perspective on the disastrous consequences of nuclear accidents by showing the chances they would happen were very small. (Thinking back, I suspect I got the job because I talked with reasonable authority about S-curves – which should have given me a real premonition of the future!) As a result, I spent the mid-80s working on fault trees for the future Sizewell 'B', doing Monte Carlo modelling of neutrons in fissile assemblies, researching fuzzy logic and the like. Unfortunately (for me) this waste of public money came to the attention of Mrs Thatcher and she shut down the fast reactor programme, throwing large numbers of us the challenge of finding something worthwhile to do for a living.

So, in the late 80s, early 90s, my mates and I sat around thinking about how we could get people to pay for the sort of stuff we did. We hit on the idea of applying the HAZOPS-type techniques we used for nuclear plant to everything and anything. We had in mind not just industries with safety issues, but every activity where there was some 'risk'. It was no time at all before we were working with our new clients to develop lists of risks and controls, using prototypical descriptions to characterise their likelihood and various impacts, drawing matrices with red, yellow and green diagonals and so on.

And so a monster was born; these activities seem to have grown out of control and beyond all sense; it's called common practice risk management and it's become one of the more persistent management fads of the times. I feel quite guilty about this though, to be clear, I'm not claiming this was really invented in AEA Technology. It was, though, in line with the *zeitgeist*.

Despite all this I still think that understanding risk and trying to do something about it is a sensible – and essential – aspiration. What's more, it's an inspiring aspiration due to the often difficult and unexpected challenges it throws up. Because of this I wanted to write a personal textbook on risk management which took a critical look at common practice and set out a way in which I think it could be done better. As such, the primary readership for this book is risk managers, their bosses and risk consultants, like me. However, I hope it will be of interest to anyone who, again like me, is intrigued by how we can best deal with an uncertain world.

This is that textbook. I'll not say more about it here – you can just skip to Chapter 1. But as a final snippet I will delve even further back into my past when I was a mathematician. The main concerns then were rigour, logic, clear assumptions and economy of concept. I have tried to stay close to those ideals here, though I am conscious it has not quite turned out the way I hoped in this respect. As a result, this book is quite theoretical. It has a few anecdotes, but it is not filled with case studies. It has many suggested tools, but few tick box checklists, and it recommends little software. It is for you to apply the ideas to whatever risk management situation you face.

You will also notice that the treatment is little uneven in respect of mathematics and mathematical concepts. I believe that all risk managers, and their managers in turn, should have more familiarity with probability concepts than they generally do. This was the topic of my previous book.[1] So, in addition to the usual discussion of probabilities, S-curves and P-numbers, I have added in random variables and their expected values. The main body of the book does not go much beyond this. Chapter 7, however, on decision making in the face of risk, is considerably more mathematical in some parts (as well as being very long). I hope that will not deter you from reading it. My aim is to make these parts skippable without losing too much.

[1] Estimating Risk: a management approach, Andy Garlick, Gower, 2007.

With regard to actually doing the calculations, I have not dwelt on standard methods; that, too, is covered elsewhere. But I have included a number of more unusual models, partly to demonstrate the range of what is possible. The keen reader might want to replicate them.

In designing this book, I have not adhered to the usual conventions for references and the like. There are relatively small number of sources I have used. For readability, they are listed in footnotes as you go through and I have repeated the references in each new chapter, but not within chapters. There are no large sections of notes and citations – destined to remain unread – at the end.

No book like this could be written without the support of the many colleagues and clients I have worked with over the years. I am grateful to them all for the ideas they have shared and the ideas they have stimulated. And it could not have been done without the support of my wife, Bernice, who humoured me in carrying on my researches when I might have stopped. (Or I might have done if the nitwits who ran the privatised version of the Atomic Energy Authority had not run it into the ground and bust the pension fund, so perhaps I should thank them too.)

I'm always keen to discuss the topics I describe in this book. You can visit *ratitles.com*, the website from which I am selling this book and the previous one. I'm also reopening my former blogging site *cloudsofvagueness.com* as a vehicle for further discussion. You will recognise some of the stuff in this book as well as have the opportunity to contribute to what I hope will be a lively and fun debate.

Andy Garlick
March 2018

Chapter 1

Improving risk management

Why we should worry about uncertainty and how we can deal with it better

---

THE RISK MANAGEMENT CONTEXT

Risk management – the idea that you can systematically and visibly take steps to deal with future uncertainty – has become quite an industry. The idea is a simple one. You write down all the risks and uncertainties you face and decide what you're going to do about them. Then you do it. So it's no wonder most big projects do this, right from the germ of an idea to the day the finished product goes into service. It's no wonder every bank is expected to stress tests its business and maintain sufficient capital to see it through bad times. It's no wonder that to be listed on the London Stock Exchange a company must ensure that:

> *"The board is responsible for determining the nature and extent of the principal risks it is willing to take in achieving its strategic objectives. The board should maintain sound risk management and internal control systems."*[1]

This book could finish here except that that there are couple of small problems. The first problem is that everyone hates it. I can assure you

---

[1] The UK Corporate Governance Code, Financial Reporting Council, April 2016.

that the welcome for the risk consultant is warm only with the idea that you might relieve someone of a tedious burden. Few enjoy being dragooned into risk workshops. Many sneer that the sophisticated analysis tells you only the bleeding obvious. Many managers convince themselves that they need only worry about the top five risks anyway so why go to all the trouble. Some attempts to list the risk and uncertainties go no further; the stage of actually doing what you've decided is forgotten. Risk management in a bank is often seen as an unproductive and anti-business compliance exercise.

A lot of things can be described in similar terms – budgeting comes to mind – but it's slightly surprising that such a fundamental and natural activity for someone who wants to achieve something gets such a bad press and is so disliked. Generals and engineers have always had to deal with what might happen, not just what they think is going to happen. In the mid-nineteenth century, for example, von Moltke was formulating his idea of strategy being a system of expedients – of which more later – whilst Brunel was writing down a detailed risk management plan to help his young assistant and future successor, Gooch, unload some locomotives. Gooch thought Brunel was wasting his time as, "circumstances were sure to alter the mode of doing it," or, as von Moltke put it, no plan survives first contact with the enemy. These are nineteenth century examples, but man has surely been managing risk quite happily since before the dawn of civilisation.

Gooch's reticence hints at the second problem. It's not entirely clear that this apparently admirable, as well as simple, idea does much good. The risk management literature is full of 'if only' books and articles. If only they had done proper risk management then X, Y or Z disaster would not have occurred. You can perm the names from Enron, BP, the financial crisis, Tesco or whatever. But as I started to write this book in New Year 2015, the long-suffering UK rail travelling public had just been hit by two major incidents. First a Christmas improvement project overran *by several days* causing the unexpected closure of a major London terminus, Kings Cross. Secondly another important London station, London Bridge, was subject to dangerous levels of overcrowding as well as significant disruption to travellers when a new operating regime was introduced during a comprehensive redevelopment of the station. Network Rail was responsible for both events and Network Rail was an early adopter of risk management techniques. And specifically, it had used the quantified schedule risk analysis (QSRA, see Chapter 2) method for some time to reduce the risk of possessions (taking the track over for project work) overrunning.

The UK's New Labour government from 1997-2010 were also enthusiastic adopters of risk management. They published the so-called Orange Book,[2] following on from a Strategy Unit report,[3] complete with foreword by Tony Blair, which mandated standard principles for use in Government departments. But the research of King and Crewe[4] indicates that the capacity of New Labour to make serious blunders was not reduced compared with previous Governments. In their 2014 epilogue they specifically mention the introduction of the Universal Benefit by the following coalition government as

> *"... a total shambles. It is as though someone had deliberately set out to produce a remake of the horror film of Gordon Brown's earlier blunders."*

In other words, despite its apparent adherence to good risk management principles, the UK government can neither learn the lessons of the past nor identify thoroughly obvious elephant traps which await the implementation of policy. King and Crewe provide some good indicators of the institutional reasons for this which we shall return to.

I'm coming back to this book in August 2017 and, albeit with some hesitation, have to mention the Grenfell Tower fire. Clearly this also represents a complete failure of public sector risk management, both from the prevention and the response points of view. The institutional failings which led to this disaster deserve – and will no doubt get – whole books of their own, but it will be important to look at them from a risk management perspective – how risk is controlled in organisations, and networks of organisations. It seems to me this is a failure of the risk culture

---

[2] The Orange Book: Management of risk – Principles and Concepts, HM Treasury, October 2004, available from www.gov.uk/government/publications/orange-book.

[3] Risk: Improving government's capability to handle risk and uncertainty, Cabinet Office Strategy Unit, November 2002, available from (sorry about this) webarchive.nationalarchives.gov.uk/+/http:/www.cabinetoffice.gov.uk/media/cabinetoffice/strategy/assets/su%20risk%20summary.pdf.

[4] The Blunders of our Governments, Anthony King and Ivor Crewe, Oneworld, revised and updated 2014.

aspect of risk management, something I shall emphasise in this book, devoting a whole chapter to it – Chapter 3.

Do these problems mean risk management is a waste of time? Obviously not: as I've just argued, managers have been doing it since the dawn of civilisation. More fundamentally, it's what managers do. They are there to improve the future: to increase the likelihood of preferred outcomes at the expense of those that are less preferred. No risk management means no management. If this is the case, does it mean we are not doing it the best way? Well, of course. Everything can be done better (unless you are an adherent of the silly 'best practice' mindset). The purpose of this book is to describe some ideas of how we might achieve that, how we can improve its image, acceptance and effectiveness.

Why do we need another textbook? There are plenty of standards and lots of guidance, including an international standard for risk management, ISO 31000. But clearly they relate to current practice, and are not actively looking for ways it can be improved, especially if improvement means going back to first principles rather than making incremental changes which do not necessarily look back at wrong paths that have been taken.

There are, of course, some texts which flag up important indicators of where risk management has not worked well and how it can be improved. Here are three examples which have strongly influenced me.

- Chris Chapman and Stephen Ward substantially changed their approach to risk and opportunity in the 2011 revision of their project risk management textbook.[5] They adopted uncertainty – in the broad sense – as the key concept and developed a theory of PUMPs, project uncertainty management processes. They also coined the slightly derogatory term 'common practice' risk management and pointed out some of the faults in techniques such as risk matrices.
- Doug Hubbard in his book *The Failure of Risk Management*[6] took a very broad swipe at many commonplace techniques and provided suggestions as to how we could do better.

---

[5] How to Manage Project Opportunity and Risk, Chris Chapman and Stephen Ward, Wiley, 2011. (Advertised as the third edition of Project Risk Management, Wiley,1997 and 2003.)

[6] The Failure of Risk Management, Douglas W Hubbard, Wiley, 2009.

- Nassim Nicholas Taleb has written a trilogy,[7] *Fooled by Randomness*, *The Black Swan* and *Antifragile*, which sets out a manifesto for dealing with an uncertain world. NNT's critique is aimed more at the financial environment than the broader risk management community, but his approach, resting *inter alia* on tried and tested methods used in the real world, strikes a resonant chord.

These authors, part of a bigger group of underpinning texts for this book, underline and expand on the points which I have thought over the years need to be addressed to improve risk management. I think there is an opportunity to bring these ideas together and build on them by making a fresh start, presenting a more informal but also more critical discussion of the discipline which practitioners can use to help formulate their own opinions on what is right for their organisations or the organisations they are advising.

My aim in this textbook is to start from scratch and develop a theory of risk management which is as minimalist as possible and use this to identify a set of tools which can be deployed to implement this theory.

The benefits I expect from this are something more comprehensible, something that can be communicated more clearly between everyone with an interest, something that is more natural and easier for risk owners – those key players in risk management – to implement. I expect that the organisational performance improvements from explicitly recognising uncertainty will be enhanced.

The aim of the rest of this first chapter is to provide a map of risk management which is stripped down to its essentials. It will start from the structure recommended in the ISO 31000 standard, but my approach will try to avoid some of the issues which have arisen in implementing this. Accordingly, the next section is a risk-based appraisal of the standard, describing the recommendations and looking at how they might go wrong. The section which follows that addresses these points and sets out an axiomatic alternative to ISO 31000 which I hope will minimise the chance that the things that *could* go wrong listed in the next section actually *do* go wrong. At the end of the chapter there is a map of the rest

[7] Fooled by Randomness, Texere, 2001; The Black Swan, Penguin, revised edition, 2010; Antifragile, Allen Lane, 2012. All by Nassim Nicholas Taleb, all UK editions.

of the book, which is essentially a toolkit aligned with my proposed perspective on risk management.

CURRENT PRACTICE – THE ISO 31000 STANDARD

I characterised risk management earlier as, "you write down all the risks and uncertainties you face and decide what you're going to do about them. Then you do it." You are not short of official guidance on how to implement this apparently simple task. The Association for Project Management has its PRAM guide.[8] The Institution of Civil Engineers produces the RAMP guide[9] and, as if this wasn't enough, the Joint Code of Practice[10] is an important document if you want insurance on a tunnelling project. I mentioned the Orange Book[11] previously and the UK Government has also sponsored the development of the MoR[12] technique in association with its PRINCE project management method. In the US, COSO has published a series of guides on Enterprise Risk Management[13] and the PMI has published its own project-relevant guidance.[14] There are also standards, most obviously ISO 31000[15] the international standard for risk management, but also BS 31100[16] which is

---

[8] Project Risk Analysis and Management Guide. Second Edition, APM, 2010.

[9] Risk Analysis and Management for Projects, Third Edition, Thomas Telford, July 2014.

[10] The Joint Code of Practice for Risk Management of Tunnel Works in the UK, The British Tunnelling Society, September 2003. Available from www.britishtunnelling.org.uk/?sitecontentid=881C32EC-21C8-41A9-8B7A-F8D530E7987E.

[11] *Op cit.*

[12] The documents for this seem to be no longer available as the work is no longer sponsored by government but has been commercialised. There are plenty of courses on it you can find online.

[13] Enterprise Risk Management – Integrated Framework, Committee of Sponsoring Organizations of the Treadway Committee, 2004. Available from www.coso.org/Documents/COSO-ERM-Executive-Summary.pdf.

[14] Practice Standard for Project Risk Management, Project Management Institute, 2009. Available from www.pmi.org/pmbok-guide-standards/framework/practice-standard-project-risk-management.

[15] Risk management – Principles and guidelines, ISO 31000:2009.

[16] Code of Practice for Risk Management and Guidance for ISO 31000, BS 31100:2011.

intended to provide additional guidance on the implementation of the international standard.

These publications all cover pretty much the same ground and potentially suffer from groupthink. I want to take this as the starting point and then challenge it. The standards, by their nature, and also by virtue of the nature of the standards bodies which produce them, tend to be more general, and less prescriptive. Their focus is more on what must be achieved than on how to achieve it. As a result, some of their pronouncements can be positively Delphic, especially to non-initiates. Taking all this together, ISO 31000 nonetheless provides a good starting point for our survey of current practice risk management, and this standard will form the basis of the discussion in this section.[17]

The aim is to give you an overview of what's in that standard, and, in particular, to describe how its worthy principles may sometimes not work out optimally in practice. You might describe this as risk analysis of risk management, and it will form the basis for the development in the next section and subsequent chapters. However I ought to emphasise that in this book I am building on the standard, not ignoring it.

The discussion is fast and loose, a recap and a commentary which assumes a certain familiarity with current practice risk management and its terminology. I think it will be accessible to most readers, though; if not, just give it a quick read – or skip it altogether and pick up the story in the following section, *Making a fresh start.*

The standard has four main components. At its centre are the risk processes themselves. These are supported by the risk framework which in turn is based on a set of principles. This whole structure is itself highly dependent on a number of definitions which give meaning to the rest. Figure 1 is designed to emphasise the importance of the definitions in supporting the rest of the structure. Each element of the figure is discussed in turn.

[17] The document discussed here is the 2009 version as referenced above. You can imagine my delight when an update was conveniently issued just as this book went to press. The changes are briefly discussed in Chapter 6.

Figure 1 Support for ISO 31000 risk processes

The risk processes

It's best to start right at the top with the processes. There are four of these in a kind of management loop: establishing the context, risk assessment, risk treatment and monitoring & review. These are complemented by a fifth – communication & consultation – which interacts with each stage and then a sixth – record keeping – which is not mapped onto the process diagram. The purpose of each of these processes is fairly easy to understand and the standard elaborates, providing useful reminders.

The business part of risk management as described in the standard is risk assessment and risk treatment. Once again, "you write down all the risks and uncertainties you face and decide what you're going to do about them. Then you do it." All the rest should be focussed on enabling these two processes. So we'll start with them.

Risk assessment

The purpose of risk assessment is to understand the risk you face and reach a view on whether you need to do something about it. The standard splits this into three tasks: risk identification to see what's out there, risk analysis to understand the potential implications and risk evaluation to decide on any further action.

Risk identification is a fun process which is aimed at expanding the horizons of the organisation. We know the future contains all kinds of off-plan events, many of which we might think could not happen at first sight. The idea is to envisage these with the help of colleagues, useful prompts, our experience of what has happened in the past and our imagination. A common tool for compiling them is a dedicated workshop designed to facilitate this thinking. At this stage it is not important that some possible events may be quite unlikely. The output is a list of risk events, issues, opportunities and uncertainties, or risks as we will call them for short, which are believed to be worth considering.

Risk identification: what could go wrong?

1. The list could be too long. Risk identification is an expansive process, so we will need techniques to bring the list back under control.
2. The list could be incomplete. Yes, of course, that's why we design our workshops to stimulate the imagination and build on previous experience as much as possible. One important source of risk is lessons learnt from past experience.
3. The list could also be incomplete because of excessively pedantic behaviour. "That's an issue not a risk." "That's what we do; are you saying we can't manage our core activities?" Etc.
4. The list could be overlapping. This is a real bugbear. Because the imagined future comprises chains of cause and effect it is easy to pick up different events along the chain as different risks, especially when we are trying to categorise or aggregate. This can lead to agonising over whether or not double counting is taking place.
5. But the biggest problem that arises at this stage is that the risks are poorly articulated; their meaning is unclear, they do not identify root causes or they do not properly describe their effect, including their effect on the objectives of the organisation.

Risk analysis aims to put some structure on this list and to provide some measures as to the seriousness of the issues identified. You have to recognise that the impact of typical risks may have several dimensions: it can cost you money, it can delay success (which will probably cost you money), it can affect your reputation (which, by the way, may cost you money, especially on longer timescales, but perhaps not as much as the reputational scaremongers tell you), it may lead to an environmental release (which, *inter alia*, may cost you money). And, of course, it may lead to someone getting killed or injured.

The several references to costing money in the previous paragraph may sound a bit facetious. Actually I'm trying to make the point that the possible futures as the risks play out are chains of cause and effect, often in quite complicated ways. When you are doing risk analysis you have to recognise this. One solution is to recompile your list of risks as major issues. The first step might be to prioritise the risk using a colour coding system.

This leads to what I am going to call qualitative risk analysis. Recognising that uncertain futures need to be characterised in terms both of the likelihood of their materialising and the impact if they do, it's easy to leap to the idea of a two-dimensional matrix. Actually it's several two-dimensional matrices, bearing in mind the several types of impact possible. In practice, my experience is that three generally covers it: cost, reputation and safety, as shown in Figure 2. Many organisations add more.

The rows and columns of the matrix can be defined by terms like 'very unlikely' or 'certain' for likelihood and 'minor' or 'catastrophic' for impact. This can be embellished with quantified ranges, and the individual cells of the matrix can be scored for importance. In doing this, it will be recognised that the more likely and more severe risks are of higher importance. Conversely we are more relaxed about the low likelihood, low impact corner of the matrices. This is illustrated by the shading in Figure 2.

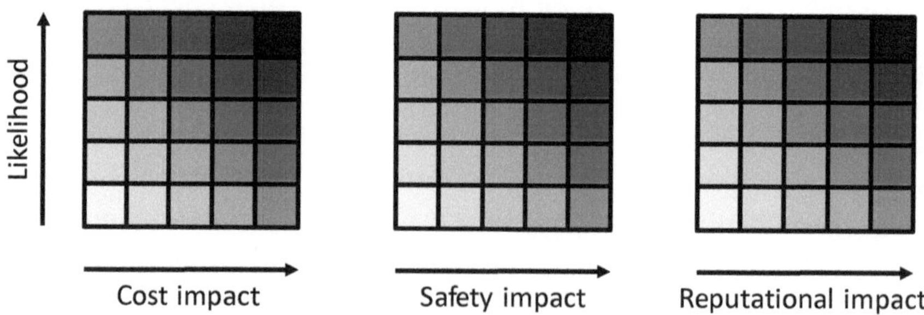

Figure 2 Risk matrices

This kind of qualitative risk analysis is liked by managers because it lends itself to traffic light colour schemes and avoids the conceptual challenges of its quantitative alternative.

Quantitative risk analysis has two major components. Firstly, the likelihood of events is measured by probabilities. Secondly, the impact of many events can be quantified and the relationships between the different types of impact listed above can be traced and modelled. This is a significant undertaking. Probability is a sophisticated mathematical concept and the systems we are trying to trace the impacts through can be complex, often surprisingly so, even when then are apparently quite simple. This was the subject of my previous book[18] and we shall return to it at some length in this one.

In principle, where the impacts can be quantified, quantitative risk analysis provides a much richer picture than the qualitative approach. But this is won at the expense of considerable effort and increased potential for misunderstanding. As a result, many organisations try to combine the two: the qualitative approach deals with multiple types of impact and comprehensive treatment of the issues identified; the quantitative technique tackles the major issues and supports the most significant decisions.

Risk analysis: what could go wrong?

1. You get stuck with the lengthy 'risk list' from the risk identification stage. You will best understand the risk you face by characterising only the major issues.
2. Crude qualitative schemes get extended and used far beyond what is sensible bearing their limitations in mind. They give a false impression of measurement to feed the adage that you can only manage what you measure.
3. Quantitative risk analysis is difficult and is not done well. There is an excessive reliance on common recipes such as 4-point quantification of risk lists or, a current fad, quantitative schedule risk analysis of a logic model of a programme. The challenges posed by the limitations of these recipes are often not tackled properly.

[18] Estimating Risk: A Management Approach, Andy Garlick, Gower, 2007.

4. Failure to recognise interdependence, or correlation, between risks.
5. Leaving something out because it is too difficult or unquantifiable. Remember this does not make it go away.
6. The results of quantitative risk analysis are misinterpreted, including the effect of these limitations.
7. The results of risk analysis are taken too seriously given the limitations of data and system understanding.
8. The scope and treatment of risk and uncertainty are poorly understood so that, for example, you hear that "it can't be a risk if its probability is 100%." In fact, 100% probabilities are an inevitable result of the proper quantification of an uncertainty issue within the commonly used 4-point scheme which will be explained in more detail later.

We kick off the decision process with the third and final element of risk assessment, risk evaluation. This is aimed at comparing the level of risk, determined through risk analysis, with some form of risk benchmark or terms of reference.

For example, the qualitative, matrix scheme can use red, yellow and green cells to indicate which risks we are most concerned about, with the corollary that no red risks can be allowed. And if we carry out a quantitative analysis we can set trigger levels of risk, for example lines in the probability/impact chart, which again will indicate an *a priori* cause for concern.

The standard uses the term risk criteria here. I am avoiding this as it implies a decision support role, that is, a definitive yes/no, which is not the intention of the standard as I understand it. This is not helped by the standard using language like acceptable and tolerable in this context. Decisions about risk are the remit of the next process, risk treatment.

I'm also avoiding mentioning two other commonly-used terms for the time being. These are risk attitude and risk appetite. Again these are not always helpful and we shall have plenty to say on this later on.

Risk evaluation: what could go wrong?

1. Risk evaluation wrongly assumes a decision-making role due to lack of clarity about how risk decisions are made. This is discussed further in the next section.

Risk treatment

The risk treatment process has two components. Deciding what to do and doing it. It seems a bit odd to group two such different activities in this way and it is odder still when you think that on the other hand the risk decision process has been split between the two major processes of risk assessment and risk treatment.

In practice to make decisions in the face of risk and uncertainty requires you first to identify the risks, then start to analyse them. To do this you will have to make some assumptions about how you are going to deal with them, which immediately leads you to the point that you have to develop a range of options for the risk treatments (aka controls, mitigations, contingencies, etc). You then have to carry out the risk analysis under all the options, including the specific further risks the options may entail, before you can finalise your decision as to what to do. The way the standard splits this detracts from the point that you need, in principle, to risk analyse all the options under consideration for all the risks. Figure 3, taken from my previous book,[19] illustrates this, emphasising the role of identifying the options.

Of course there are formulations which help with this rather theoretical approach. You could perform the risk analysis taking account of all the risk controls you have already got planned, or 'normal controls' or whatever. Having evaluated the risk you can consider if there is more you can do (or less?) to reduce the biggest risks, carry out a cost benefit analysis or the like and decide whether or not you are going to do them. But often it is a little more nuanced than that and you need to revert to the more fundamental risk decision process.

There are a few prompts to help you think about the risk treatments. You can do the activity in a fundamentally different way which avoids the risk, you can reduce the likelihood by tackling the root cause or you

---

[19] *Op cit.*

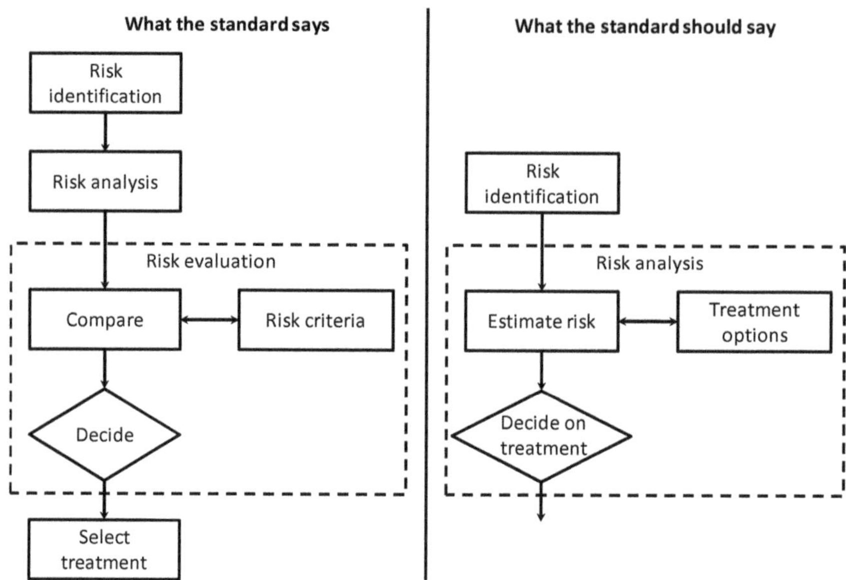

Figure 3 Alternative perspectives on the risk decision process

can do something to reduce the impact, a contingency plan. You can try to get someone else to take the risk through a contract or insurance, or you can just put up with the risk, even if it is big, because in the context of the whole enterprise it is worth it. Or you can go home, have a beer and forget the whole thing because it isn't worth the risk. Or, and you don't always see this, you can go home, have a beer and wait and see how things develop. Or, and sadly you see this too often when it's pointless, you can ask for more information, go home and worry about it another day.

The guidance for making the decision itself is likely to arise elsewhere in the organisation. Accordingly this is discussed in some detail later. Maybe you have to reduce the risk to some prescribed level, or maybe you have to do whatever is cost effective to reduce the risk. But you need to keep the big picture in mind. Typically the risk treatments will affect several risks and you need to make sure this is represented properly. Piecemeal decisions will not always lead to the optimal risk control plan. To take just a simple example, we know that one possible plan is to have a contingency fund. The risk treatment is to spend some money if the risk materialises on putting right its effects, keeping a team running for longer or whatever. But how do you determine the size of the contingency? Do you make provision for all the risks happening? Or just those that are more likely? You realise you have to look at the risk profile as a whole to make a sensible decision about that.

Risk decisions: what could go wrong?

1. Failure to consider all the options, including 'do nothing', 'wait and see' and 'get more information'.
2. Overconfidence in the effectiveness of controls, especially 'transfer it to someone else'. This is never 100% effective and rarely 50% for that matter.
3. Inappropriate decision criteria. Basically we take risk because we have to in order to gain the rewards we seek. So the basic decision process should weigh up risk and reward. But the literature is full of stuff about intolerable risks and the like which is sometimes appropriate, but often not.
4. Inappropriate risk analysis. For example it is tempting to tackle the treatment decisions risk by risk. This can cover up important interdependences and enhances the tendency to think small rather than strategically. Maybe the best treatment is to appoint a competent project manager.

There is little to say about implementing the risk control plan: you just do it. Actually this has very little to do with risk management as doing what you decide to do is a basic management function. It will be a feature of what follows that we carefully separate what you have to do specifically for risk management, such as risk identification, from what is not dedicated to risk such as implementing the plan.

Implementing risk treatments: what could go wrong?

1. You don't. In spite of what I've just said, or rather because risk activity takes place in its own bubble, there is a tendency for the risk exercises to stay on the shelf and the controls not to be incorporated into the actual plan of action.

Monitoring and review

What I have described up to now are the simple actions of, "you write down all the risks and uncertainties you face and decide what you're going to do about them. Then you do it." Outside of this you have the first very important process which turns it into a management loop: monitor and review. Monitoring is about taking measurements of what is going on and deciding if it is departing from what you have planned for, or hoped for. Review is deciding what to do if it is. Often I shall just say review, with the monitoring being understood as an essential part of the process.

There are two distinct functions within this. Firstly, you have to review risk management. How is your level of risk evolving? Is it still OK? Do you need to do something else? If so, what? Secondly, you have to review your risk management processes. Are they working OK? Do they identify the risks which materialise? Are we taking the right decisions? And if not, how shall we change our approach?

It is important to keep these two functions separate as they monitor different things, ask different questions and lead to different actions. Importantly they also happen on different timescales, or should do.

Reviewing risk management should be an embedded, heartbeat function. To avoid confusion with other risk management reviews I'll call it reviewing risk performance. To monitor risk performance you need (of course) risk performance indicators, also called KRIs, key risk indicators. These are forward-looking measures that suggest whether the likelihood of the risk is changing, or if the impact could be different from what we expect.

KRIs are strangely neglected in some areas of risk management. They are well developed in others such as operational risk management in financial institutions. There, structured sets of KRIs with associated trigger levels are often put in place. But it is very rare to see a set of KRIs in a construction risk management plan. One problem is separating the KRIs from forward-looking KPIs. Arguably you shouldn't as they are looking for the same thing.

Once you have the KRIs and criteria for starting to worry about your risk performance, it is straightforward in principle to re-enter your risk analysis and risk treatment processes to update your understanding of current levels of risk and to reappraise your options: monitoring is the new bit, review has already been dealt with.

Reviewing risk performance: what could go wrong?

1. Unsuitable performance indicators (KRIs). More work needs to be done to determine a set of suitable KRIs for specific situations and they need to be integrated within overall performance measurement.
2. Specifically there will be no KRIs for risks which have not been identified. But you still need to watch out for unanticipated stuff happening which needs to be observed and added to the risk profile in a suitable way.
3. Failure to distinguish risk performance review clearly from risk process review. The standard (and other risk guidance) does not properly do this which tends to detract from the importance of monitoring risk performance.
4. Insufficiently fast and adaptive progress through the risk performance loop. There are at least two reasons for this. Firstly, as just noted, it is quite a neglected area of risk management. Secondly, the importance of adapting is underemphasised in process driven organisations. The myth that you can just formulate and plod through a plan is adhered to. Nothing much happens when you slip off-plan until suddenly there is chaos. One of my favourite analogies for this is the OODA loop developed to model fighter pilots during and after the Second World War. OO is 'observe and orientate,' roughly corresponding to risk assessment. DA is 'decide and act,' that is, risk treatment. The fighter pilot who survives, it is said, is the one gets through his OODA loop quickest. The organisation that survives, we might assert, is the one that goes through its risk performance review loop most quickly. This is a restatement of von Moltke's system of expedients and we shall come back to it later.
5. Failure to look sufficiently hard for new risks, rather than just following up on the old ones.

The risk process review is much easier. Having a defined process means that you can audit how the process is being implemented: that all the matrix cells are filled in, that the risk treatments are being carried out and suchlike.

More importantly you can check that lessons are being collated and learnt from. Evidently the risk performance review provides learning opportunities. Lessons from where risks have materialised in the past should be entering the processes through risk identification. They can also inform likelihood estimates as well as assessments of the effectiveness of the risk treatments where relevant.

Finally the review should provide an assessment of whether risk decisions are taken in line with policy and whether in doing so they continue to best serve the needs of the organisation.

Reviewing risk processes: what could go wrong?

1. It may get tangled up with the risk performance review. It is clearly separate and most likely should take place on more relaxed timescales.
2. It may focus purely on which boxes are filled in rather than the effectiveness of risk controls, whether lessons are being learnt or whether risk decisions are optimal.

Establishing the context

The final substantive risk process is the one that kicks it off, establishing the context. This is concerned with carrying out the preliminary work which ensures the other processes meet the organisation's needs as well as those of the specific business units or departments which the processes are used in.

What the standard requires here is an understanding of the external and internal contexts generally, and then framing the context for risk management. Much of this may have been covered in defining the risk framework – see next section – which will already have considered the internal and external context, though perhaps in less detail, and have formulated the attitude to risk which informs how risk decisions are taken. I discuss all of this as part of outlining the risk framework.

The most important part of the risk management context is the assignment of responsibilities for carrying out the processes and here there are two key roles. The first of these is the risk owner. This is the person who is responsible for making decisions about how risk will be dealt with. Given that risk often comes in lists we can appoint an owner for each item on the list. The second role is the so-called 'risk manager'. This title is in quotation marks because the person in this role bears no organisational responsibility for the management of risks. The 'risk manager' is there to ensure that risk is managed: that processes are in place, that risk is identified, that risk is suitably analysed, that risk owners are appointed, that they develop treatment plans and that these are implemented.

That 'risk managers' don't manage risk is an oft-repeated truism in the risk management game and yet we still carry on using the job title. Better titles would be 'risk facilitator' or 'risk advisor'. My guess is that we continue to use the manager word as it strokes the ego of 'risk managers' who clog up the proceedings of professional meetings with laments about not being taken more seriously at the top levels of their organisations and aspirations to join the C-suite (no, me neither) as Chief Risk Officer or something, in a bid for recognition in their humble consultative and training role.

Other roles within the risk management processes include risk analyst - someone with the appropriate geeky skills, especially to do the quantitative stuff – and action owner – the person who sees through elements of the risk treatment plan.

Finally the risk objectives, processes and responsibilities should all be documented, for example in a risk management plan.

Establishing the context: what could go wrong?

1. The objectives of risk management can be set too restrictively, for example they can become too narrowly tied to organisational objectives, or reflect only event risk rather than uncertainty more generally.
2. Risk decision criteria may too formulaic, either limiting the taking of larger risks which might be beneficial for the organisation or allowing apparently small risks to be taken which have the

potential for major impacts, on the organisation's reputation, for example.
3. The risk management approach developed may inhibit flexibility or the necessary adaptive behaviour.
4. Responsibilities for risk management can become confused, especially in respect of the 'risk manager' who is sometimes expected to assume risk owner responsibilities.

Communication and consultation

An important principle of modern risk management is that it should be visible. That means that what is done, the results of the risk analysis, the decisions made, the risk control plan, should all be available to be scrutinised and challenged by an appropriate audience. This audience (or stakeholders) should also be consulted on how the processes are run and what decisions are made.

It's not entirely clear that it's helpful to regard this as a process. The arena for communication and consultation comes wreathed in a murky fog of divergent interests, up and down a management chain, as well as between silos in an organisation, and between organisations and their stakeholders, including their customers, their neighbours and their owners. As a result the most effective communication and consultation is informal. Issues are resolved though 'adult conversations', negotiation and concession, alliance behaviours and the like. It's often not ideal for issues to be resolved through formal early warning registers, claims for compensation and rigid interpretation of contracts.

Leaving this point on one side for the time being, there are clearly areas where communications can be progressed. The lists of risks can be published, as can the risk analysis, the decisions and the risk treatment plan. Organisations often develop risk databases to contain all this material, and the database will produce the relevant reports to support all the processes from an internal perspective as well as to communicate them to stakeholders. This should include the facilitation of the various risk management activities and processes within an organisation, and, indeed, with its external stakeholders.

The processes themselves can also be published, for example in the risk management plan.

Communicating and consulting on risk: what could go wrong?

1. The risk database, often procured as an off the shelf product, drives the definition of the risk management processes. Obviously it should be the other way round so that they can embed themselves as seamlessly as possible in the organisation's existing processes.
2. The risk reports to support internal processes such as risk performance review are not suitable. For example they may focus on flaky concepts such as the Top 5 risks rather than the real issues of importance.
3. Regarding communication and consultation as a process encourages a formulaic approach to resolving important organisational issues which require intense personal engagement.
4. The need to communicate may inhibit the open and honest sharing of sensitive information, for example in workshops. Most organisations are reluctant to record that the client is a devious, untrustworthy, incompetent idiot, even when this is clearly a major source of risk to be dealt with.

The risk framework

I have dwelt at some length on the risk processes which lie at the heart of risk management. The risk framework is the mechanism by which the organisation puts these processes in place and seeks to ensure they are effective. Note that this is the first time that 'the organisation' has appeared as an essential part of the model. The risk processes would (or should) be carried out by any individual to deal with the uncertainty they face, though clearly the communication part is more relevant in multi-actor environments such as organisations. Now we have to face the challenges of doing the same thing coherently across an organisation which may have different business units, many partners or stakeholders and many employees, perhaps with different ideas about how things should be done and what risks should be taken, and perhaps with misaligned objectives.

According to the standard, the risk framework is composed of foundations and organisational arrangements. The foundations comprise policy, objectives and mandate & commitment; the organisational arrangements include plans, relationships, accountabilities, resources, processes and activities.

Building these foundations and implementing these organisational arrangements are the subjects of another management loop. The key point is that the risk management framework has to be reviewed, and improved where possible. The management loop is kicked off by the foundational matters and then goes through the familiar cycle of design, implementation, monitoring & review and continuous improvement.

I struggle to understand how the framework part of the standard deals with process. One picture is that an organisation has several disparate risk processes going on. A bank will have a risk process for its trading floor, another for its commercial lending and yet another for its branch security. They will all adhere to the process guidance I've described and in one sense they have a common goal: preventing the loss of £10m, whether by an over-exuberant trader, a default on a loan to build a factory or a robbery. So the bank could develop a framework which enables each relevant department to design and implement a suitable risk management process and report back on its performance, all in a coordinated way.

But the standard is not worded like this. In fact, it uses 'risk process' in the singular to refer to the processes of the organisation as a whole. The framework section also covers responsibilities which, for the most part, are attributes of the processes themselves. What's more, nowhere does the standard explicitly address the design of the risk process(es), something which you might expect to be a fundamental topic.

To ensure our discussion is comprehensive I will assume that the framework is responsible for identifying the need for individual processes and (to use the jargon) for providing their requirement specifications and checking that they have been met. The individual areas, what I shall call departments, can then go off and design compliant processes, implement them and report back on their risk profile and performance reviews.

Starting with the mandate and commitment stage, it is hard to overemphasise how important it is for senior management to be totally committed to implementing risk management. It's important they assign adequate resources, it's important they set out policy and objectives for risk management, it's important that they make the necessary appointments, but what's most important is that they live the principles of risk management and that they inculcate this throughout the organisation.

Mandate and commitment: what could go wrong?

1. Senior management think risk management is for everyone else.
2. Senior managers focus on process – "Who was at the risk workshop?", "Are there any red risks?" – rather than content. In practice a constant feature of their conversations throughout the organisation should be enquiry into the detail of specific risk issues and specific treatments.

Designing the risk framework is, as I noted, primarily about understanding the requirements for risk processes throughout the organisation. This starts with understanding the organisation and its context – a high level version of what is needed for each individual process and moves on to define a policy.

As for risk review, it is worth thinking separately about the policy for risk management and that for risk itself. The risk management policy can state that the company carries out risk management, in line with the standard perhaps, and assign responsibility for making sure that happens. It might also describe at a high level how this is done, especially the link with organisational objectives and the breakdown by department. An important policy objective should be to make the risk processes fit well with other processes the organisation runs. This is sometimes known as embedding.

The policy will also need to set out how internal and external communications will be implemented. From the internal point of view, it may be challenging to integrate the reports of each department so that a clear picture of performance is created in a way that is both honest and accurate, but not over-elaborate. Externally, too, the organisation has to present a clear picture of the uncertainties it faces and how it is dealing with them, especially to its 'owners', actual or prospective. Among other things, it needs to be able to show how it is complying with governance requirements such as the corporate governance code needed for London Stock Exchange listing I mentioned at the start of this chapter.

If there is to be a policy document for risk itself, it will need a different name, which, in the absence of any guidance in the standard I will call the risk attitude statement. This provides a high-level view of the organisation's risk profile and, for each type of risk, state how the organisation feels about the issue and how it should be tackled strategically. Evidently this only gets fully into its stride when the risk assessments have been completed to a reasonable level.

Designing the risk framework: what could go wrong?

1. The policy is either too prescriptive or not prescriptive enough.
2. The risk attitude statement is either too prescriptive or not prescriptive enough. Senior management over-controls how risk is dealt with or takes too light a supervisory approach.
3. Failure to distinguish between process and content means that the risk profile is not reviewed often enough. Alternatively the organisation gets too bogged down in process.
4. Insufficient attention is given to embedding the risk management processes so that they remain an irritating extra chore on top of doing the day job.
5. In fact, it is inherently difficult to embed an additional process, a key point which is addressed in this book
6. The organisation is unable to integrate the risk management activities of its parts into a clear and comprehensive view that can be acted on effectively by senior management or its stakeholders.
7. The risk policy is inconsistent with the organisational culture.

The remaining elements of the management loop are quite straightforward. Implement the framework, monitor and review it and (continuously, of course) improve it. This all needs plans, timescales and responsibilities in just the same way as any other organisational initiative. Once again it makes sense for the monitor/review step to separate process and content. It is likely that you will want to review the risk exposure more frequently than the framework. And at this level too, it is important to be adaptive and get round the review loop quickly.

One aspect of this is to reach a view on the effectiveness of risk management in the organisation. Such a view would be informed both by the results of the process review and those of the content review. Contemplating the risk profile is valuable, but an apparently satisfactory picture can conceal two issues. Firstly, no estimate of risk is objectively correct. The risk estimation process is very subjective and may well omit important issues. It is the risk process review that gives you some confidence that the risk management work is as good as it can be and has been carried out in line with some accepted view of good practice. Secondly, even an accurate risk assessment, if it existed, would admit the possibility that something could go wrong, albeit with low likelihood. Maybe you get unlucky.

So you will conclude that risk management is effective if the risk management activities comply with your risk management policy and the risk profile is in line with your risk attitude statement.

Completing the framework loop: what could go wrong?

1. The effectiveness measures may provide a false level of confidence.
2. Things will go wrong despite your best risk management efforts.
3. The loop is not circled quickly enough to adapt to changing circumstances.

The risk principles and definitions

The standard starts with a set of principles. However, on closer examination, these do not form a very compelling basis for the definition of the framework and hence the processes. They are all correct statements but come across as a mixture of truisms and vague aspirations. You could imagine they would naturally be met by any coherent risk management approach although they do, perhaps, help provide some perspective into the scope and methods you would use. But it is hard to get excited about them as fundamental principles and in fact they will emerge naturally from the approach taken here. In effect, these are not foundational principles, but indicators of good practice risk management. They are reviewed in detail in Chapter 6.

So far I have used many specialist terms. I hope that their meaning has been clear based on a common language understanding or, if not, I have tried to explain them. The standard is supported, as you would expect, with a large vocabulary[20] of defined terms. Some of them are helpful, some less so.

For example, risk is defined as 'the effect of uncertainty on objectives'. This is helpful as it underlines that risk management is all about dealing with uncertainty; it legitimises the u-word. However the notes to the definition are less helpful. Note 1 clarifies 'effect' as 'a deviation from the expected', thus introducing the idea of an 'expected' future completely unnecessarily as this point. Instead of mercifully leaving uncertainty to be understood in its natural 'we don't know the future' sense Note 5 states, "uncertainty is the state … of deficiency of information related to, understanding or knowledge of an event, its consequence, or likelihood." This sentence is a syntactic disaster, introduces another unnecessary concept ('event') and is plain wrong in that an event with a likelihood about which there is full knowledge nonetheless admits of uncertainty. I'm being pedantic, of course, but I do think that alarm bells ring when you hit such sloppiness at the first stage of a foundational approach. And more positively, building foundations which avoid the perils of unnecessary elaboration, lack of clarity and logical error holds the prospects of a better way which, who knows, may help avoid some of the issues we started this chapter with, and elaborated in this section.

Risk definitions and principles: what could go wrong?

1. Pursuing unnecessary principles or working with misleading or meaningless definitions may burden risk management with pointless or unhelpful activity which in turn may detract from its effectiveness.

---

[20] Strictly speaking the definitions come from another standard: Vocabulary for Risk Management, ISO Guide 73:2009, but as they are repeated this is largely irrelevant, except to note that the standard has to work with the material provided which has a broader scope of application than just ISO 31000.

Interim conclusions

In this section I have provided a brief and personal overview of current practice risk management based on the international standard for the discipline. This standard is a major achievement, compiling the knowledge and experience of many experts and practitioners. But as the 'what could go wrong' boxes have outlined, it is not without its problems in practice. As you might expect, those things that could possibly go wrong have indeed gone wrong somewhere or other.

Like Chapman and Ward,[21] I think that a large body of common practice has developed that is not necessarily good practice, let alone best practice if you believe in that ephemeral concept. This is not the fault of the standard, except to the extent that it does not warn against these practices.

The plot of this book is now clear. As a book about risk management its intention is to build on the work set out in the standard and other documents, but seeking to address the shortcomings identified.

Accordingly, the next step is to rebuild these concepts from the bottom up, aiming for simplicity, but also using logic and rigour as a guide. In the next section I will give an outline of the framework I propose, pointing out the key deviations. In the subsequent chapters I will go into the detail of each step, defining what I think is a more natural approach to risk management which, in turn, will be more effective.

MAKING A FRESH START

The previous section took us on a fairly comprehensive trip though the essentials of current risk management thinking. Now we come at this material in a different way, starting from a stripped down or natural approach and adding formal risk management perspectives as required. The narrative will aim to avoid some of the issues which have arisen in in the previous section. I hope to point out how you can minimise the chance that the things that *could* go wrong with risk management listed in previous section actually *do* go wrong.

---

[21] *Op cit.*

In developing this approach, we shall use a small number of 'axioms', things which I would regard as self-evident, though you might not.

Natural (risk) management

A good starting point is the management loop. In fact, this is our first axiom, the management loop axiom:

> *The commonly accepted iterative approaches to management (plan-do-review) form a suitable basis for the definition and description of good practice management processes.*

We'll start with the OODA loop. I've already mentioned this in the previous section as the Observe, Orient,[22] Decide, Act cycle originally developed to describe and improve the performance of fighter pilots. It's equivalent to the plan-do-review cycle which is more commonly used in management (for example, the Deming cycle) if we add a stage we might call 'measure' in honour of the platitude about measuring and managing. Figure 4 shows the correspondence. We also note that the measure/observe stage is what is referred to as monitoring in the standard.

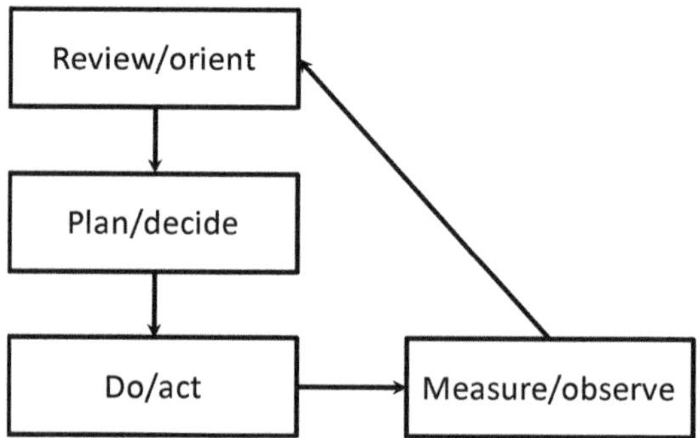

Figure 4 The basic management loop

[22] I have some difficulty accepting 'orient' as a verb, and I am not the only one, according to a quick straw poll. However it seems, according to the Oxford Dictionary, that it is not only correct usage but that 'orientate' is a 19th century neologism, so I will stick with the short and simple form.

There are a few reasons to prefer the OODA loop concept to Deming.

- The *orient* stage is identified[23] as being a very rich process bringing together many areas of background and personal information in contrast to the rather bland *review*. It emphasises the important of context, as we have already met in the risk management processes, but in a way that focusses on the next stage.
- The OODA loop was explicitly developed to emphasise the importance of agility and adaptability. Speed through the loop and frequent adjustments to the plan are key characteristics which you can contrast with the plodding nature of drawing up a plan and then following it, with a nervous breakdown and indecision when something changes. Identifying emerging developments, whether internal or external, and responding to them are key aspects of good performance.
- The OODA loop is also adapted to competitive situations – winning dogfights! Risk management typically models uncertainty as making the best of a random environment. But many contexts are essentially competitive – the risk of not winning work for example – and many more are situations where we are dealing with customers or other stakeholders whose responses, while not necessarily being competitive, are also not random. Instead they represent the individual and collective results of their own OODA loops. The big difference is human behaviour, directed at specific objectives, rather than randomness. This game theoretic aspect of risk management is not widely considered. Part of the OODA loop story is confusing your competitor with frequent changes of plan, throwing dust in their own OODA process, and, while this is not a primary topic of this book, we shall return to it much later.

This also raises the point that the OODA loop is primarily about the actions of individuals rather than organisations, something we shall need to think about in the rest of the book.

I have introduced the OODA loop as an informal path to improved performance which is also aligned with the formal management theory represented by the Deming cycle. I think this creates quite a powerful

---

[23] For example, in Wikipedia.

picture of what you might call *natural management*. Of course there is nothing explicit here about risk or uncertainty, but equally obviously we need to ensure these concepts are included in circuits of the loop, which from now on I will christen the OODeming loop, in line with Figure 4:

- planning/deciding needs to take into account the uncertainties which we have identified, including the formulation of contingency plans
- doing/acting on what we decided to do needs to include the implementation of the control measures and contingency plans as circumstances demand
- measuring/observing needs to identify how the way things are turning out varies from what we expected from the actions we took
- reviewing/orienting needs to take on board the reasons for these variations as well as other changes in context which are different from what we assumed in the previous cycle.

What is key here is that these are things to be recognised in the mainstream management activities, they are not part of their own risk management loop. We call this the no risk process axiom:

> *There are no risk management processes, just management processes that recognise and accommodate uncertainty.*

That is why this book is about tools for risk management, not risk management processes and risk management cycles per se.

This discussion also emphasises the importance of natural management whether or not the context is risk. The fighter pilot does not write down the options he is considering, though I guess he has plenty of measurements to look at. The reviews are also not formally structured or reported, albeit they take account of a rich context. The organisation needs a little more formality, as we shall come to next, but the organisation also needs to attend to the instinctive side of risk management, making sure that each stage is carried out naturally in as effective a way as possible. This depends both on the individuals *and* the organisational culture. The organisational culture has to ensure that risks are identified and planned for, and that emerging issues are factored into reviews in an unforced way. The next step is obvious: everyone must carry out their duties with the explicit recognition that the future is uncertain. But what does this mean? And how is it made explicit?

One possible answer is that everyone talks about it. By this I mean that managers discuss with their teams what uncertainties they face and what they are doing about them. This discussion is comprehensive and relentless. It involves gaining assurance that people are doing what they say they are doing. It is a conversation which extends throughout the organisation, changing in scale and scope to match the forum. If these conversations don't happen, risk won't get managed. You can't say the same about filling in risk registers.

What we have here is very significant. We have arrived at the point that risk management is, in the first instance, about behaviour: how, and how often, people talk about risk, and what they do about it. It is about behaviour, not about process, not about management frameworks. This gives us a completely different perspective on risk management from that of ISO 31000 and we need to describe how to get the behaviour right. This is achieved (by definition) through the organisation's culture with regard to risk. Risk culture needs to be a significant topic in a risk management textbook and we shall expand on this in Chapter 3. It should arguably be the dominating topic, but because the realisation of its importance has come relatively late it is still relatively undeveloped.

Explicit risk management

Is that it? If we can create the right culture so that managers are thinking about and dealing with risk in the right way, perhaps there is no more to do. We have a self-managing organisation with built-in risk management. It may be that that's all that needed. For example, I'm an independent consultant, working through a small company, and I like to think this is what I do - except it's just me so, there's not much communication. My main form of performance measurement is to check on the proximity of body and soul from time to time. It's worked OK up to now.

There are good reasons why some organisations think they need to do more:

- maybe distributed decision making about uncertainty is inherently suboptimal; maybe decisions taken locally cannot give the best outcome for the organisation in spite of appropriate guidance and instruction

- maybe the results of delegating decisions about uncertainty are not trusted, in spite of the creation of a good or excellent risk culture
- maybe they need to predict what the impacts of risk and uncertainty might be expected to be
- maybe performance information about risk is regarded as essential to the organisation's scorecard
- maybe external stakeholders want visibility of what is being done about uncertainty.

For some or all of these reasons the organisation may need to:

- maintain risk databases which record the controls and planned actions to deal with each identified uncertainty
- carry out and record formal risk analyses to provide estimates of the level of risk, and to support decision making
- provide forecasts which include the effect of risk and uncertainty
- monitor risk performance and review risk decision making and the implementation of the controls and actions
- and finally, monitor the implementation of these processes and review their effectiveness for risk management.

All of these suggest we need to supplement the natural approach to risk management and introduce what I call the risk management axiom:

> *The performance of your organisation will be improved if it is governed with the explicit recognition that the future is uncertain.*

We'll come back to 'governed' shortly, but what are the implications of 'explicit'? This is the idea that, although being natural and having an appropriate risk culture is important, indeed necessary, you need to go beyond this. Some things need to be written down in quite a formal way, especially when it comes to risk and uncertainty because of its very broad scope. This is *explicit risk management* which adds a layer of formal activity around the natural risk management core.

Accordingly, we'll add a couple of extra activities into the OODeming loop. Firstly, there is the additional internal activity of forecasting performance. This was already hinted at when I mentioned departures from what is expected. What is expected is recorded in the forecast and I have also added an activity called synthesising which brings together

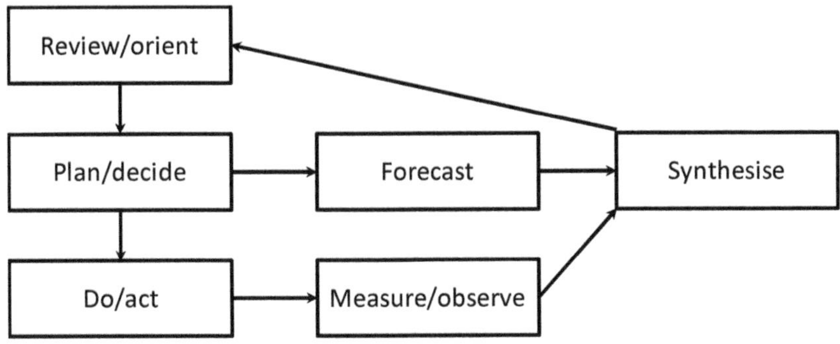

Figure 5 The enhanced management loop

the measurements and the forecast to form an integrated view prior to reviewing/orienting. This short circuit of the management loop enables managers to measure 'variances from forecast', in principle at least. Figure 5 shows the effect of adding in these two extra activities.

This now suggests that most management processes in organisations have a set of management documents which would include plans, forecasts, performance reports and records of reviews. The performance reports will compare forecast with actuals and provide some explanation of variations.

What should these documents say specifically about risk? Plans will make allowances for risks and uncertainties. They will include risk control measures, potential opportunities and make provision for contingency arrangements, that is, actions to be taken if risks materialise. This means they will imply a residual risk profile, that is, provide a characterisation of risk which takes account of all the measures that are planned to enhance the likelihood of better outcomes. The forecasts will reflect the plans and will therefore be uncertain themselves, in line with the residual risk profile. This is of course at odds with the idea that forecasts are single numbers. This is the cause of immense confusion, not to say a certain amount of stress, and we shall be coming back to this point at some length in Chapter 4.

It would follow that differences between actual performance and forecast performance are difficult to pin down if the forecasts are uncertain, but if we take for granted for the moment that such differences can be identified, then they can be attributed to risk materialising, hopefully in a way which is consistent with the residual risk profile. This is also discussed in more depth in Chapter 4.

Finally, the reports should indicate what we have learnt from the risks which have materialised and the uncertainties which have crystallised, what new external risks have emerged or dematerialised and what our approach is to dealing with the new context. They may record the conversations that have taken place and the agreed actions.

In moving beyond 'natural' to 'explicit' we have focussed on risk. That's not surprising as this is a book about risk, but I think that risk is also a uniquely important driver for the development. This is because of the complexity of uncertainty in most organisational contexts. Any business will inevitably be taking on a wide spectrum of risks of different types, impacts and likelihoods and it is unreasonable to think that any manager will be able to comprehend the overall risk profile. Many managers and entrepreneurs are running organisations and businesses which rely on risk taking to meet their objectives, and are very good at keeping track of the risks and their potential impact. But it is hard to do this in a thorough way, and any comprehensive and accessible risk profiling tools in particular will greatly assist the manager to navigate the sea of uncertainty they face.

That is why we need the risk management axiom to move us beyond natural risk management.

(Risk) governance

There is a glaring hole in the discussion so far: there has been no mention of objectives. Managers plan, decide, act and measure in such a way as to meet a set of objectives which are generally set from outside the OODeming loop, and from higher up in the organisation. Managers have bosses and directors have shareholders, so even the most natural and freewheeling of OODeming loopers will have to take some instruction and report back on performance. There are many potential terms for this director-executor, master-servant, client-vendor relationship, but to emphasise its formality we'll refer to the processes associated with it as 'governance'.

There are three clear aspects to governance.

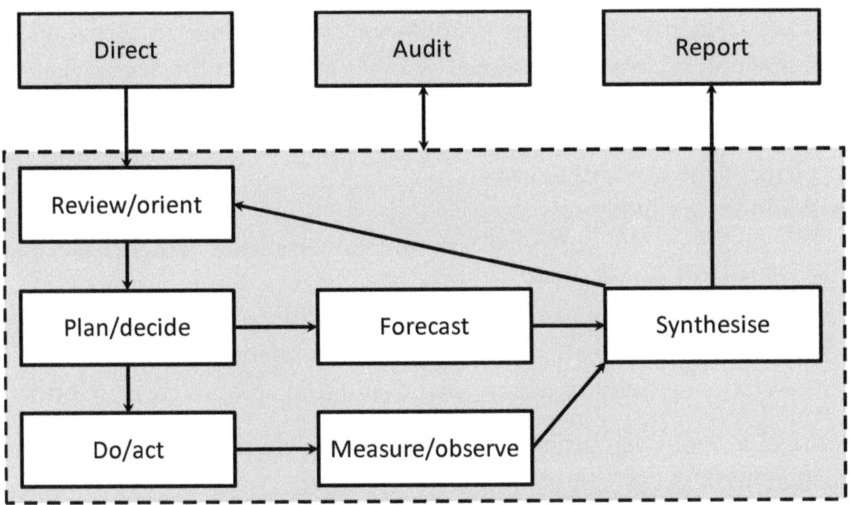

Figure 6 Adding governance to management

- Providing direction: as well as including setting objectives, there will likely be guidance on how these are to be achieved, what the constraints are and other matters.
- Receiving performance reports based on the measurements that the governed managers have made, the deliberations that have taken place during review/orient and an updated view on if, how and when the objectives might be achieved.
- Getting assurance in advance that these results will be in line with expectations, that the forecasts are 'realistic', the measures 'accurate' and the whole management process is efficient. We call this audit.

This is illustrated in Figure 6 which draws a box around the OODeming loop to emphasise its existence as its own system.

These three functions provide a further, governance layer to the natural and management layers we have already identified. These governance layer processes have a number of features which are specific to risk.

- The directions are likely to provide some guidance on what the approach to risk management should be, which risks can be taken, which should be avoided and which should be referred back up for discussion and approval at the governing level. They will also set out the policy with regard to the use of risk management tools.

- The performance reports should explain variations in terms of the risks which have materialised, whether they were foreseen, what the updated risk profile is and how this impacts the updated plan. They may contain information which is likely to change the high-level plans of the governing entity.
- Auditors are likely to:
  - challenge the menu of risk and uncertainties which have been planned for,
  - challenge their assumed likelihood and impact,
  - challenge the control and contingency plans,
  - challenge why risks have materialised in spite of these controls.

Again, risk tools will be helpful in facilitating these aspects of the governance process.

At this point it is worth noting that there is a commonly accepted model of governance which is based around three lines of defence:

- first line of defence: operational processes
- second line of defence: risk management
- third line of defence: internal audit.

This model is intended to clear up any confusion between the functions of audit and risk management. It's clear that I don't agree with this distinction in the sense that I think risk management – especially in its natural risk management guise – should be a function of operational management with no distinct existence of its own (apart, maybe, from facilitating operational management in doing its job with regard to risk).

What is under discussion here is whether there should be a separate risk management function, which might, say, report independently on risk to that part of the organisation creating and, presumably, managing that risk. This appears to be an unnecessary complication which I'd regard as part of audit. I'll be returning this in Chapter 5.

Multiple loops and the scale free organisational model

The previous discussion focussed on the governance of a single management activity. It's likely that the governing system operates to its own management cycle. This adds planning/deciding and forecasting to the

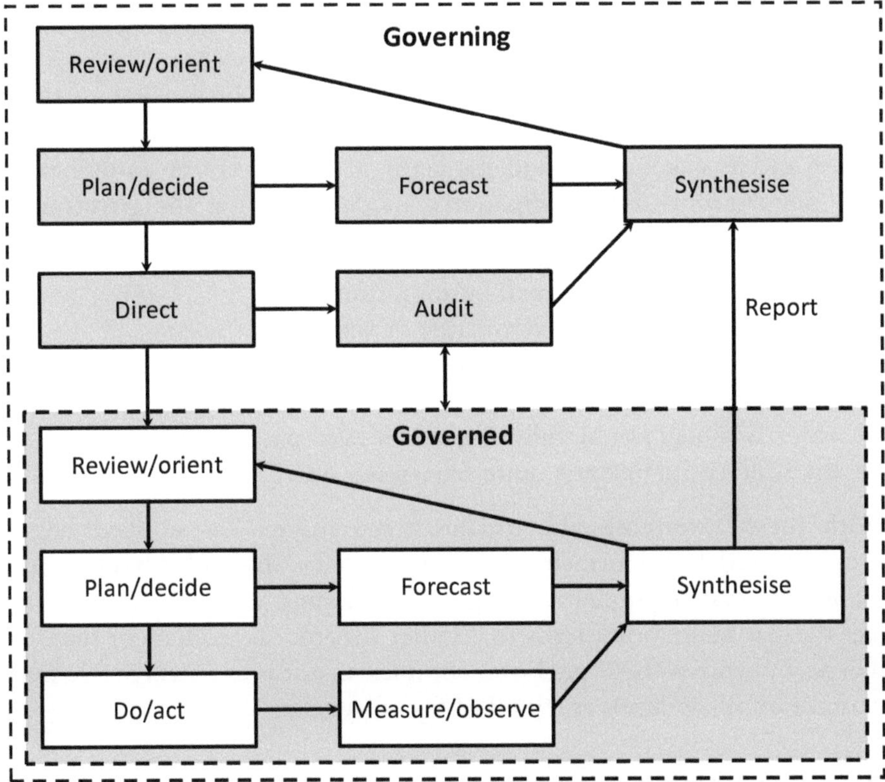

Figure 7 The complete governing loop

governance level, as well as synthesising and reviewing/orienting. Objectives can cascade down through the organisation as part of directing.

It can be seen from Figure 7, which shows the completed set of loops, that *Direct* is part of the *Do/act* element of the governing unit and, in the same way, *Audit* is part of *Measure/observe*. In addition, *Synthesise* will accept not only the performance measurement reports synthesised by the governed unit, but also the records of the audits as well as its own performance reports, if relevant. We could also add in the reports of the reviews within the governed unit.

This presents a modular view of the organisation. This is helpful in understanding the organisation and also in promoting its efficiency and effectiveness: each module being essentially self-managing within its governance framework. It's worth saying this is not the only way to draw these charts as the point about reports has just illustrated. Each organisation will have its own detailed cycles and associated timescales. However I will stick with Figure 7 throughout the book.

It's a fairly obvious extension to think about hierarchies of such loops, and these could be quite extensive, both up and down the organisation and its stakeholders, and also across it. This opens up a number of rich opportunities for organisational modelling using the governing-governed relationship:

- companies may have several business units
- clients may have many contractors or vendors
- governance and management processes may be less well defined in some cases
- objectives may not be fully aligned, or even partially conflicting
- the scale could become quite fine, going down to individuals even.

With these extensions, the organisational model has stopped being simply a model of management and governance. Instead it has become a complex system model reacting to and dealing with uncertainty. In fact the last bullet point leads to a rather theoretical refinement that for practical purposes the model is so complex that it is essentially scale free, existing on many levels as a kind of fractal system.

Recap and definitions

This section has attempted to develop a framework for risk management within general management which is based on a number of universally accepted (or acceptable?) truths or axioms.

The first one is straightforward, the uncertainty axiom:

The future is uncertain.

This means the future could play out in more than one way, each with its associated level of performance, and management must take steps to ensure that those futures with higher levels or performance are favoured.

I regard the words uncertainty and risk as more or less synonymous. If there is a difference, then it is

- **Risk** – the implications of uncertainty for a specific organisation.

The next axiom is what I called the risk management axiom:

> *The performance of your organisation will be improved if it is governed with the* explicit *recognition that the future is uncertain.*

I don't believe this needs further definition though it is worth looking the words up in a dictionary – see box below. In other words, the risk management axiom stands in plain English, on its own. We do need a couple of points of clarification though.

Some definitions (from the Oxford Dictionaries[24])

1. **Governance**: The action or manner of governing a state, organization, etc
2. **Govern**: Conduct the policy, actions, and affairs of (a state, organization, or people) with authority
3. **Management**: The process of dealing with or controlling things or people
4. **Manage**: Be in charge of (a business, organization, or undertaking); run
5. **Process:** A series of actions or steps taken in order to achieve a particular end

'Governed' is used instead of 'managed', partly because, as the definitions make clear, you govern an organisation but manage a risk, but, more fundamentally, because the word reflects the seriousness of the requirement which needs to be performed with authority. If you don't do it, you are not conducting the organisation's affairs properly.

'Improved' means by comparison with any mode of governance which future uncertainty is not explicitly recognised. 'Explicitly' is the key word here.

Given where we are obviously going, to expand on the implications of 'explicit' recognition, we perhaps need to accept that the costs of this are worth incurring in the light of the 'improved performance'. As the

[24] oxforddictionaries.com

discussion up to now has made clear, this is pretty much an article of faith. I do indeed regard risk management as essential to management and not just some kind of add-on which needs to demonstrate its ROI. Obviously you need to do it as efficiently as possible but there is little point in embarking on some contrived exercise to quantify the savings from the risks that didn't happen to demonstrate value for money or the like.

'Performance' is a vague term in general but should mean something specific in the context of each individual organisation. We are making an implicit assumption that the governance of the organisation is directed at improving its performance. If this is the case, it follows that its governance, the method of conducting its policy, actions and affairs, must explicitly recognise that the future is uncertain.

We can define these steps to be risk management, or more precisely

- **Risk management** – those aspects of the policy, actions and affairs of the organisation which are specifically related to the explicit recognition of future uncertainty.

In other words it's only risk management because you are explicitly recognising future uncertainty. If you would do it anyway, it's not risk management.

The third axiom, the no risk process axiom, is:

There are no risk management processes, just management processes that recognise and accommodate uncertainty.

This is somewhat more controversial; it is the most important way in which this book parts company with ISO 31000 and most common practice, generally accepted, risk management approaches. Because of this I have changed the perspective of risk management activities into the deployment of a set of tools in the course of, and to support, mainstream management and governance.

As a result, we need the final axiom, the management loop axiom (slightly extended from before):

The commonly accepted iterative approaches to management and governance such as the OODA loop or the Deming cycle form a suitable basis for the definition and description of good practice management and governance processes which accommodate uncertainty.

Thus the four axioms and two definitions of this section are all that are required to set up our new and improved risk management framework. By contrast with ISO 31000 I think the framework:

- is easier to understand
- is much easier to embed within organisational management processes
- raises the profile of an appropriate risk culture.

STRUCTURE OF THE BOOK

This discussion has combined four simple axioms together with the OODeming management loop. It has also identified three layers within which risk management tools can be deployed: natural risk management is wrapped in a management layer which in turn is wrapped in a governance layer.

Accordingly the rest of the book provides more detail and tools in each of these areas:

- Chapter 2 is concerned with natural risk management: how you can characterise your risks and decide what to do about them, how you can be agile and adapt to changing circumstances. It also addresses whether and why a supporting management layer is needed.
- The emphasis on natural risk management also highlights the importance of an appropriate risk culture in organisations to supplement the fundamentally personal perspective of Chapter 2. Thus risk culture, and the need to ensure mature, comprehensive and relentless conversations about risk, are discussed in Chapter 3.
- Chapter 4 resumes the narrative by addressing the management layer, how we forecast the impact of risk and uncertainty, how we measure risk performance and how we build this into our management reports and reviews.
- Chapter 5 is then focussed on the governance layer and the tools available for providing direction, auditing and reporting from a risk perspective.
- This concludes the central thread of the book and Chapter 6 returns to common practice risk management to compare and contrast, covering the basic principles and the risks identified in the first section

of this chapter so as to present a consolidated picture. It discusses the construction industry in more detail as an example.

- Throughout the book I refer to the fundamentals of decision making where risk and uncertainty are important. This is a key topic and not as well understood in the risk management community as it should be. Chapter 7 gives a full discussion of some foundational issues.
- Finally I give a personal view of the future of risk management in a very short Chapter 8.

Chapter 2

Tools for natural risk management

Understanding the risk you face at any point in time, and deciding what to do about it

The previous chapter presented a picture of risk management in layers. What I have tried to idealise as natural risk management is wrapped in an explicit management layer and then a governance layer. Natural risk management is part of the day-to-day managerial task. This chapter is focussed on natural risk management and the tools managers can use to ensure they take risk and uncertainty on board in everything they do.

As such, there is no organisational context at this stage. Discussion of organisational risk culture is deferred to the next chapter and organisational process matters to those that follow. This means that, although we have used the term 'manager', we are referring to anyone who wants to deal well with risk in the activities they undertake: a car buyer balancing affordability, reliability and environmental impact or a gap-year student planning a round-the-world backpacking adventure, just as much as a minister planning infrastructure investment to stimulate economic growth in a deprived region.

These tools will be listed against the OODeming loop structure. As well as representing good practice, this emphasises the advantages of agility and adapting to circumstances. However loops need an entry point and to accommodate this we shall start with an initial orienting step, and then go through deciding, acting and observing before coming back to updated orientation and changes to the plan. This entry point is aligned with the ISO 31000 approach of 'establishing the context' which is really the first iteration of risk review.

The core of natural risk management is about understanding the risk and deciding what to do about it. There is less emphasis on the managerial tasks of measurement and review. We noted in Chapter 1 that these activities are essentially part of the explicit management layer, so this chapter does not discuss the tools available to support these management activities to any great extent – this is deferred to Chapter 4 – but it does talk about the circumstances in which these explicit tools become necessary.

Accordingly, there are four main sections to this chapter which describe tools for

- establishing the risk context
- risk analysis
- risk decision making
- the requirement for risk measurement and review,

with a summary and signposts at the end.

In doing this I have identified the separate activity of risk analysis as part of the *Decide/plan* element of the loop. Risk analysis can be defined similarly to what is in the standards,[1] though it occupies a relatively small box in the ISO 31000 flow chart

- **Risk analysis** – gaining an understanding of your risk sufficiently to support decisions about what you are going to do.

TOOLS FOR ESTABLISHING THE RISK CONTEXT

This is not a highly technical activity but is nonetheless an important preamble for more detailed risk analysis. It will include:

- scoping the activity to be risk analysed
- identifying the objectives and performance indicators
- identifying the policies and guidance which are relevant to the activity

[1] "Process to comprehend the nature of risk and to determine the level of risk."

- identifying the current plan including tasks (that is, sub-activities), resources, timescales
- identifying the controls and other risk management measures (called risk treatment in the previous chapter) which are currently planned
- identifying interfacing activities, especially, for example, predecessor activities such as the previous project development stage which may bequeath substantial risk documentation
- identifying relevant external political, institutional, economic, business, social, technological, environmental and other factors
- identifying relevant internal cultural, contractual, capability and capacity, and other factors
- identifying constraints, including legal and regulatory constraints
- identifying relevant guidance, codes of practice, etc
- identifying the stakeholders, and their capacity to influence the activity
- identifying similar or related activities which have been, or are being, carried out
- forming a first idea of the sort of uncertainties the activity faces.

It should be clear that all this data collection is aimed at the last point: providing the raw material from which the risk can start to be understood. Each of the items identified can be a source of risk.

I would suggest that you use the items above to create a checklist for the information to be collated. A document which contains all this information is a useful start for risk analysis and it can be updated at each review so that it remains live. For example, this could form part of a document known on many projects as the risk management plan. I would prefer the term risk analysis context, whether it is part of the risk management plan or a standalone document.

ISO 31000 proposes that more information than this is collated as the risk management context is established. This relates mainly to proposed methods for risk planning and also risk criteria, that is, the means that are to be used for decision support. I think that in respect of the methods this is *in principle* jumping the gun. As I shall outline below, the methods should be driven by the problem at hand, not some one-size-fits-all corporate solution. *In practice* it may be the case that the risk is sufficiently well understood that the methods can be described as part of the risk analysis context. This should not be taken as a general rule.

Similar considerations apply to risk decisions: don't decide too early how it's going to be done.

TOOLS FOR RISK ANALYSIS

There are three main elements to this. First of all, I discuss how you can explore the uncertainty you face in a defined undertaking. Then I describe how to gain a more nuanced and comprehensive picture of the effect of this. The picture is qualitative but it would be useless without some appreciation of how it would change under different assumptions about the actions you might take to modify the uncertainty.

Thirdly, I show how this picture can be made richer and more useful by quantifying it. We call this risk modelling. This leads on to the next section where I explore how you can make decisions about which of the modifying actions you might take.

But before any of this we need to take time to think about the nature of uncertainty itself.

The nature of uncertainty

> *"Our knowledge of the way things work, in society or in nature, comes trailing clouds of vagueness."* Kenneth Arrow

This quotation expresses the risk management challenge very eloquently. It is a favourite of mine (I used to run a blogging website on *cloudsofvagueness.com*) for the way it evokes our comprehensive inability to predict what is going to happen even in situations which are notionally under our control. It reminds us that real life exists in a different world from that of accountants and project controllers which is inhabited by plans, budgets and forecasts. It's important that we understand the scope of this vagueness so we start with a short discussion of what might be involved.

There are many taxonomies of uncertainty. Some are not very helpful for risk management, but one that is are the four types itemised by Chapman and Ward.[2]

---

[2] How to Manage Project Opportunity and Risk, Chris Chapman and Stephen Ward, Wiley, 2011.

- **Event uncertainty**, the classic paradigm of a thousand risk registers. You define an event which or may not happen such as a fall from height, a default on a loan, loss of a key person or encountering a sand inclusion when constructing a tunnel. The events are generally bad news, as here, but there is nothing to prevent something nice happening like arriving on site and finding the electrical cable you expected has already been diverted somewhere else.
- **Inherent variability**, a number you do not know with certainty – the cost of getting your front door painted, the exchange rate in 2 years' time, the number of loan defaults, how many key people leave, the extent of the sand inclusion. This is what is known to some people as uncertainty and, where the examples relate to the events just mentioned, you can see that in many cases it is the more important concept. The variability can be upside or downside compared with some baseline.
- **Systemic uncertainty** is not, in truth, a separate category, but it is nonetheless vitally important. It is the recognition that there is correlation between the other sources of uncertainty you may have identified. For example, if the cost of getting your front door painted is higher than you thought, the same may apply to the cost of getting your back door painted. There are potentially many causes of this: a poor estimator, an increase in the cost of paint or heating up in the global market for door painters. An inappropriate contracting strategy for local authority services may well mean waste bins are not emptied as well as the expedient felling of street trees. And of course, there is that risk taboo of 'bad management'; if they mess one thing up they will probably mess up a lot of other things. You might credibly demonstrate that the chance of a nuclear reactor safety system not working is one in a hundred. But no-one would believe you if had three such systems and claimed that the chance of all three failing is one in a million, in spite of systematically eliminating the dependences between them; there is always some common cause which will sneak under the radar. Systemic uncertainty really means overlapping risk descriptions and it poses a significant challenge for risk analysis which can get ignored if too much activity is created by long risk lists, for example.
- **Ambiguity** represents types of uncertainty which cannot easily be characterised by events or numbers. It results from a lack of

definition. It is what comes closest to the clouds of vagueness that trail from our knowledge. The cost of a railway signalling system is inherently variable even if you know you are going to buy system X from vendor Y. It is more of an ambiguity if you have yet to decide what technology to use for a railway which is planned for ten years' time. And it is a real ambiguity, maybe not even worth identifying separately, if you are planning a city fifty years in the future with a maglev transportation system.

Chapman and Ward's book is about projects and I think you can add another source of uncertainty to their four.

- **Ignorance** is where ambiguity shades into unknown unknowns and black swans: things that we do not know about or cannot conceive of with the information available to us. Making provisions for things you don't know about is a commonly recurring question in risk and is a concept worth spending a little more time on.

Glib appeals to 'unknown unknowns' are one of the tedious aspects of the risk manager's life. I find Rumsfeld's peroration[3] on the topic completely incomprehensible in terms of what it is supposed to mean in the context of Iraq and weapons of mass destruction. I think a more important point comes at the start where he states, "reports that say that something hasn't happened are always interesting to me." This might also be termed (after Sherlock Holmes) 'the dog that didn't bark'. The failure of something to happen which might have been expected is just as useful a clue as something happening which was not expected.

But unknown unknowns is about things which cannot be anticipated, and turning to black swans, Nassim Nicholas Taleb sets three criteria in his book:[4]

1. could not have been foreseen
2. high or serious impact
3. can be understood and rationalised in retrospect.

Anything can be rationalised after it has happened, and criterion 2. just says we are not so interested in black cygnets. So the main point is

[3] See Wikipedia for instance.
[4] The Black Swan, Nassim, Nicholas Taleb, Penguin, 2010.

number 1., which also corresponds to unknown unknowns and we can term the phenomenon UU/BS.

Taleb's view is that there are many of these black swans out there, that you can't predict them and as a result you need to be resilient in a way that is independent of specific, foreseen risks, and, in particular, protect yourself against any high downsides. This is essentially a decision rule and we'll discuss it later, but Taleb makes a strong case that any kind of exploration of your risk is a waste of time because what actually happens will be dominated by the black swans you inevitably miss. That may be true as a general rule about life, the universe, etc, but if you are the project manager of a door painting project or a bank manager extending your loan book, or even a nuclear engineer, I take it as an article of faith that you will gain some value from thinking about the specifics of the uncertainty you face. You may also see point 1. as a failure of the imagination and you should certainly strive to think through what might happen, however apparently far-fetched or unlikely.

If the central question here is whether you should make any specific provision in your risk analysis for UU/BS, I believe there is nothing in this discussion to suggest that you should do so. I'm against adding in a bit of money for things you haven't managed to think of. But you do need to remember that unknowns and black swans may occur, and you should certainly look out for them so that you can adapt to them as early as possible.

Understanding these categories of uncertainty is important, but the main point of this section is to remind you that you need to cover all sources of uncertainty in your analysis, especially the early exploration. Ignoring ambiguity will not make it go way, and it will not make it leave your project or business alone. In thinking about your uncertainty, you must not fall into the trap of just recording event-based risks.

Exploring your risk

Having compiled the background material into a risk analysis context document you are ready to go on to the next stage which is to explore your risk landscape. The idea is to identify all potentially significant sources of uncertainty without making too many premature decisions as to how real or significant they are. It should be an expansive process, broadening your horizons, before embarking on the following reductive stages. I had a customer once who said he needed his risk manager to be his scout, looking out for all the things which might ambush him. That's not a bad metaphor to bear in mind, though, of course, he needs to do his bit.

I think that it is also necessary at this stage to consider what you are actually going to do about the uncertainties you face. This does not mean building up a complete risk management plan but to get to the next stage – characterising your risk – you need to have some kind of context about what risk treatments you will routinely put in place, or are currently planning to do, and also start to sketch out further measures. Levels of risk do not exist in a vacuum. We discussed the risk treatment strategies in the previous chapter, and the risk control plan you adopt will depend on your risk attitude, either your personal attitude or that of the organisation. These are discussed in Chapters 3 and 5 respectively so we will not dwell on the topic here.

The classic way to explore risk and risk control is to hold a risk workshop. That is what I shall describe here. But it is not the only way. Some risk analysts think they can do it on their own, based on their experience of other, similar activities. A colleague once painted a picture of a pompous facilitator locked up in a room with 20 or so bored people with better things to do. "In any case we know all the risks and we can always review them later." I don't think that's necessarily a bad approach, especially with the emphasis in this book on going round and round the management loop rather than focussing on kicking it off.

Another technique is to do a series of interviews (management interviews in the jargon) essentially with the same people as would have been in the workshop. So I'll describe how I run workshops and the same principles will apply to the other approaches. However, it's worth saying there is nothing to beat a bunch of people working together in a workshop atmosphere to push the borders on identifying the uncertainties an activity faces.

First of all, try not to be pompous. That should not be difficult when you'll be meeting a bunch of new people who not only know far more about what's going to be looked at than you do, but, as my colleague says, have no wish to be there.

Secondly, don't have 20 or more. Managers can often think of reasons to extend participation, generally on the grounds of covering all expertise bases, which is alleged to help buy-in. There is a limit to the number who can meaningfully participate, and people can and should contribute outside their silos. This is what makes it work, and again you can always review later.

This brings me back to preparation. Given the challenges you face it is vital that you get up to speed as far as possible on whatever is to be looked at and the people attending. I am happy to have briefing meetings, and peruse specifications, drawings, programmes, contracts and the like to an almost unlimited extent to help a workshop go well. This highlights an important difference between me and the colleague I mentioned. I am usually working with a new client in a new business for the first time whereas he is embedded in a client organisation which does projects of a broadly similar type. Once again context is everything.

I also usually issue a brief a week or so ahead of the event if there is time. This covers objectives and logistical items, and contains a process outline and agenda. However, its main purpose is to give the impression I know what I am doing. I'm not sure how effective it is in this regard, especially as I have no hesitation in ignoring the agenda. I normally finish the brief with sets of prompts driven from different perspectives such as stakeholders, project activities and programme, systems, and so on. Of these, stakeholders is the most valuable as it is generally they that mess up your project. These prompts can be extracted from the risk analysis context document. This document starts to pay its way while you are developing the brief.

And so to the meeting. The first item after intros (which are worth spending a little time on to develop the context) and reviews of the brief is to make sure everyone is on the same page with regard to what's being risk analysed. Be careful. As a rule, everyone will say they know what it is, and the top dog almost certainly will, but in practice there may well be some disagreement or misunderstanding over what the project or programme comprises. I once started a risk workshop at 6 o'clock in the evening. It was the sort of organisation where they could only find time for risk outside normal hours. We then spent the next two and a half hours clarifying what the project was. By the time we got to risk, everyone's evening was well and truly ruined, but this part of the discussion was definitely useful.

Coming to risk identification, I use a very simple device which I think works well but I have not seen elsewhere. I just go round the table asking everyone to name their biggest concern. We have the usual discussion around phrasing it properly as a risk and I generally allow a bit of debate, especially around the early stages until everyone gets into their stride. I record the results on Post-Its (make sure you get the super sticky sort) with a large print, marker pen headline and small print details for me in normal pen. We go round the table two or three times, and then review the prompts that are in the brief. By the time everyone has run out of steam you have maybe 50-70 Post-Its.

This discussion is the key phrase. You have to make it relevant and you have to probe. You are constantly trying to find a balance between asking questions which take you somewhere useful and those which just make you look silly. (Yes, contrary to accepted facilitating wisdom, there are silly questions, at least for the facilitator.) You are trying to uncover areas which some participants might prefer not to face up to and you are trying to maintain momentum without cutting back on useful discussion. You have to concentrate on what's being said, record it, formulate a plan for where you're going, and remain adaptable, all at the same time.

You then spend a nervous lunch trying to sort the Post-Its into coherent issues whilst minimising discussion with people whose smartphones have not created enough to occupy them. This 'affinity mapping' stage (not my term – it was invented by someone I used to work with) presupposes that the next stage is to try to develop the outline risk management plan.

Having grouped the Post-Its into issues you can invite a discussion of how they are to be tackled. This can be recorded on flipcharts and stuck on the walls. (My second playschool tip is to have a roll of plastic film you can put on the wall and write on – for example Legamaster Magic Chart. This is essential if you are in a law firm's offices, a bank's or the like. They generally have smart meeting rooms aimed at impressing clients with elegant, Blu Tack-unfriendly decor and expensively-curated art installations. Engineers and designers offices are less of a problem.)

The idea of this discussion is to gather the data to produce a complete picture of the uncertainties and what is planned to deal with them. These plans may be routine, or they may have been invented during the workshop to deal with some unforeseen issues as they were surfaced. If the latter, it will be necessary to keep a close eye on management later on to ensure they will deliver on what they have said they are going to do.

At this point the workshop can stop. Hopefully the team has found the discussion enlightening and useful and not such a drag as they were expecting. I have found some clients who enjoy the discussion alone; they don't care about the written output. The point for them is that a conversation framed by risk can be very useful.

But now the nightmare starts. The disorganised collection of material has to be turned into something coherent. The conventional way to do this is to create a risk register, broadly speaking a list of the Post-Its described according to formulas like: 'there is a risk that due to X,Y happens, leading to Z','there is uncertainty in the amount of A','there is an issue that M','there is an opportunity to O'. Each item in the risk register should be clearly articulated in terms of what might happen and how it might play out (for example, by clearly separating cause, event and impact). The action plan can then be added as a separate column, whilst noting that this can be inefficient if many risks have the same or similar management plan.

Risk registers are not the universal solution to presenting how you have characterised your risk. But they work satisfactorily for recording risk workshop proceedings and we shall come to other ideas later.

The workshop agenda I've described covers only the identification of risks and the associated management plans so that you can move to the next stage of prioritising them to assist in thinking about any further actions. It is possible to embark on this during the workshop as well. Many people do this, but I am very sceptical of the benefits. Firstly, it will extend the workshop. These days, people are, rightly or wrongly, reluctant to give up more than a couple of hours for this kind of exercise. Extending them to gather data about how seriously the issues are viewed is useful, but not essential. You need to be clear about the objectives of the session and the trade-off between taking up people's time and getting more information. There will be more on this in the sections that follow.

Here is a list of other things I don't normally do, in addition to not prioritising.

- **No beautiful assistant.** In principle it would be good to have someone else to record events and maybe take over. But in practice it's difficult for others to appreciate the nuances, follow my changing plans and generally not get in the way of getting the most value out of limited time. Anyway I can't afford it.

- **No recording on screen.** Again this gets in the way. Everyone follows the typing and gets bored. It detracts from the organised chaos.
- **No voting.** If you are going to prioritise, you can get little pads which enable people to express their views on where each Post-It should be located in probability-impact space (as in Figure 2). I'm tempted to say the stupidity of this is beyond words, but it's not really, so let me just point out that it's completely contrary to the core idea: to have a workshop where people share and pool their ideas and experience.
- **No remote participation.** No teleconferencing arrangements are as immediate as being all together and working together in a room. I once did one with two participants sitting in Sweden. The ambiance and demeanour were pure Wallander and I was lucky to escape with my sanity.
- And as an extension of this, **no virtual or modularised workshop.** Some time ago I was persuaded by a new customer to hold the workshop in stages throughout the day with different specialists. We collected quite a decent set of risks, but they all seemed somehow mundane, the sort of things I could indeed have written down myself. As the work proceeded after the workshop many turned out to be non-issues or were not recognised by other people in the team. I'm pretty sure that the eventual risk profile suffered from not having been kicked off by a diverse team engaged in a meaningful discussion.

You have to remember that it is exactly for this that we hold risk workshops: this final criticism applies to the alternative techniques I mentioned earlier of DIY plus review or management interviews. You need to be alert to these issues if you take these approaches. Of course, if, like my colleague, you know it all already, there's no need.

I'll finish with an important cultural point here. In the UK it's not difficult to draw people out on what might go wrong and enjoy a faintly ghoulish discussion of the implications. The truth is that this is what makes risk workshops successful. But in other countries it might not be acceptable to own up to the possibility of things going wrong, especially in front of a local big cheese. In others the idea of chance (as opposed to the will of god or whatever) may be difficult to work with. You'll need to adapt to circumstances, but equally you'll need to stand firm on the core idea that risk management requires openness of both information and thought. If you cannot share freely what you know and what you think, it won't work.

Characterising your risk

Before we think about how to use the results of a risk identification exercise it's useful to consider what concepts we might use.

Concepts for characterising risk

In Chapter 1 we defined 'uncertainty' and 'risk'. In the previous section we discussed, without elaborating, list of risks and uncertainties (and issues and opportunities). What do we mean when we talk about 'a risk' or 'an uncertainty'. In linguistics, if you're interested, we have moved from the mass noun versions of risk and uncertainty to the count noun versions. The two versions have an important distinction:

- the mass noun definition of 'uncertainty' is, as I have noted before, the plain language, dictionary definition: the state of being uncertain, of not knowing
- the count noun definition of 'an uncertainty' needs to be a technical one: a specific aspect of the future that can be described, observed and measured.

An uncertainty is the number of inches of rain tomorrow. Another is whether or not Manchester United will win the Premier League next year.

This may seem pedantic. But I think the distinction is crucial for a proper discussion of how to do risk management. Perhaps this is best illustrated by the observation that to characterise an uncertain future requires a list of uncertainties. In other words, to make progress with risk management we need to identify a list of aspects of the future that can be measured. The trick is to do this in the right way, but we won't dwell on that here. Chapman and Ward solve this problem by talking about 'sources of uncertainty'.

There is a similar distinction between the mass noun, risk, and the count noun, a risk. ISO 31000 and most other documentation live with these concepts, seemingly without ever noticing the error.[5] So if 'risk' is the 'the effect of uncertainty,' then 'a risk' is 'an effect of an uncertainty.' Note how I have used the count form, and uncertainty, in this. It provides a useful distinction: if we think about risk we are already thinking about the effect; we are going to the next stage.

These definitions have no sense of upside or downside, of threat or opportunity. Some people like to make this distinction, but it's unnecessary, and unhelpful. You will not hear of threat again in this book, and opportunity is dealt with in a different guise. The effects of a risk might be good, or they might be bad. And in many cases they will be both.

If the organisation is a forum for all-embracing discussions about risk and what to do about it, we need a language. We need to be able to characterise the effect of uncertainty in some way, and also be able say that if we take a certain action the effect of uncertainty will be different, preferable, perhaps. The obvious way is to talk about 'risks' which may or may not happen, that is, effects which may or may not materialise. And if we want to do something about the risks we probably want to take steps which mean undesirable effects do not happen, or at least are less likely.

There are two big points in the previous paragraph. First, it implies that the way to characterise future uncertainty is with a list of risks. Secondly, we have introduced the idea of likelihood. The notion of risk lists – or risk registers - as the way to characterise risks is very common and has also come in for criticism, some justified and some not. The most fundamental criticism is that the future is far too complex to be described by any manageable list of risks. We will discuss problems with risk registers shortly.

The second point is the use of 'likelihood' as part of the characterisation of risk. Likelihood is a slightly evasive concept. Tracking the definitions tends to create circular trails involving the unhelpful 'chance' and the highly mathematical probability. However, experience shows that it is worth keeping the likelihood concept separate. The definition is along the lines of (my) likelihood (of risk X) is a qualitative expression of (my)

---

[5] It is indeed an error, not a stylistic quibble. If you insert the definition for 'risk' into all the sentences of the standard which contain the word, many do not make sense.

degree of belief (that risk X will happen). A number of points arise from this:

- We need to be clear what it is we are making a statement of likelihood about.
- Likelihood is a subjective, personal property, so in principle you need to say in whose opinion it is that the likelihood is high, low or whatever. It could also be the consensus opinion of a group or organisation.
- It is qualitative and arguably is simply a comparative concept: risk X is less likely to happen if we do Y.

This last point is the contrast with probability which is a *quantitative* expression of one's degree of belief as we shall come to in the next section. Probability is a highly mathematical concept supported by a deep theoretical foundation. But it is still subjective when we choose to apply it to real world problems. The usefulness of likelihood as part of risk management terminology is that it is informal, plain English[6] and easy to understand. Few people understand probability properly.

Finding better ways to articulate and communicate the uncertainty that a person or organisation faces is a perpetual and unresolved issue for me. I shall return to this point several times in this chapter and in others. It seems clear that for the time being we should embark on our exploration of uncertainty with the assumption that it will be a list of risks characterised, albeit vaguely, by expressions of likelihood and, ideally, probability. Let's see where this leads.

Qualitative schemes

Having explored the boundaries of how you might be impacted by uncertainty the next step is to start to draw up a profile of how this might play out. Risk modelling attempts to do this in a quantitative way but, before coming to this, there are other semi-quantitative or qualitative approaches which are sometimes useful and are in any case very common.

---

[6] Likelihood as used here should not be confused with its use in statistical inference, for example in maximum likelihood estimation, etc. I understand that in some languages the distinction between likelihood and probability cannot be articulated.

Very high	Very likely to happen	Probability over 75%
High	More likely than not to happen	Probability between 50% and 75%
Medium	May happen	Probability between 20% and 50%
Low	Unlikely to happen	Probability between 5% and 20%
Very low	Very unlikely to happen	Probability less than 5%

Figure 8 Likelihood categories

In Chapter 1 we touched on the idea of risk matrices, together with some illustrations. These are grids on which the risk issues are plotted according to a rough idea of their likelihood and impact. To do it properly you start by identifying suitable intervals of likelihood and impact. Say you want a 5x5 risk matrix. You identify five categories of likelihood in terms of probability, see Figure 8 for example.

You can do something similar with impact as illustrated in Figure 9. So if you know the probability of it happening is 10% and it will cost £1m you can plot it in the (Low,Medium) square of the risk matrix.

Very high	More than £10m
High	Between £2m and £10m
Medium	Between £80k and £400k
Low	Between £16k and £80k
Very low	Less than £16k

Figure 9 Impact categories

This is known as a qualitative scoring scheme. There is a list of reasons why this is a good idea.

- It looks simple.
- You can colour code it, for likelihood, for impact and for the elements of the risk matrix itself, red for high impacts and likelihoods, green for low ones so you get a diagonal pattern as illustrated in Chapter 1 (Figure 2); this recommends it to managers.
- You can do it quickly.
- You can cover several types of impact: financial (as above), schedule, reputational, safety and environmental and so on; each one can have its own table of descriptive material, the extent of media coverage for reputational impact and the like.
- You can do it with different assumptions about what risk management actions you are going to take so you can start to see the benefit of these actions.

Unfortunately there is also a rather compelling list of reasons why you might think carefully about this approach.

- It destroys information – if you know it is 30% probability of £1m just draw that on a chart, and if you are uncertain you could just draw it as a blob not a point.
- Many issues are not easy to represent in this way, for example, the same issue may materialise as a high probability of a low impact and a low probability of a high impact – this can be a line on a chart but is hard to represent on a matrix, you end up with one or the other and waste time agonising over which.
- Dealing with probabilities can be problematic as you cannot have a probability without an event and event risks are only one of four types of uncertainty listed previously (and you also need to decide whose probability it is as they are subjective, as we shall discuss extensively later).
- Inevitably people think in terms of high/medium/low without considering the precise details of the scoring scheme; that's why it's an attractive method, but also prone to inconsistency and systematic error.

- Many project managers are disappointed if they have no red risks so they like to have a tailored impact scale to remedy this; this is a peculiar idea and one that is inimical to consistency in an organisation.
- Too much effort is dedicated to scoring different sets of assumptions such as inherent versus controlled risk.

This latter point will be discussed in some detail shortly but schemes which require systematic consideration of the risk with and without certain controls detract from more important matters as we shall also see.

These criticisms have been aired by both Chapman and Ward[7] and Hubbard.[8] Chapman and Ward rechristen the risk matrices from PIDs (probability-impact diagrams) to PIGs (grids) as a mark of disrespect. Hubbard attributes the failure of risk management, no less, in large part to overuse of these, and similar scoring schemes.

In spite of these adverse comments such schemes can be useful to give an overview of the risk profile, especially when the different dimensions of impact are explored, but these methods have gained in usage far more than they should, partly because it is simple, partly because it makes for exciting-looking software and partly because it purports to provide measures for management.

One particularly egregious development arises from labelling the categories 1 to 5. Each cell in the risk matrix is then labelled as the product of the likelihood label and the impact label. This number, the product of two labels, is now regarded as a measure of the seriousness of the risk. It is hard to think of anything more inane, but many organisations do it.

If you do decide to pursue the qualitative approach, then one way to fill in the matrix is to do it in the workshop. It is generally not hard to build a consensus about the right scores for each item in the risk register. However, you should bear in mind that proper articulation of the risks is a job I have reserved for after the session so as to ensure it is done clearly and well. Plus, as I have already said, unless you are in the unusual position of having lots of time, it is generally better to use the time available to explore the uncertainties in more depth. So I am not a great fan of populating probability impact matrices in workshops. Of course, house

---

[7] *Op cit.*

[8] The Failure of Risk Management, Douglas W Hubbard, Wiley, 2009.

rules may require this and you need to have a slick patter to do it quickly and paper over the many conceptual cracks this implies.

I think a good alternative approach is to do it yourself. With a bit of experience you can process a list of risks quickly and consistently. After all it's a very inexact science and little of much importance hangs off the results! Don't forget you will have the chance to come back to this at the next review when the team can pick up any glaring errors. If you are getting round your OODA loop quickly, as you should, you ought to be able to validate your assumptions quite soon. Of course the same applies if you do decide to do it in a workshop.

As a final point on this, it's interesting how people seem to manage to prioritise risks quite happily into High, Medium or Low or whatever without the two-dimensional probability-impact crutch. They seem to be able to take both likelihood and impact into account in an assessment and I think this is an approach which could be pursued further as an efficient means of prioritising risks for attention.

Modelling your risk

One of the reasons I'm reluctant to spend too much time on qualitative methods is that it's often as easy to go straight to a full quantification and this is what I shall now discuss. One potential problem is that some hard-to-quantify aspects may get forgotten, but as long as you don't lose sight of this, quantification provides a much richer way to characterise your risk.

Probability

It is obviously desirable to be able to be able to paint your risk profile in numbers. This will enable the clearest possible view of the risk exposure and potential improvements through management actions. Whilst it is reasonably straightforward to quantify many impacts of risk occurring such as cost, delay, safety incidents, etc, it is more problematic to get a perspective on the relative likelihoods of the different possible impacts. In the previous section we mentioned probabilities without dwelling on their meaning and it is, of course probabilities that we use to quantify uncertainty. So now we need to spend a little time discussing what probability is and how it might help. I'm going to spend some time on this as, in my experience, people have some funny ideas about probability, even – shock! horror! – experienced risk managers, let alone their bosses.

Probability theory is a branch of mathematics which has been developed since the sixteenth and seventeenth centuries,[9] starting with the provision of a means of describing and deciding about games of chance. The central construct is to itemise all the ways the future might turn out (called a sample space in the jargon). An event is any subset of this list of items and we assign a number to each event. These numbers – or probabilities – have several properties:

- they are non-negative
- the probability of any event which is the combination of two mutually exclusive events is the sum of their probabilities
- the probability of the whole list of possible futures is 1.

So if you have a dice which you throw once there are 6 possible futures. You might have the probability of a 1, 2, 3, 4 or 5 being 10% and of 6 being 50%. The probabilities add to one. The probability of an odd number is 30% and of an even number is 70% (also adding to one). If you make the further assumption that the dice is perfectly symmetrical then the probability of each number is 1/6 and the probability of an odd number is 50%.

So far this is just a numbers game. The relevance to the real world is that if you throw your dice a large number of times the long-term ratio of the number of 1s, say, tends to a limit which satisfies the axioms of probability (the three bullet points above).

These axioms can be used to develop other results such as that the probability of throwing two 1s with two throws of a perfectly symmetrical dice is 1/36 (or 1% for the loaded dice I mentioned first). This development of probabilities to describe very large numbers of repetitions of a random process was described in some detail in my previous book.[10]

The only other concepts I want to mention here – because of their importance in the future development – is the idea of a random variable

---

[9] For a fascinating account of the history see Against the Gods: The Remarkable Story of Risk, Peter L Bernstein, Wiley, 1996.

[10] Estimating Risk: A Management Approach, Andy Garlick, Gower, 2007.

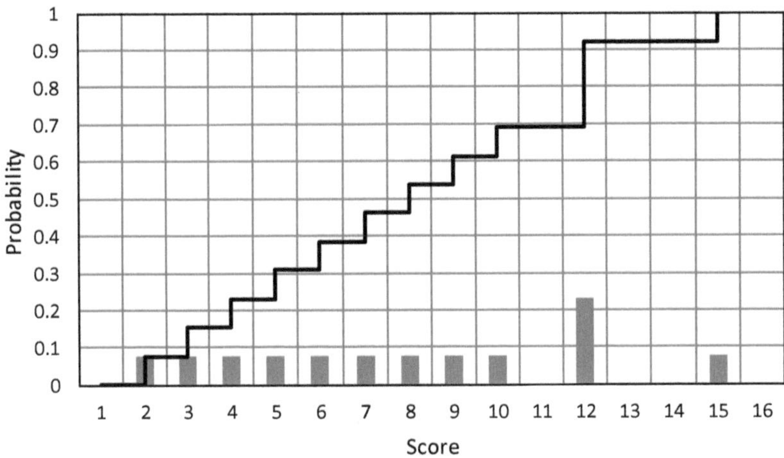

Figure 10 Histogram and cumulative probability distribution of the card draw random variable

and a cumulative probability distribution. A random variable is a number associated with each future (what we mathematicians call a real function on the sample space). If you draw a card from a pack you would have no difficulty scoring 2-10 but would have to adopt a convention for J, Q, K, A, say 12 for picture cards and 15 for the ace. The score, which is an example of a random variable, has a probability distribution (1/13 for each of 2-10 and 15, and 3/13 for 12). This can be drawn as a histogram but you can also draw a *cumulative probability distribution* as a series of steps, see Figure 10. At any point, the graph shows the probability that the score is less than that number. For example at 9.5 the cumulative probability is 8/13 (0.62).

There are only 11 values for the card draw score, so this is a discrete random variable. If you measure the time for a radioactive sample to emit a decay particle, this is a continuous random variable. If you have a million atoms each with a half-life of a million seconds, you might wait about a second on average – actually it would be 1.44 seconds as it happens. You can now draw a histogram based on intervals or smooth this to something called a *probability density function*. But you can also draw a cumulative probability distribution just as for a card draw. Instead being a series of steps it is now a smooth curve. Both are shown on Figure 11.

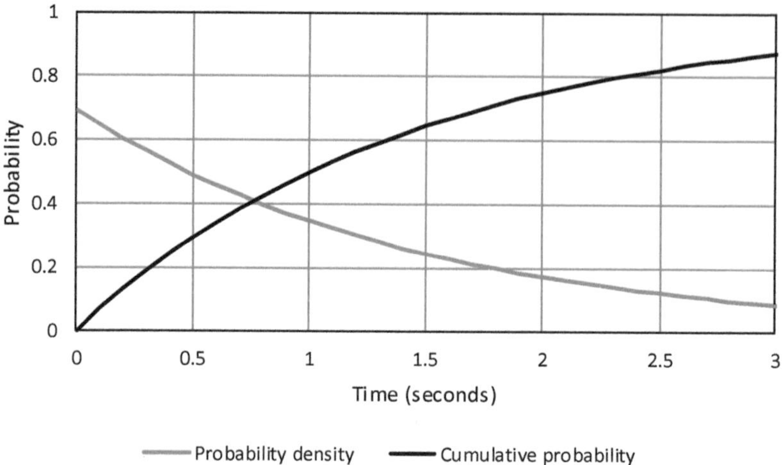

Figure 11 Probability density function and cumulative probability distribution of first atomic decay

If you measure the time until 10 particles are emitted, this is also a continuous random variable centred on 14.4 seconds (ten times the average for one emission). Now the probability density and cumulative probability functions have slightly different shapes as shown in Figure 12.

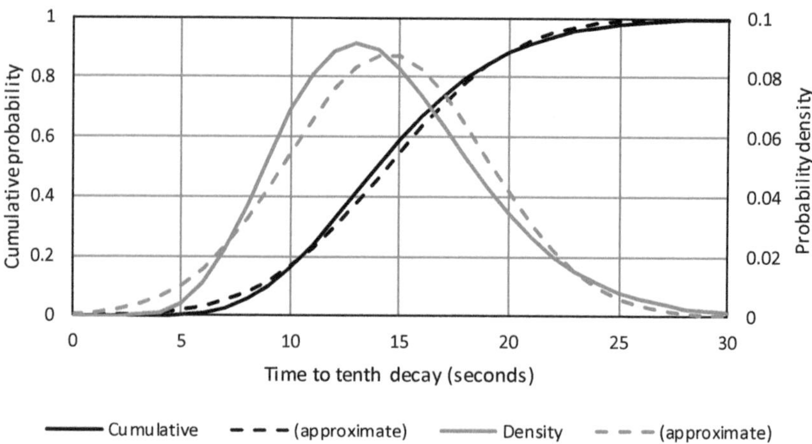

Figure 12 Probability density function and cumulative probability distribution of tenth atomic decay

You can ignore the dotted lines marked 'approximate' for the time being. The grey probability density function has a shape often known as a bell curve. However we shall avoid this type of presentation, mainly because few people really know what a probability density function is. The black cumulative probability distribution is known as an S-curve (for obvious reasons in the case of Figure 12). I warn you now that quantitative risk analysis is death by S-curves: they are a powerful and reasonably comprehensible tool.

There a few other common terms associated with random variables and probability distributions which are useful in risk management. I have summarised them in the box on the next page.

Now this kind of mathematical modelling is fine for atomic decay and playing poker, but what, you may ask, has it got to do with the success of my project or the departure of a charismatic CEO. The answer is not a lot seeing that we don't have anything remotely like a random process and we are subject to human whims rather than laws of nature. Yet we persist in using the mathematics of probability for characterising risk. How does that work?

There is in fact a justification for doing so, but not one that most people would recognise, and one that requires a considerable amount of spadework to put in place. A fuller description of decision-making and the role of probability is contained in Chapter 7, but the key features are as follows:

- Probabilities are fundamentally subjective, even where they describe random processes. This means that any statement of probability must include a mention of whose probability it is.
- If you are trying to make decisions under uncertainty and you wish to satisfy certain plausible 'rationality' criteria your decision must reflect the use of 'decision weights' on each version of the future that impinges on the decision and a quantitative measure of the attractiveness of the outcome if that future materialises. Specifically you should select that option which maximises the product of the decision weights and the attractiveness measures.
- If then you call the decision weights probabilities and the attractiveness measure utility you end up with a restatement of the classic decision rule under uncertainty of maximising expected utility. In

The three Ms: key probability terms

There are a number of important terms in probability which often get misused. Some people even think they can employ their own definitions, despite 300 years of rigorous mathematics.

1. **Mean** The mean of a probability distribution just signifies the probability-weighted mean. It is also called the *average* or *expected value*. The mean of the card scores is 8.08 and for the single atomic decay it is 1.44 seconds, as noted. Expected value is a really useful parameter in spite of its slightly confusing name: it is not really any more expected than anything else. But the expected value of a sum of random variables is the sum of their individual expected values. This is really useful where sums are relevant such as for money.
2. **Median** This is the value of a random value which is as likely as not to be exceeded. It is not necessarily equal to the mean. You can read it off the S-curve. For example, the median for the cards is 8 and for the single atomic decay is 1 second (why?). What the S-curve represents can be described as a set of confidence levels, P*n*. P20 is the value which has an 80% probability of being exceeded, and consequently a 20% probability of the random variable being less than P20. P80, a very popular parameter for some reason, is the opposite: you are 80% confident that the value is less than P80. The median is the P50.
3. **Mode** This is also known as the *most likely* value, that is, the location of the peak of the probability density function. It is not necessarily equal to the Mean or Median, though it is for symmetrical probability distributions. The mode of the cards is 12 and the single atomic decay is zero.

For a symmetrical distribution like the tenth atomic decay the three Ms are all (approximately) equal at 14.4 seconds. You can read more about probability in my previous book.[11]

[11] *Op cit.* Or someone else's if you must.

other words you should decide on your subjective probabilities and take the course of action which has the highest mean attractiveness (as defined in the three Ms box which defines the specialised, but useful, expected value term).

- So you can talk about probabilities for the non-random process situations you are trying to characterise, but you need to recognise that these probabilities are at a level of subjectively which is even more extended than for the dice throwing, atomic decay games. They are just arbitrary decision weights which you use to ensure you are rational under certain assumptions. These assumptions are described in Chapter 7 along with a discussion of why you might not want to go along with them and a description of circumstances in which 'irrational' decisions are made.

The probability game is pretty much the only one in town and we shall go along with it. The presence of theoretical shortcomings will not take away the need to make decisions, and we need to crack on with making them the best way we can. But we should not lose sight of what we are doing, and whether suspending rationality might be a better way forward – for more see Chapter 7.

So for the rest of this chapter, I am going to take the probability concept for granted as a way of characterising uncertainty.

Modelling inputs and outputs

The idea behind risk modelling is that you create a model linking inputs and outputs. Both the inputs and the outputs are uncertain, but you have the idea that you know something about the input uncertainties and the model will enable you to tell something about the output uncertainties. I described this in some detail in the previous book[12] and successive chapters dealt with different types of model, as listed in Figure 13.

Perhaps the simplest and most common of these models is the risk register with 4-point quantification of cost. The total cost is the sum of the costs incurred under each risk *plus a baseline cost estimate*. The 4-point quantification means that each risk has associated with it:

- a probability of something happening (the event)

---

[12] *Op cit.*

Context	Inputs	Nature of model	Outputs
Reliability and other binary models	Component failure probabilities	How system can fail, (eg fault tree)	System failure probabilities
Cost and other additive models	Component cost	Sum of costs	Total system cost
Time and programme	Activity durations, resource availability	Logic linked programme	Project duration and time to meet key milestones
Safety	Frequency of precursor events and escalation probabilities	How events can escalate (eg event tree)	Frequency of accidents
More general models	General parameters	Model of cause and effect (eg influence diagram)	Output risk

Figure 13 Typical risk model types

- the minimum cost impact if it does happen
- the most likely cost impact if it does happen and
- the maximum cost impact if it does happen

(which you might also call a 1+3 quantification).

In cases where there is no event, just a variability (see nature of uncertainty above) the probability is 100% and you have a 3-point quantification of the variability (which might include upside as well as downside relative to the baseline). The S-curve of a typical 4-point distribution is shown in Figure 14.

The baseline is very important to this sort of modelling. Typically it is a cost estimate put together assuming all goes well. If an event happens, it will generally be an adverse event which increases the cost relative to the baseline. However, this does not have to be the case, and, certainly where there is variability, the estimator may not insert the very best case into the baseline, so there may be scope for upside.

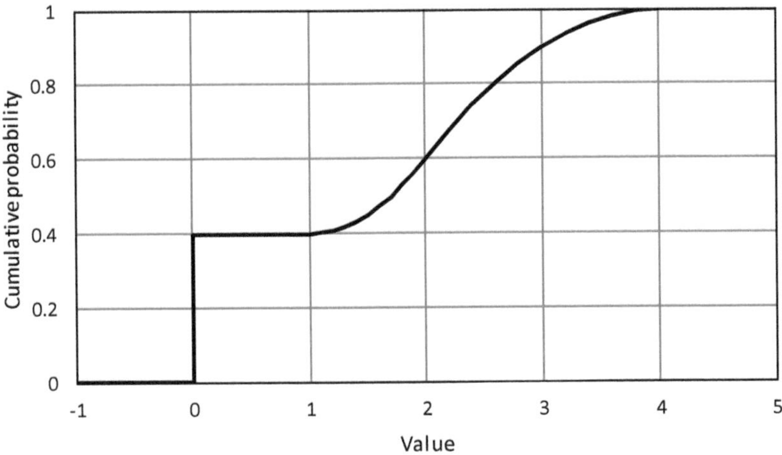

Figure 14 Typical 4-point quantification S-curve

Contrary to what is commonly accepted, neither uncertain nice events and upside variability constitute opportunity. An opportunity is where there is scope to do something different in the hope or expectation of a better outcome. As such it is a risk control measure which affects the risk profile, not a contributor to the risk profile. You will often see qualitative risk matrices extended to include 'opportunity' as a mirroring in the likelihood axis. This is not a good concept: it is essential to recognise that most opportunities are things that you do different, maybe entailing their own risks. It is a fact of life that we build plans and then look at the risk that the plans do not go as well as intended. There is an inbuilt preference for plans in which everything goes well with anything off-plan being downside. Opportunity is about changing the plan to be even better.

One of the stupider remarks you will come across with 4-point quantifications is "if it's 100% probability it's not a risk, it should be in baseline." Normally this is stupid for one of two reasons.

- In the case of events, you may be sure the event will happen, but if the estimator has not recognised it in the baseline, it needs to stay in the risk analysis until he has.
- Not all uncertainties are event-based risks, as noted earlier.

Expanding on the second point, some people are very wedded to the 4-point formulation, with probabilities less than 1, as a necessity for inputs whilst accepting smooth S-curves as the norm for outputs. This is not particularly sensible. If you think about a model with an S-curve output you can envisage that it contains models of contributory issues that successively break the model down into more detail. As it gets more detailed you will tend in some cases to move toward event-based components. But it is the smooth S-curve probability which is the norm and you have to get to something very detailed before events and discontinuities become evident. And after all, even a 4-point model has an S-curve, albeit one with a rather peculiar discontinuity (see Figure 14).

I think that in fact you could get by with either 2-point models for events (probability and impact) and 3-point models for variability (minimum, maximum and most likely).

What's more, a very useful simplification is where the most likely is equal to either the maximum or minimum. This is known as a fully-skewed triangle distribution and has a number of useful properties. Indeed in most cases, where there is both an event and the minimum is zero, then it should also be the most likely, otherwise the density function has some odd properties. Figure 15 shows the S-curve for such a risk with a 50% probability and a maximum impact of 10.

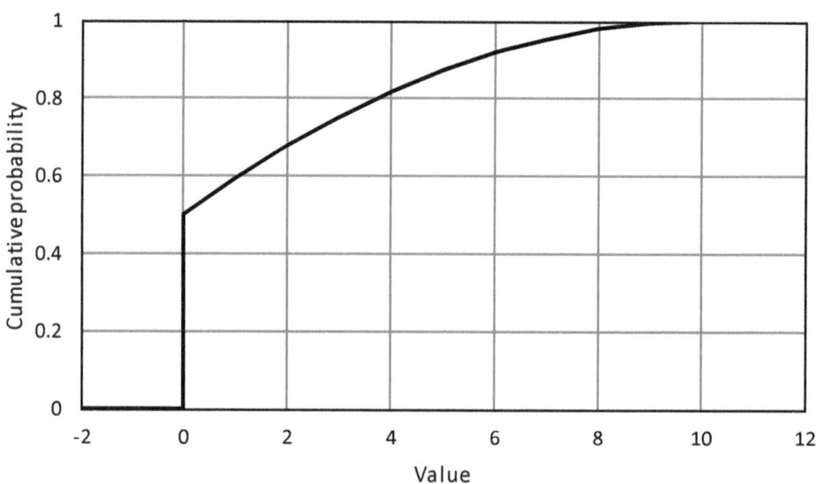

Figure 15 Fully skewed 4-point quantification

Neither Figure 14 nor Figure 15 show the probability density functions. This is because they contain infinite spikes representing the non-zero probability of a zero impact. Apart from that, the non-zero impact could be represented by a triangle with maximum at the most likely (or modal) position. In the case of Figure 15 this is at zero, also the minimum, giving the fully-skewed shape.

Where do the numbers come from for the models? Now is the time to say with great certainty that a risk workshop is not the place to put numbers on the risks. Quantification is definitely best left to a focussed and controllable group of relative experts who know what's involved and can be trusted to take a workmanlike approach – with your facilitation, of course. The alternative will most likely be a disastrous and uninformed debate which wastes everyone's time. The numbers represent some sort of consensus between those present. Specifically it will be *their* subjective probability distributions.

There is an idea that the best people to quantify are domain experts who are also calibrated. Domain expertise means they are in a good position to quantify impacts and calibration means they have a good appreciation of probability and can use it to express their confidence about propositions. Calibration can be measured and improved by reference to testing on a range of topics. For example you could ask people to answer a set of pub quiz questions, and to provide confidence levels for their answers. If they were well calibrated you would expect them to get 90% of the questions right in which they had expressed 90% confidence in their answers. I am not convinced of this. Firstly, it's far too difficult in most risk analysis situations to get people calibrated. Secondly, I have a residual feeling that there is only a remote connection between probabilistic literacy, if there is such a thing, and the subjective probabilities in most risk analyses. So I think that a much more pragmatic solution is an experienced facilitator.

For example, I was trying to quantify the uncertainty in production rates with a novel piling method and was told something like it might be 10% worse than the estimate in the worst case. "What? Even though you've never done it before?" "Oh, yes, definitely no slower than that!" Needless to say, I just put 50% in and I think it actually turned out worse than that. I think you need more than a bit of calibration to correct experts' overconfidence.

The next key point is what to assume about the risk controls during quantification. I've mentioned already that many organisations like to work out their risk exposure making multiple assumptions which might include:

- inherent risk – no controls at all, whatever that means
- risk with 'normal' or routine controls in place
- current risk – with the controls you actually have in place already
- target risk – risk with all the planned controls in place.

They like this because it provides some sort of justification for all this risk activity: you can see how much has been saved by reducing the risk. But my position is (a) obviously you should be doing it anyway and (b) that risk analysis and modelling is subjective enough as it is, so that it is pointless to spend time doing more than one risk analysis: just work it out for what you're planning to do. An exception to this is where you are trying to do a cost benefit analysis of a specific control.

Perhaps the most important factor to bear in mind during quantification is the possibility of dependence between the risks in the register. In the case of the 4-point formalism this might arise because the occurrence of the events is correlated or the impact if they do happen. The best way to deal with this is to explicitly model causality and effect. Some risk modelling packages allow you to insert a correlation coefficient, but it is not clear to most people what this means. I have never found the correlation tools useful and I think they detract from thinking about the mechanism which leads to dependence. Often it's better just to correlate fully and get a pessimistic result which frequently is in any case not unduly pessimistic.

Which brings me to how to calculate the model. The easiest and most common technique is *Monte Carlo*. This means simulating many futures using the input probability distributions and creating output probability distributions from the results. Packages in the form of spreadsheet add-ins are available to manage this. This was extensively covered in my previous book and I shall not repeat the ins and outs here .[13]

---

[13] *Op cit*, except to note that I now generally use the RiskAMP add-on tool which is very cheap and very efficient. You can find it on-line at riskamp.com. Its correlation tools are very weak which I regard as a good thing!

The discussion up to this point has focussed on the inputs to the model, but now we come to the model itself. The most straightforward type, the second item of Figure 13, is the additive cost risk model in which some form of quantification is applied to a list of risks, and the output is the sum of the inputs.

Risk modelling is more an art than a science. It does not make sense to model all the sources of uncertainty you have thought of, but this is what tends to happen in the additive risk register approach. Broadly speaking there is no point in modelling details which lie within the bounds of uncertainty of more important issues. This is expressed by Chapman and Ward[14] in their maxim that you should identify all the sources of uncertainty but model only a few.

There is a slight potential problem with this maxim if you have a baseline which is systematically optimistic. Although small individual risks may not have much impact their collective effect could be important. In many models the process of adding up the expected value of all the risks to get the expected value of the total is all the processing that happens. The other aspect of uncertainty, concerned with working out reasonable ranges within which the future might fall, gets lost. Both are important and the solution may be to consider the consistent neglect of small downside risks in the baseline as a single issue: call it optimism bias say! I think this is more plausible than believing that you can get a better, 'more accurate' number by having long lists of risks, all quantified. What happens is that the probabilities get stupidly small as the number increases, and the result bears no relationship to any 'reality' except to the extent that a senior manager looks at it and thinks it might be 'about right'. The issue of single point estimates for risk is important for bringing other information on board as part of the outside view (discussed shortly) and in creating forecasts, covered in Chapter 4.

The other issue with adding up lists of risks is that you can easily ignore the dependences we have just discussed. There is a powerful result in probability theory, the Central Limit Theorem, which tells you that the sum of a set of *independent* random variables is distributed approximately normally. You constantly see this in looking at Monte Carlo analyses of risk registers: you can do the sum in your risk list itself (see

---

[14] *Op cit.*

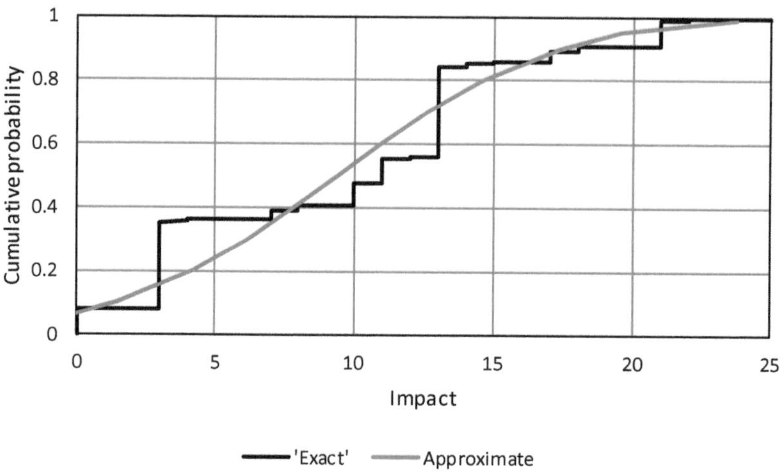

Figure 16 Approximate distribution from Central Limit Theorem

the box on page 75). These distributions often look unnaturally narrow and this is caused by the independence of the random variables. The way to explore this is to look for causal relationships between the variables, and modelling these will lead to broader and more credible distributions, by which I mean they better express the beliefs and judgement of the risk analyst and the experts she is consulting.

Figure 16 shows how the Central Limit Theorem works for four disparate risks which are actually 2-point quantifications: a probability and a single impact (the details are in the box). This discussion again underlines Chapman and Ward's point that it is only worth analysing the main sources of uncertainty. Because variance is a square measure (again as explained in the box) the width of the distribution, or what we are calling the range, is dominated by a few risks.

Finally mention of 'credible' distributions raises another issue. You sometimes come across analysts who think that with sufficient work you can create a long enough risk register and objective enough probabilities that you will have an 'accurate' risk estimate. Any shortcomings in the risk analysis are just down to laziness. This is an illusion. As I have emphasised a number of times, probabilities are just subjective decision weights. The terms 'accurate' or 'realistic' should be banned where risk analysis is concerned.

The Central Limit Theorem and 4-point estimation

If you have a set of independent random variables then, subject to certain assumptions about having enough and not being dominated by one or two, the sum is distributed approximately normally, that is, it is described by the classic bell curve also known as a Gaussian. In my previous book I coined the term 'direct method' for avoiding the Monte Carlo calculation. This is based on the mean of the sum being the sum of the mean and the variance of the sum being the variance of the mean.

(*Variance* is a standard statistical term and means the average of the square of the difference from the mean. It is a measure of the width of the distribution of a random variable, or, as I put it in the main text, the range. The variance is the square of the *standard deviation.*)

If you know the mean and the variance of the individual risks in the list you can add them up and draw the normal distribution that has the corresponding mean and variance. For the record if you have a risk with a 4-point quantification with parameters $(p, x_{Min}, x_{ML}, x_{Max})$, then the mean, m, and variance, v, are given by

$$m = pm_D$$

$$v = pv_D + p(1-p)m_D^2$$

where m_D and v_D are the mean and variance of the 3-point impact element which are given by

$$m_D = (x_{Min}+x_{ML}+x_{Max})/3$$

$$v_D = ((x_{Min}-x_{ML})^2+(x_{ML}-x_{Max})^2+(x_{Max}-x_{Min})^2)/36.$$

Go forth and calculate. The chart, which is taken from my previous book,[15] shows the results for the sum of four risks: (50%,10), (20%,8), (10%,4) and (80%,3). The approximate normal distribution shown has a mean of 9.4 and a standard deviation of 6.2. This underlines that the Central Limit Theorem applies whatever the shape of the contributing distributions, as does another example: the dotted lines in Figure 12 which show the normal approximation for the time until the tenth atomic decay. The approximation for the S-curve is quite good, but the skew in the density function is, of course, missed.

[15] *Op cit*, page 218.

Schedule risk

Another common approach to risk modelling is used for projects. A common dichotomy is to contrast project and business-as-usual organisations.[16] Given the rate at which things change, it's hard not to see everything as a project, with objectives to be achieved within a given budget and timescale, and it's schedule, of course, which has come to define what is special about projects. As a result, one of the more preposterous fads to have hit risk management in recent years is so-called QSRA, or quantified schedule risk analysis. The basis for this is a project schedule consisting of logic-linked tasks. Risks impact the schedule by affecting the duration of the various tasks and from this you can infer the probability distribution of the time at which the project will be completed, or intermediate milestones are met.

It's a simple idea, which is sometimes useful, but its incorporation into common practice far exceeds what is sensible. Some of the pitfalls are the following.

- Schedules for decent-sized projects run to tens of thousands of activities so a typical risk could impact many of them.
- Project planners generally do not put their schedules together to facilitate risk analysis, typically embedding many constraints so that the baseline programme looks OK, but such that it will not respond appropriately to the application of the risks.
- Planners often make some allowance for risk and uncertainty by extending activities with time risk allowances (TRAs). This generally causes confusion in sorting out whether the risk allowed for here is also included in the risk register or not and this is often conflated with commercial interpretations ofTRA: does it belong to the client or the contractor?
- When things go off-track the schedule may not be able to model the perturbed sequence of events properly. This may involve additional, contingent, activities, for example.
- Typically specialist software is used to link to the scheduling software. One example is Primavera Risk Analysis. PRA has an outmoded uncertainty model for risk analysis which causes endless problems for

[16] See for example Project Delivery in Business-As-Usual Organizations, Tim Carroll, Gower, 2006.

the analyst who is taking a sensible, but non-standard approach to risk modelling.

- Conversely the approach for which the software is designed may be misleading. For example, PRA encourages the comprehensive application of duration uncertainties to activities to produce histograms and tornado charts which are – conceivably – interesting, but serve little real purpose.

QSRA has become so widespread that it is frequently required by client project control personnel (another profession in which common practice is mistaken for good practice). As a result, many pointless exercises are undertaken which sometimes walk past the true nature of the risk which needs to be modelled. These exercises will often require substantial re-jigging of the programme to ensure the project logic can freely drive the end dates.

Alternatively, it may be necessary to prepare a dedicated programme for risk analysis. While in principle this may be as simple as chopping out the lowest level activities in the programme, leaving a smaller but higher-level programme, this is fraught with difficulties in terms of maintaining the logic. It is often not obvious how to maintain the correct behaviour when ten tasks are being shrunk into one along with their attendant logic structure.

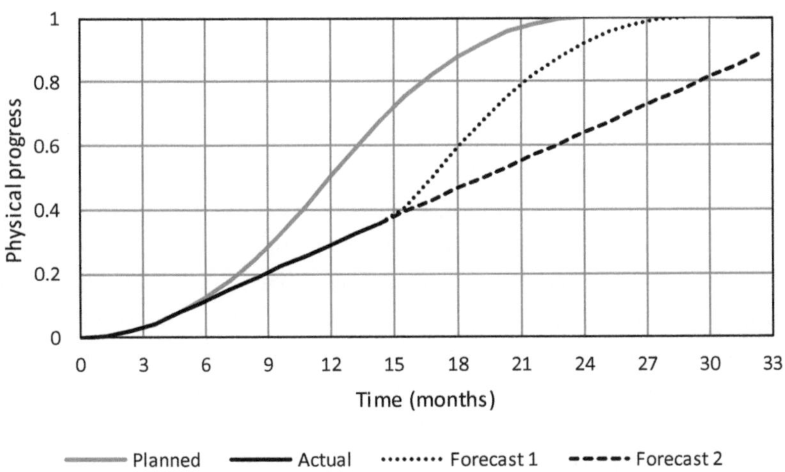

Figure 17 Progress to date and possible futures

A slightly different approach which I have found to be useful sometimes is based on the rate at which progress is made and is illustrated in Figure 17. This shows planned progress as a function of time and actual progress falling away. It also indicates two possible futures: the planner's forecast shows progress magically resuming at the originally planned rate; the risk analyst's forecast shows it carrying on as in the past. This diagram is emblematic of many projects. The risk model will aim to encompass these futures and others in a probabilistic way.

Rather than go into the details of each individual task, this technique allows you to concentrate on production where this is the most relevant factor: what are the risks to production, including for example, poor productivity, and what effect will they have on making progress overall.

This type of model can be implemented more directly than the activity duration method with its many activities and logic links. Typically you would use a spreadsheet model with Monte Carlo add-on rather than a cumbersome QSRA tool. The approach can be enhanced in various ways as required. For example you can look at the rate of progress by discipline (earthworks, concrete placement, mechanical and electrical, fitout, etc), depending on where the production issues are. And you can also start to build in some logic if one discipline cannot get too far ahead of another.

At this stage you may be asking how you measure progress in big projects, bearing in mind its disparate disciplines, contracts, work areas, etc. There is a standard approach called Earned Value which I shall describe in more detail in Chapter 4 when we get to forecasting and budgeting.

I'm not recommending this approach as a substitute for QSRA, just something that is sometimes more appropriate, depending on the nature of the project and the main types of uncertainty you want to take on board. The point I want to make here is that risk modelling is a skill which requires you to think first about what issues you have in your system, how these might play out, and then how you could put some quantities around it to paint the risk by numbers. This then leads you to a decision about how the model could be implemented. It may be that a list of 4-point risks is ideal; it may be that shaking the skeleton of a linked logic programme is just what is required. But this may well not be the case in which case you will be looking at a blank sheet of paper – or more likely an empty worksheet – which you will have to fill in with some pictures of cause and effect which lead to an Excel worksheet being populated with Monte Carlo functions.

If you do not do this you run the risk of embarking on some common practice, formulaic modelling, doing a duration uncertainty analysis on some massive programme with a big 'so what' about the resulting black box. Indeed if the answer's not bleeding obvious, it was probably not worth developing!

Plus remember the emphasis at this stage of Chapter 2 is on getting the risk modelling up and running. There will be plenty of time later on as we iterate through our OODeming loop to revisit the model and refine it. You will often find plans for grandiose, aspirational risk models being held up because of lack of data, unavailability of plans, inability to convene workshops or to get sensible answers out of them. In contrast I believe that at any point in time it should be possible to quantify the uncertainty about an undertaking with whatever information is available. I think that's a good aspiration to adhere to: there is generally no shortage of people to tell you you've got it wrong once you've put it together.

Ranges, point estimates and the outside view

In dealing with risk and uncertainty we are acknowledging that we do not know what the future holds. We want to recognise that there is a range of outcomes. You could argue that understanding the range of futures is the key objective of risk analysis. However in many applications of risk analysis we are interested in single numbers. This arises from the fact that we put together plans in which everything goes well and then recognise that some things will go badly and we need to make an allowance for that: add 10% 'contingency' to the budget, say. It's not really a contingency because you know you'll have to spend some or all or more of it. We address this in the context of forecasts in Chapter 4, but it is also important for risk analysis.

The notorious *optimism bias* is a case in point. When Gordon Brown was Chancellor, he got fed up with projects that cost a lot more than their sponsors had estimated. This was attributed to 'optimism bias' and Brown commissioned some research which provided average values to add to the sponsors' cost and duration estimates to provide a working value. These values varied, depending on the type of project, and were known as optimism bias, though they would have been better called optimism bias correction. They corrected the optimism built into the sponsors' plans without explicitly recognising that the optimism arose from not recognising the risk that might be present.

Associated with this was the idea of the inside and outside view of a project initially developed by Tversky and Kahneman (who had originally coined the term optimism bias and the related term *planning fallacy*) and promoted by Bent Flyvbjerg. Flyvbjerg[17] famously called forecasters fools and liars, inviting their clients to fire them, ask for their money back and even sue them. Risk analysts who, like it or not, are in the forecasting game should feel uncomfortable about this.

Notwithstanding these hazards, the inside view is that of the sponsor and perhaps her risk analyst who are biased in such a way as to understate the risks. The outside view is to look at other similar projects and get an estimate based on them. It was exactly this technique that led to the Treasury optimism bias correction factors. This in turn leads to the reference class forecasting technique of which optimism bias is an example. Reference class forecasting means using previous similar projects to create an estimate for your next one. This makes the tacit assumption that the risks that affected your previous projects will also affect your next one, and vice versa for those that didn't.

This approach is naturally an affront to risk analysts (and of course their employing sponsors) who think it is too crude. I was part of an exercise to try to replace this optimum bias with 'proper' risk analysis.[18] What this lacked though was a coherent technique which enables you to move from the point values of a reference class to the spread implicit in a risk model: the outside view is a great idea, but it doesn't necessarily tell you the range of outcomes.

While this is partly because there is no generally accepted technique, you can also argue at length over what comprises the reference class. For example, in carrying out a life expectancy risk analysis for myself, you might think my male relatives would form a good reference class. As it happens my father and both grandfathers all dropped dead at age 73 from

[17] Quality control and due diligence in project management: Getting decisions right by taking the outside view, International Journal of Project Management, 31(5), page 760, 2012. Available from www.sciencedirect.com/science/article/abs/pii/S026378631200138X

[18] Managing cost risk and uncertainty in infrastructure projects: Leading practice and improvement, Report from the Infrastructure Risk Group 2013, available from the website of the Institute of Risk Management, www.theirm.org.

bad hearts. Encouraging from the risk analysis point of view, but this is not necessarily what I want to hear. If I broaden the reference class I remember that my mother and both grandmothers all kept going well into their 90s, so I'm tempted to include them in the reference class.

One way to meet the implied challenge is to note that the 'inside view' risk analysis and 'outside view' reference class are different types of data shaping our knowledge of the future. There is a statistical inference technique called Bayesian updating which, as its name implies, takes a risk model and updates it in light of further data. In this case the risk model could be the starting point and the reference class observations are the updating data. The essential point is that the probabilities in the risk model are taken as unknown, and in fact have their own probability distribution. (It is essential to the Bayesian approach that your degree of believe in a statistical hypothesis is represented by a probability – probabilities of probabilities if you must.) It's an amusing calculation to choose a mortality model and then update your prior beliefs with the different potential reference classes: I get an extra ten years of life expectancy by adding in the women. But this is too formulaic, the risk analyst needs to look into the details of cause and effect.

What risks happened in the reference class? What lessons have been learned? What risks did not happen? What new risks are there. What is needed is an analysis of the consistency of the risk model with the experience that the reference class represents. If this consistency can be demonstrated, then the risk model is good to go, and the risk of being called a fool or a liar or of getting sued should be under control.

Notwithstanding the details, there are some key points which come out of this discussion.

- You need to recognise that there is a systematic optimism error in plans which assume all goes well.
- As well as this optimism bias there is an uncertainty range arising from the fact that we do not know what will go wrong and to what extent.
- We need to bear both of these factors in mind in risk modelling.
- You need to remember the outside view as well as the inside view. If your analysis is inconsistent with what has been experienced on other similar activities you either need a good reason why, or you need to make it consistent, which amounts to the same thing.

General risk modelling

This section has discussed cost and schedule risk modelling in some detail. It also provides some pointers to other types of risk modelling which are described in my previous book.[19] What I would like to be able to do here is to provide you with a universal method for constructing risk models. Unfortunately I can't. I have had, reluctantly, to accept that the best way to collate all the information about risk and uncertainty is to use a risk register, but what do you do with it?

I need to enlarge on the risk register point. Over the years as I've worked with them, I've felt increasingly unhappy. Every time I sit down to create or edit a risk register I do it with a sense of gloom because I know I'll spend hours agonising over the best way to do it, in spite of which I shall end up knowing I've failed. Arguably it's the risk register that is the real worm at the heart of risk management and I shall not be happy until I've found a better way to articulate the risk profile, either better registers or something else.

First let's take a slight deviation. Matthew Leitch has a novel take on risk management which he calls "working in uncertainty." On his website of that name[20] you can discover his approach. Its main characteristic is an emphasis on actually managing risk rather than jumping though the ERM[21] hoops. Matthew rightly identifies that all this activity can actually detract from working towards a better future in the face of uncertainty. His approach starts with the natural controls we all routinely put in place for risk and then invites us to think about what more we could do. He asks us to change our language and to adopt a much more natural approach.

Leitch has a page[22] devoted to a critique of the risk register concept. He makes many valid points and he also provides some suggestions as to what to do about characterising risk for quantification. But this book is about my experience and while I'm on a similar hymn sheet to Leitch, it's not quite the same one. I'm not so opposed to the 'risk'-type jargon and I'm not so against the idea of listing the controls against the risks.

---

[19] *Op cit*, Chapters 8 and 14.

[20] www.workinginuncertainty.co.uk.

[21] Enterprise risk management, a term which encapsulates the management fad aspect of risk and common practice risk management.

[22] http://www.workinginuncertainty.co.uk/risk_listing.shtml

So what's wrong with risk registers? Here are some symptoms.

It's difficult to decide what the risk event should be. Each event has a string of causes and a string of consequences. It's not obvious which one should sit in the centre of the bow tie and any attempt to do this is bound to be arbitrary. Some people find the bow tie concept very useful, and indeed it helps, but that's as far as it goes. The more general concept of a linked fault and event tree helps more, at least conceptually, but is only part of the story. The extent to which the trees are inconveniently linked across the system tells you something about the problem.

Even when you've decided, it's really hard to articulate it accurately so everyone understands and it's comprehensive enough to cover all the things that aren't covered by other risks. When reviewing a risk register people will gladly say, "well if you read it, it doesn't cover that," (so they don't have to quantify 'that'), blithely ignoring that 'that' has now disappeared into the ether and may never return.

Risk registers grow indefinitely as you identify more and more features which are significant enough not to be forgotten about. This conflicts directly with managers' wishes to keep it simple, stupid, "I can't manage more than 5/10/30 things at a time." As they grow it is increasingly difficult to ensure the risks don't overlap.

Risks defy categorisation. Risk standards are full of well-meaning advice on how to do this. Clients love to ask for their risk broken down by geographical area, system, subcontractor, or whatever. You can humour them – even when you know they are about to embark on the ultimate folly of divvying up risk contingencies accordingly – but it doesn't generally make much sense.

What's going on here? What you are trying to do is characterise the possible future states of a system. The risk register approach tries to do this by categorising these states in terms of whether or not a specific event (the risk register line item, or more specifically, the risk event) occurs in that state. Put that way, it doesn't sound a very good idea. If you think more directly about the components of the system you can see how the problems come about. Each component can be categorised several ways (as above) and each component can be broken down indefinitely. The system model becomes a series of hierarchies, each of which can be decomposed to an effectively infinite level of detail. You start thinking fractally. Each element of the model can interact with other elements of the hierarchies in ways which are quite unstructured. I think the principal driver of the risk register problem is the fact that such models do not in fact aggregate.

I'll try to explain what I mean by this. Imagine an influence diagram. Each node reflects a characteristic or component of the system and the influences cause changes to propagate between the nodes. If there is an element of randomness or uncertainty in the node states then this will create risks which may propagate deterministically over the remainder of the network, or, more likely, will propagate in a way which creates additional randomness. It's a big influence diagram so to make sense of it you try to group the nodes into supernodes. Each supernode has more complex behaviour reflecting all the nodes and influences within it. And it is linked to the other supernodes by 'superinfluences': complex pipelines which aggregate all the influences linking the various nodes in each supernode. This approach and its obvious generalisations seem like the only way to make progress in characterising risk. But it just doesn't work. There seems to be no way in general which enables you to make high level sense of the low-level detail. The devil really is in the detail. Understanding risk means understanding the minutiae of the system, not just looking at generic risk categories.

I spent quite a lot of time some years ago thinking about an object-oriented approach to risk analysis. During this work I developed the concept of risk maps which aim to build these influence diagrams in systematic and practical ways. I think they help, but I have to admit they are not the whole answer.

So risk in a system is about simple things happening in the microdetail of the system. This is what makes complex systems so risky in general. The safety risk paradigm which years ago promoted the risk register / risk process works because it gets down to the right level of detail in a fairly simple system. These simple things propagate right across the system affecting the important outputs. You cannot aggregate and hope to understand the risks. It's important to say that I'm not trying to be esoteric here. All I want to do is itemise the big uncertainties that exist when we embark on a project in such a way that:

- it's a comprehensive list (of the big uncertainties defined in some way)
- it's comprehensible
- it's capable of being built into a risk model which can be quantified.

You might call this the intelligent risk register. It should include not just the risks but interdependences between them, not just the risk but the relevant significant means of control. It is not extended just for completeness, but it does pick out the risk hotspots. The intelligent risk register is more like the narrative on risk that might be part of a prospectus for a financial deal.

Let's just have a look at one example. You want to know the cost risk for a project. The estimated cost of the project is built up on a cost breakdown structure. You can easily define a comprehensive list of risks by defining each one to be the uncertainty in one of the elements of the cost breakdown structure. But the first real risk you write down is inflation. That affects all of them. The next one is delay. Well that's caused by a host of other risks, not characterised by the cost uncertainties. The next might be bankruptcy. But you've got ten key subcontractors. Can you treat them all the same (like we generally do)? And so on.

All of this shows risk workshops in a good light. They may be crude, but what they are really good at is picking out individual strands from the neurotic mess that is the risk model. So let's stop pretending risk workshops are a way to write down all the risks. They do something different but just as valuable: they start to give us an insight into the sort of things that matter for that business or organisation or project. Since they are not comprehensive they are not necessarily much good for creating a risk model, but they do help us craft the model alongside other more comprehensive, but less insightful, techniques. Anything that gets us away from the idea of quantifying each line of a risk register with its Central Limit Theorem pitfalls can't be bad.

Then what? Working with your intelligent risk register, you can map out the sources of uncertainty you want to model initially, reflect on how they may play out, figure out how that might be quantified and start to build the model. You need to avoid formulaic approaches. One advantage to this is that the answers to questions which seek to drill down should naturally come out, or, if not, reveal a good reason why. I find this technique works with clients, even if I cannot give a prescription for how to do it. Which may be a good thing!

RISK DECISIONS

It's a truism that risk management is all about the decisions you take; it's only they that change things. But I think this is overstated. The key thing is to understand your uncertainties and how they might play out over time. When you've done that the decisions are generally no-brainers. Perhaps that is one reason why decision theory has a low profile in risk management.

What's more, the decisions you take will depend on your attitude to risk. This attitude will provide guidance about how to make risk decisions which will reduce the need for detailed analysis. Your individual risk attitude is discussed in the next chapter and I come to the organisational risk attitude in Chapter 5.

As a result, I do not have much to say about this here. In some ways this is a cop out as natural risk management involves taking decisions constantly. But the point I want to emphasise to all natural risk managers is that there is a simple picture which ought to be incorporated as the headline in all risk attitudes, but rarely is. The simple picture is that we take downside risks because the rewards are worth it. These rewards might be the reduction of another risk. For example, a contractor might take the risk of bidding a project at a price that risks not making a profit. The contractor takes this risk to reduce the risk of not having any work.

Thus, the decision depends on our assessed likelihood of the risk materialising. As explained earlier, the 'rational' way to do this is to use subjective probabilities. Because these subjective probabilities are decision weights there is no great scientific truth involved. We decide to take the risk because we think it is worth it: the risk is not weighted sufficiently to decide otherwise.

You need to come to terms with this slightly unwelcome truth.

Many years ago I was involved in a debate about whether it was possible for a steam explosion to happen if a molten nuclear reactor core fell into a pool of water. The potential impact was a very rapid conversion of the water to steam and a pressure wave which might destroy the containment building of the reactor leading to a massive release of radioactive material into the environment. Many experiments seeking to replicate the possible effects were carried out, but it did not prove possible to rule out a powerful explosion, unlikely as it seemed. There was debate as to whether the probability was one in a hundred, one in ten thousand or one in a million. In normal probability terms this was a fundamentally meaningless debate. The fact that reactors continued in operation might have been interpreted as implying a decision weight of around, say, one in ten thousand or less. But in truth the decision was one which amounted to a view that the evidence allowed a decision weight of this order, nothing more scientific than that.

There is an enormous body of knowledge on making decisions in the face of risk and uncertainty. I have given a broad overview of this in Chapter 7, which in spite of being a broad overview, is very lengthy. This covers:

- how you ought to decide, in ideal circumstances, that is, how to decide 'rationally'
- how people actually decide, that is, how they are 'irrational'
- how you might decide practically, that is make decisions that are good enough in the circumstances, that is, using 'bounded irrationality'.

I think the risk manager should be familiar with this material and the underpinning arguments, including why you might put quotes around 'rational'. Outside Chapter 7, I have preferred to use the term *coherent* which carries less emotional baggage (except for economists for whom the accusation of incoherence is the greatest insult). The overall lesson from Chapter 7 is you need to aim to quantify the risk using probabilities. That is why it is described in such great detail in this chapter. But you also need to recognise the pitfalls of this approach. This means adopting a toolbox approach with heuristics and apparently arbitrary prescriptions.

I will describe this in more detail in the relevant section of Chapter 5 which deals with the attitude to risk, and which can apply equally to the organisation and the individual.

Beyond this, there are a couple of tools in the toolbox which might appear to contradict the idea that the decision criterion is to take risk if the ensuring benefit appears sufficient:

- precautionary principle
- risk appetite.

Precautionary principle

This is the idea that you want to be extra careful about taking risk. It is particularly applied in the safety and environmental fields, and especially in regulatory or compliance contexts. Regulation is a specialist topic, not covered in detail in this book. It is different because you are not making decisions about your risk, but other people's. It is natural that in these circumstances you will want to be precautionary; that's the purpose of regulation.

For example, it is a requirement in UK workplace safety legislation that risks be reduced to a level that is as low as reasonably practicable. This precautionary wording was interpreted long ago in the courts as meaning that there should be a gross disproportion between the costs of further risk reduction and the value of this reduction. As a decision criterion this means that you have to use a very high disutility for adverse health and safety outcomes in taking risk reduction decisions.

So far so good; this fits in with the picture of maximising expected utility, albeit in a 'grossly disproportionate' sense, but further guidance issued by the Health and Safety Executive places limits of 'tolerability' on the risk of death of individuals both in the workplace and as members of the public affected by an employer's activities. From a mathematical perspective the decision weight has become infinite.

This needs a little disaggregation. Firstly, in safety risk we are often dealing with situations where the randomness paradigm is more appropriate than is generally the case in organisational risk management. We have statistics about the prevalence of fatal accidents in the construction industry, hospitals, etc. We have enough information to be able to estimate how much more likely a fall from height is if there is no handrail, or an MRSA infection if immigration controls mean there are no cleaners. Perhaps we can convince ourselves (probably more than we ought) that we have reasonably accurate risk estimates. In that case the idea of decision weights goes away.

In fact, the decision criterion here is nothing to do with uncertainty. It is an ethical position that it is unacceptable to have people whose risk from a specific source is greater than some value. It is assumed you can calculate the risk (based on randomness principles) and take a deterministic decision based on social consensus. It is possible that the costs of achieving this ethical objective are completely disproportionate to any practical value of the benefit, but our starting point is that this is not germane to the decision. We might also note that the limits on individual risk do not, for example, apply to soldiers on active service. This raises interesting ethical points about what risks we are prepared to tolerate.

Risk appetite

The concepts just discussed have been extended into the non-safety risk context. You will sometimes hear a level of business risk described as 'intolerable'. You will see risk matrices coloured in with red at the top right with an imperative to make sure that such risks are mitigated to a more acceptable colour. From this has grown the concept of risk appetite which sometimes has associated with it the idea that not only do you have to put up with some risk, but that you actually need to, and your appetite will guide you to the right level.

This is nonsense. The basic premise for individuals and organisations is that they will have to take risk as the lesser of two evils, based on an assessment of the full risk picture. You have to navigate between the risks of pricing yourself out of work and of pricing at a loss, between the risk of investing in a potential new product and of having an outdated product portfolio no-one wants to buy, of alienating customers with a provocative advertisement and having no customers with a boring one. These are the risks you have to eat, but – as a generalisation – you have no 'appetite' for them.

These risk decisions are generally made with no ethical dimension, though of course in business you are never entirely free of the spectre of your workforce (and you) being out of work with no means of support for their families. Or maybe your neighbours suffer from your pollution. But the starting point should always be the maximisation of expected utility. You can add the complexity later.

Of course it may be that to implement your strategy you might want to limit the risks that are taken on board in the lower levels of the organisation. It is here that red risks might look a bit inedible. But really the message should not be 'no red risks' but 'no red risks without asking me'.

The idea of the risk appetite has become mixed in with risk attitude and KRIs and we shall return to this in more detail in Chapters 4 and 5.

In summary then, where the decision is not bleeding obvious, your starting point should be to develop subjective probabilities and maximise your expected utility. These are simply code words for ensuring the reward outweighs the risk. Then you can apply your toolbox and worry about compliance, doing the right thing and so on. I aim to codify this in Chapter 5.

NATURAL RISK PERFORMANCE MEASUREMENT AND REVIEW

One of the premises of this book is that the best way to start thinking about risk management is to build on the natural way we have approached risk and uncertainty over thousands of years. This is an almost unconscious approach in which we take on board at least some of the ways an uncertain future might play out and take sensible steps to limit the downsides, create opportunities we can exploit, and so on.

The first step we might take in improving this is to try to be more comprehensive in thinking about the sources of uncertainty. This has been the main topic of this chapter, and I have developed it far beyond what the casual natural risk manager could envisage. Nonetheless the point remains that a systematic approach to identifying the risks and what can be done about them is at the core of successful management. What is also core is to maintain an awareness of the situation so that you can adapt your plan to what you see: the observe and orient stages of the OODA loop. But whilst you can envisage natural risk managers maybe writing down a list of things that might happen, and even recording possible contingency plans, they don't generally convene formal risk reviews and prepare formal risk performance reports for consideration at them. This is the transition from the natural to the managerial which is the topic of later chapters.

So the question arises of whether it is ever right not to make this transition and deal with everything at the natural level. Take me as an example. I have run my little business for a number of years with no risk register, no risk mitigation plan and no risk reviews. Given my specialist topic, you might regard this as highly hypocritical, but I would argue it's just not necessary. When I read Nassim Nicholas Taleb's book[23] on resilience and beyond, I was pleased to see that I was more or less running my life on antifragile lines. I like to think risk is adequately inculcated in the way I do things. I spent five minutes over breakfast this morning thinking about my data security and, as a result, have an action to take when I'm back in the office which closes out one potential loophole.

My daughter has a more complicated business life involving bars and restaurants. She's a natural risk manager too, but it's hard to argue she wouldn't benefit from a more managerial approach, if she had time for it. In fact entrepreneurs tend to be natural risk managers and indeed risk management lies at the core of their attitude. They recognise that the risks they run could blow up on them at any moment.

The natural approach would be to keep a constant, mindful measurement and review processes going. You would make a mental note of what is happening, what the emerging issues are, how they might escalate and what can be done about them. Maybe you would glance at your risk model from time to time, but ideally you would not need to – you would know what it contains anyway. In doing this you would be constantly aware of the importance of risk conversations with people in your business and with stakeholders. Incessant risk conversations are a key element of natural risk management.

This is complicated by the need to keep control of a coherent risk management plan. It's not just about stopping risks materialising, it's about changing the plan if they do. Returning to the military analogy of Chapter 1, a good risk strategy needs von Moltke's system of expedients so you can respond effectively to what happens at first contact with the enemy. Natural risk management is more challenging than you, or the entrepreneur, may think.

So you need to question whether there is more you could do to reduce the chance of your risk blowing up. And the more complex your activities the more the answer to that question is yes, providing it can be done in a helpful way.

This means there are two factors which push people and organisations to a more explicit managerial approach:

- greater size and complexity of the challenges future uncertainty poses

---

[23] Antifragile: How to Live in a World We Don't Understand, Nassim Nicholas Taleb, Allen Lane, 2012.

- less comfort with risk and risk taking in organisations which have a managerial rather than entrepreneurial culture (which is most of them).

The challenge for the manager who wants to keep things natural is to make sure their affairs don't get too complicated. Or put another way, to recognise when they are too complex to manage naturally. I'll tell my daughter when she has time off from her risk conversations.

WHERE NEXT?

This chapter has primarily been about how to think about and deal with the risk and uncertainty issues you face. It has not dealt with explicitly organisational issues, though the presence of the organisation was felt in terms of a certain necessary formality which we shall enlarge on in Chapter 4.

The discussion was based on a management loop model designed to ensure the approach to risk adapts to changing circumstances whether internally or externally driven. Inevitably perhaps, by far the most extensive part of this chapter has been concerned with gaining an understanding of the uncertainties, their implications and the impact of the actions which could potentially be taken to deal with them. This is the deciding/planning element of the loop. By contrast, acting/doing, observing/measuring and orienting/reviewing are covered fairly briefly, mainly because they are pretty self-evident in nature at the natural level.

Deciding/planning for risk is generally a very sophisticated activity. It introduces probability, a highly mathematical concept, and then relegates it to the status of a subjective decision weight. The theory of decisions in the face of uncertainty is extensive in terms both of how you should take decisions, how people actually do take decisions and what is a good pragmatic approach. Most importantly, the uncertainties surrounding any given enterprise are very complex and it is easy to get bogged down in this. Chapman and Ward's encomium[24] to identify all sources of uncertainty but model a few is sensible, but not necessarily easy to implement or to provide a prescription for. It is also difficult

[24] *Op cit.*

when we choose baselines that are very optimistic so that the many, relatively trivial, unmodeled sources may collectively be important.

This explains the apparent imbalance in this chapter. But we are still left with a challenge which I think remains largely unsolved. How best to communicate the risk model? Without a doubt a risk register is a very poor communication tool. I say this in spite of having been asked to waste forests by providing a copy for the Board, or whoever else, a thousand times. I know very well that they do not look at it beyond the first few items, let alone gain a comprehensive understanding of their risk exposure. I believe that part of improved risk management is an easily understood common picture of the risk profile and the key determining factors. Only then can the team work together to improve it. I have put many years of thought into this without, as yet, coming up with a killer idea, either for analysis or communication.

The prospects for resolving this are not good. Whilst it is relatively easy to present a cost plan which can be drilled down into in many different ways, the same is not true of a project programme. It's the case that you can take a programme with tens of thousands of activities and define rolled up activities which show you in broad terms what sort of thing will happen when. But it much harder to understand the underlying rationale. Printouts of high level programmes do not show the logic links for the simple reason that they operate at the lower levels and are very complex. As a result, it is very difficult, as I mentioned earlier, to get a decent programme for your QSRA model, and it requires, of course, a great deal of poking around in the entrails as befits this voodoo activity. It's interesting that many project managers generally still work with pdfs of Gantt charts rather than *.xer* files of the programme. Maybe solving this problem will provide a lead for risk modelling which suffers from very similar difficulties.

This discussion builds on our conclusions in Chapter 1 to suggest that there are three key steps you can take to improve risk management.

- **Reduce complexity** Chapter 1 mentioned that a structure of management loops enables organisations to be more modular and allows business units to be self-managing. Obviously you need to make sure they fit together coherently which is a significant challenge, but it's a step in the right direction. These governance issues are discussed in Chapter 5.

- **Improve the culture** You can aim have everyone in the organisation more risk aware, more comfortable with uncertainty and better at taking decisions concerning what to do about it. This is what I shall come to next in Chapter 3.
- **Make it explicitly managerial** This is what I described in Chapter 1, completing the management loops in a formal way, but driven by a minimalist approach rather than the full ISO 31000 panoply which we now see as common practice. The key to this is no risk management processes, just risk tools. I take this up again in Chapter 4.

Chapter 3

Tools for risk culture

Meeting the challenges of organisations and the people in them

The previous chapter described an approach to risk management which did not in essence depend on any organisational context. The idea was that it would apply to you as an individual, your family life, the business you work in, the political party you campaign for and so on. It applies to organisations but it does not address itself to the specific challenges that risk management in organisations presents.

We start dealing with those challenges here by looking at the issues which arise from the key characteristic of organisations: they are collections of people, each with their own perspectives, ways of thinking and objectives, but all directed, we hope, at achieving a set of common objectives. In the next chapter we shall move on from this people-centred view to look at the process and system requirements that organisations create.

The way future uncertainty is dealt with by an organisation depends on the *behaviour* of its people, that is, their decisions, actions, communications, investments, and so on. This behaviour arises from something we can call *culture* which is the aggregation of people's values, beliefs, attitudes, knowledge and understanding. If we know something about the culture, we can begin to predict the behaviour. If we can change the culture, we can expect to change the behaviour.

This behaviour-culture paradigm provides a basis for analysing the people aspect of risk management in organisations. It hardly needs to be said that this is not a field in which hard results are available. This would not be a realistic aspiration, but we are also faced with a lack of a common understanding on what we should try to achieve.

In this book I have taken the starting point that to avoid some of the pitfalls of common practice risk management we need an approach that is as natural as possible, building on the instinctive ways that people and organisations manage risk. Not only is this more natural, but it also allows faster, more agile adaptation to changing circumstances. This places the emphasis on a high level of risk awareness and coherent risk decision making, criteria we shall return to in more detail. But if you read Erik Banks's book[1] on risk culture you will find that it is much more directed to achieving a culture that ensures the prevailing risk management processes are adhered to. This is a completely different emphasis, albeit an important one.

As a result, the discussion here is much more exploratory and less definitive than in other parts of the book. There is still a lot of work to do but I believe that this is a key challenge for improving risk management as we de-emphasise the role of unembeddable process and reemphasise more natural approaches.

One aspect of risk management where the challenge has been largely met is safety. Our thinking on safety culture has advanced considerably over the last couple of decades so that considerable improvements in performance have been achieved and teams in which conversations about behavioural safety are the norm are now commonplace. We shall look at this as well as the recommendations made by Banks shortly, but first we start with one of the most significant contributions to our understanding of risk culture which is the report on the topic prepared by the Institute of Risk Management[2] (IRM).

Our review will therefore begin with a fairly full review of the IRM report, ending with a critical appraisal, before moving on to examine some of these other aspects and reaching overall conclusions.

---

[1] Risk Culture: A Practical Guide to Building and Strengthening the Fabric of Risk Management, Erik Banks, Palgrave Macmillan, 2012.

[2] Risk Culture: Resources for Practitioners, The Institute of Risk Management and Protiviti, 2012. Available from www.iia.org.uk/media/.../irm_risk_culture_-_resources_for_practitioners.pdf.

THE IRM AND RISK CULTURE

The IRM report is essentially a reader on risk culture. It covers a baffling array of models and assessment techniques without aiming to provide a single story. This is useful for the enquiring reader, but it is also very difficult to extract a coherent viewpoint. This can be quite frustrating as you struggle to see the relevance of some of the material.

In spite of this, the report does have some themes that are maintained throughout, the main one being the IRM risk culture aspects model. This comprises eight aspects which are useful prompts both for assessing risk culture and for seeking to improve it. We shall spend some time on these cultural aspects.

Before coming to this we need to worry over some definitions, particularly how they work for individuals and for the organisation as a whole.

The IRM briefly mention the so-called ABC model: in which culture arises from repeated behaviour and behaviour is shaped by attitude. To make this work they define attitude as

> *"the chosen position adopted by an individual or group to a given situation, influenced by perception,"*

behaviour as

> *"external observable actions, including decisions, processes, communications, etc"*

and culture as

> *"the values, beliefs, knowledge and understanding, shared by a group of people with a common purpose."*

I think this approach needs some adjustment. It's unclear what a 'chosen position' is supposed to be or why we need to add 'influenced by perception' to the definition. It's not clear that a decision or a process is an 'observable action'. It is clear that there is more to culture than things that are shared. What makes it interesting is that most organisations run *in spite of* differences in individual values, beliefs, knowledge and understanding.

As you will have gathered from the preamble, I prefer a much simpler BC model where behaviour, as for IRM, is what is observable, what you can see, essentially what people say and what they do. And culture is all the stuff that shapes this behaviour and, again, I have already lumped 'attitude' in with this. In this picture, decisions lurk uneasily between culture and behaviour, not really being part of either, but, like the IRM, we'll regard them as part of behaviour.

In fact, I'm not going to provide definitions at this stage as there are other sources to review.

What is interesting about this is the contrasting macro and micro scales. To test the culture of an organisation we aim to define some high-level characteristics that we can measure and attempt to manage. But culture is in fact the aggregation of values, knowledge, etc of individuals although we are unsure how to aggregate them in a practical way. The situation is potentially analogous to attempting to understand the behaviour of a gas where statistical mechanical modelling of individual molecules can lead us to a thermodynamic macro-understanding. The only trouble with this concept is that one rogue trader can bring down a bank by unwisely deciding to cover up his losses, hoping to recoup them in further trading. An individual, human preference, when faced with a number of unattractive options, is to choose that option which carries some faint hope of survival. This can have significant organisational consequences. Risk culture is not easy.

Risk culture and individuals

What can you measure in individuals that reflects on their attitude to risk? Here are three things described by the IRM. They consist of consultant-style charts that need little explanation.

Risk predisposition

This is said to be determined by two aspects of personality:

- spontaneous and challenging versus organised, systematic and compliant
- cautious, pessimistic and anxious versus optimistic, resilient and fearless.

From this you can develop a 'compass' with nine types of risk predisposition, including the undifferentiated 'typical' group. This is all shown in Figure 18.

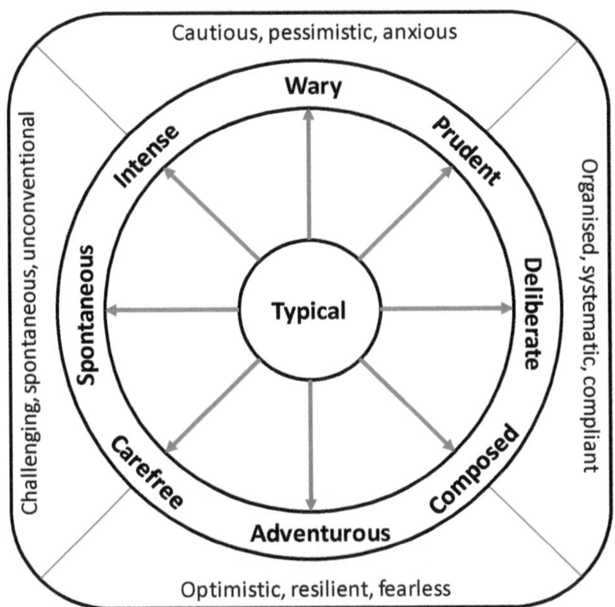

Figure 18 The Risk Type Compass[3]

This can be mapped onto a single dimensional risk tolerance scale, moving from top to bottom. Interestingly the best place for you – or your people – to be in an uncertain world is probably 'composed', meaning organised and optimistic.

Ethical and moral disposition

This can be assessed through various techniques, but the IRM emphasises Moral DNA profiling[4] which looks at ten moral values (including courage, prudence, trust, fairness, honesty) to arrive at a score for three ethical consciences (obedience, care and reason). These vary with age and environment (home versus work) which indicates they may not be the ethical anchors which you might expect or want.

The focus of this assessment is the quality of judgements and decisions. Needless to say, the moral high ground is seen as the place to be to do this best.

---

[3] Trade mark and product of Psychological Consultancy Ltd, www.psychological-consultancy.com.

[4] See more at moraldna.org.

Social predisposition

The cultural theory of risk, as developed by Douglas and Wildavsky, provides a social explanation of our perceptions of risk and preferences for how it should be controlled. These perceptions are shaped by our position in the so-called grid-group matrix. High grid means we are subject to strong social hierarchies and high group means we belong to and work as part of a larger group. Based on this you can develop four prototypical attitudes to risk management.

- **Fatalist/Pragmatist** The future is highly uncertain. Therefore strategic planning is not beneficial and all you can do is react as circumstances change.
- **Hierarchist/Manager** Risk experts are needed to help in assessing how much risk to take on and whether there is an appropriate reward balancing the risk.
- **Individualist/Maximiser** Risk provides opportunities to accrue profits. Therefore large risks should be accepted if the gains they offer are sufficiently rewarding.
- **Egalitarian/Conservator** Avoiding losses is more important than improving profits. Therefore it is best to avoid, control or mitigate risks.

What is interesting about this is that all four of these attitudes are seen as useful, at least in the account I have given so far, even though the theory was developed to explain, and even justify, competition or conflict between groups. This creates an interesting challenge for the manager.

Organisational culture – the double-S

The IRM report takes the reasonable view that "people make the place," and so building on the social and psychometric measures associated with the individual risk predispositions of the previous section makes sense as part of exploring the organisational risk culture. All the charts there could be developed as scattergrams, bar charts, organisational footprints or whatever. You might look for a balanced social predisposition, a high ethical disposition and a prudent accounting department, but an adventurous product development team.

However there is more to the organisation's risk culture than this, and the first point to make is that the risk culture is a facet of the organisation's culture overall. It makes sense to explore this first and then think about those aspects of this culture that has a particular bearing on risk management.

The study of organisational culture is a well-developed discipline and the IRM reports some of the findings in terms of the language of culture, the existence of hidden cultures and subcultures, the impact of strong and weak cultures, how this is all affected by social and national cultures and so on. The levers for changing culture are also reasonably well understood. These academic foundations are available to develop our understanding of the risk culture in an organisation and how to manage it.

One starting point is to examine the double-S location of your organisation: sociability versus solidarity. Highly social organisations have a people focus with people working for each other spontaneously. High solidarity organisations have a task focus with common tasks, shared goals and mutual benefits.

Based on this you can develop four organisational styles: communal, mercenary, fragmented and networked. Each of these is seen as having strengths and weaknesses from the risk management viewpoint.

The IRM cultural aspects

Building on this, but more specifically, you come to the IRM eight aspects model:

- Tone at the top
  - leadership (linked to solidarity)
  - dealing with bad news (linked to sociability)
- Governance
  - accountability (solidarity)
  - transparency (solidarity)
- Decisions
  - informed risk decisions (solidarity)
  - reward (sociability)
- Competence
  - resources (solidarity)
  - skills (sociability).

It is unclear from the report how the cultural aspects were developed, but we can accept that they are the outcome of considerable work and provide a good framework for thinking about how we influence the risk culture. Specifically, unlike some of the other concepts introduced so far, the IRM risk cultural aspects model is more than just a descriptor because it is unambivalent that an improved risk culture is represent by an improvement in any of the eight aspects.

The cultural aspects provide a useful tool to assess your risk culture and this is described in full in Appendices 1 and 6 of the IRM report.

Attending to solidarity

The IRM report contains separate chapters on 'building solidarity' and 'building sociability'. This implies that to manage your risk culture you need to be high on both elements of the double-S, essentially moving towards a communal culture. As I noted, it is more complicated than this and the IRM cultural aspects provide the signposts. What you have to do is make sure your risk culture is both matched to the organisational culture and effective. The IRM makes the assumption that the solidarity aspects can be improved by making changes to the risk system:

> *"This section assumes that risk culture is an outcome influenced by the risk system. However, equally it can be said that in practice the relationship is tightly coupled and that risk culture influences the nature of risk governance processes and frameworks. We will demonstrate that risk culture needs to be managed or monitored so that it can support the risk governance system, otherwise it risks distorting the system."*

This statement is somewhat Delphic and, to the extent it can be understood, it is not aligned with the philosophy of this book, where our starting point is to rely on the risk culture to help us get things right *without* the support of process. However I'll let this ride for the time being and we shall have a closer look at how the IRM see this relationship. This amounts to a programme for each of the five solidarity aspects as follows.

- **Risk leadership** Leaders should:
  - articulate how the organisation can most effectively balance risk taking and value creation
  - articulate expectations with regard to risk management
  - reinforce the risk strategy and culture in any communication

  - explicitly define the desired risk culture and values
  - establish a top-down process for risk, capital allocation and strategy to maximise shareholder returns
  - set risk-related objectives and challenge the status quo.
- **Accountability** is part of governance for which the IRM prescribes:
  - a clear escalation process in line with the risk appetite framework
  - clarity as to who (or which committee) makes specific decisions and how they are documented/recorded
  - a common currency for risk exposure
  - a committee structure
  - appropriate policies, standards, boundaries, triggers, decision templates, etc
  - a clear mandate for risk management and enforcement of the previous points.
- **Informed risk decisions** The IRM paradigm is one in which managers and boards demand information prior to making decisions. Of course this information should include risk information and, according to the IRM, "risk awareness becomes a 'watermark' though decision making in the sense that leaders are educated to demand and expect information on the risk implications of any strategic options or initiatives to provide a balanced business case." It's difficult to quarrel with this, but on the other hand it paints a slightly unnerving picture of managers who do not have an innate understanding of their risk exposure, but instead need to be fed information from underlings. Who carries the can when it goes wrong?
- **Resources** This is focussed on the risk team which is seen as key in the three lines of defence model. The IRM considers that it is important to have a respected second line, comprising the independent view of the risk managers.
- **Transparency** The IRM sees transparency as synonymous with having effective risk tools to communicate the risk profile and the action plan for risk. Among these are typically risk registers, risk appetite, a capital management framework, stress testing, scenario analysis and reporting tools.

Attending to sociability

Apart from a brief nod at the start of the relevant chapter, the IRM report abandons any pretence of developing a narrative against the three cultural aspects said to be concerned with sociability. Instead it presents its thoughts against four headings as follows.

- **Risk disclosure** – escalation and reporting of risk events. It is essential that we take the learning opportunities offered by all events and we need a process to do. There are cultural barriers in persuading people to report what has gone wrong and we need to recognise that there are different types of event ranging from the classic safety accident or trader loss, through near misses where no serious impact was actually experienced, to the poor practices which might form the basis of whistleblowing. Openness and freedom from blame are essential indicators of a good risk culture.
- **Performance management and reward** If dealing with uncertainty is a managerial responsibility, it stands to reason that objectives should be set with risk in mind and payment schemes should reflect risk performance. The IRM report introduces a 'concern for risk' competence defined as, "ability to demonstrate a strong awareness of risk, how risk aggregates, how to communicate uncertainty effectively and to incorporate risk into management decision making." Specific attributes can be developed and incorporated into a performance assessment scheme. Likewise your pay might depend on how uncertainty crystallises, but in fact the IRM demonstrates a scheme which is about the actions you take to control risk. One very important objective here is to disincentivise the taking of too much risk to enhance short term performance.
- **Awareness and communication** This has two aspects, firstly the communication of the culture development programme, reinforced by a stakeholder influence plan and, secondly, getting better awareness of risk and risk management itself, for example by links to the organisation's values.
- **Learning and development** Yes, it's a good idea to train people in risk. As part of this the report defines another competence – 'risk' – as, "awareness of the impact of uncertainty on decision making and understand the importance of evaluating risks as part of decision making. Ability to weigh up alternative strategies, considering short term and long-term implications as well the balancing of risk and reward. Maintaining a positive and open attitude to risk taking based on informed judgements. Willingness to take calculated risks in order

to achieve business benefits, whilst managing the risk issues involved. Willingness to challenge others and question positions being taken on risk."

Finally this part of the IRM report includes yet another risk culture dashboard, this time one that attempts to measure embedding. The seven aspects of this are sponsored, owned, decisive, communicated, integrated, valued and sustained.

Implementation guidance

The IRM report concludes with a sensible ten-point plan for implementing a risk culture improvement programme:

- evaluate the current culture
- consider how many risk cultures might be present
- analyse the findings of the evaluation
- define the desired future risk culture
- consider the consequences of the required culture change
- scope out a risk culture change programme
- risk assess the culture change programme
- plan how this will be developed in practice
- evaluate progress as the basis of continuous improvement
- recognise that the journey is as important as the destination.

This suggested programme is referenced to many of the other tools referred to in the report to support carrying out each stage and to identify the risks to what you are trying to achieve. It is recognised that culture change is a slow activity and the programme will accordingly be an extended one.

Critique

The IRM report is a major step forward but also a challenging read. I started off by describing it as a reader, not a textbook. As a result it covers considerable ground and what it has to say is not synthesised, and indeed in some areas is not internally consistent. The array of assessment tools and models is unnerving and commitment to the 'IRM risk cultural aspects model' is shaky. I found it was difficult to emerge from reading the report with a clear picture. But this comprehensive horizon-scanning is its strength, in spite of the challenges it presents.

More seriously from the viewpoint of this book, the IRM takes the ERM paradigm as the unique framework for good practice in risk management. Indeed, since the report, the IRM has branded itself as, "the leading body for professional Enterprise Risk Management." This means the role of risk culture is seen as a supporting one for the development of prescribed risk frameworks, risk systems, risk processes, risk appetites and all the other ERM paraphernalia. This book takes a different approach. It identifies a need for stronger risk culture exactly because of the shortcomings in traditional ERM with its embedding difficulties and abandonment of a natural approach to dealing with future uncertainty.

It's not surprising then, that much of what is in the report seems a little misdirected. There is an overemphasis on academic studies and consultant tools which in many cases are not specifically aimed at risk, and there is an overemphasis on ensuring compliance with elaborate and contrived risk management systems, with additional complexity arising from over-regulation. Correspondingly there is an under-emphasis on what I think are the core purposes of a good risk culture: the quality and prevalence of the understanding of risk throughout the organisation and the coherence of the decisions about risk. We'll return to this theme later in the chapter.

However, the cultural aspects model, and its associated assessment tool, are clearly useful, both to understand the current culture and to devise a programme to improve it. It does not go much beyond the usual risk maturity tools, something the report more or less admits, but that is not necessarily a criticism.

RISK CULTURE IN THE FINANCIAL INDUSTRY

Erik Banks's book[5] is very focussed on the financial sector, though, as he rightly points out, it should be applicable to all organisations. One aspect of this worth mentioning is that the treatment of risk culture is set against a background where there is a delusional belief that risk can be calculated,

---

[5] *Op cit*, earlier this chapter.

where rational decisions can be supported by data analysis, where capital reserves can be maintained against the worst downside. Our friend Nassim Nicholas Taleb puts the lie to this and this is what makes risk management interesting, and inspires this book.

Another consequence of the financial sector setting is that the treatment is very rooted in the convention that business managers do deals, make money, etc, and that there is a cadre of risk managers who keep them in check, either as policemen to be complied with or as valued colleagues offering sensible advice.

Banks's book also comes at risk culture from the point of view that it is there to ensure the risk processes are adhered to, compliance if you like, or more positively embedment. This is clear from the introductory chapter:

> *"This is in effect the idea of risk culture – a state where risk management processes are so intuitive and so embedded in the fabric of an institution that they exist subconsciously and are practiced as a matter of course."*

As I have noted a number of times, this is not the approach we are led to in this book. The issue I have highlighted is that common practice risk management is practically unembeddable and therefore we need to strengthen risk culture, not to embed risk processes but to make them unnecessary (in an ideal world). Nonetheless there is a lot to learn from Banks's train of thought.

He starts by defining risk culture in a more practical way than the IRM:

> *"We consider* risk culture to be *an internal sensibility, reflected in the thoughts and actions of all of an institution's employees, that reflects knowledge of, and respect for, risk."*

Banks goes on to define an assessment framework, an assessment of what goes wrong when risk culture is poor and a set of imperatives for improving it. The ten-point assessment framework is very similar to the eight IRM aspects, as shown in Figure 19.

There is a remarkable congruence between the two approaches and, what's more, it is predictable that the two additional areas in Banks's will be dealt with in some way within the IRM framework. The relationship between business managers and risk managers is so important within

Banks's key metrics		IRM cultural aspects
1.	Leadership tone on risk	Tone at the top – risk leadership
2.	Governance processes related to risk	Governance – accountability
3.	Transparency on risk strategy, appetite and exposures	Governance – transparency
4.	Resources devoted to risk management	Competence – risk resources
5.	Technical risk skills	Competence – risk skills
6.	Decision-making processes, timeliness and success	Decisions – informed risk decisions
7.	Business/risk management relationship	No direct equivalent
8.	Communications frequency and clarity	No direct equivalent
9.	Incentive mechanisms related to risk taking	Decisions – reward
10.	Risk-related surprises	Tone at the top – dealing with bad news

Figure 19 Assessment framework compared with IRM aspects

financial institutions that it has to be covered in detail. This is central to the three lines of defence paradigm which the IRM elaborates on as part of risk resources and building the risk function.

As I argue elsewhere, I think the emphasis on the three lines of defence is misplaced in a natural approach to risk management: business managers should not need someone else to tell them about and share responsibility for the risks they are running. This is the key function of any manager. But perhaps it is the only way to run a bank.

The other metric with no direct IRM equivalent is the frequency and clarity of communications. This is part of the *Governance – transparency* aspect and is a key element of attending to sociability (which, as I noted, has slightly deviated from the eight aspects model). Communication is also a key component of transparency and dealing with bad news.

It follows from this congruence between the models that the diagnoses, predictions and treatments are pretty similar and I will not reiterate them. Banks provides a helpful lexicon of the manifestations of a poor risk culture and their consequences which I reproduce here as Figure 20.

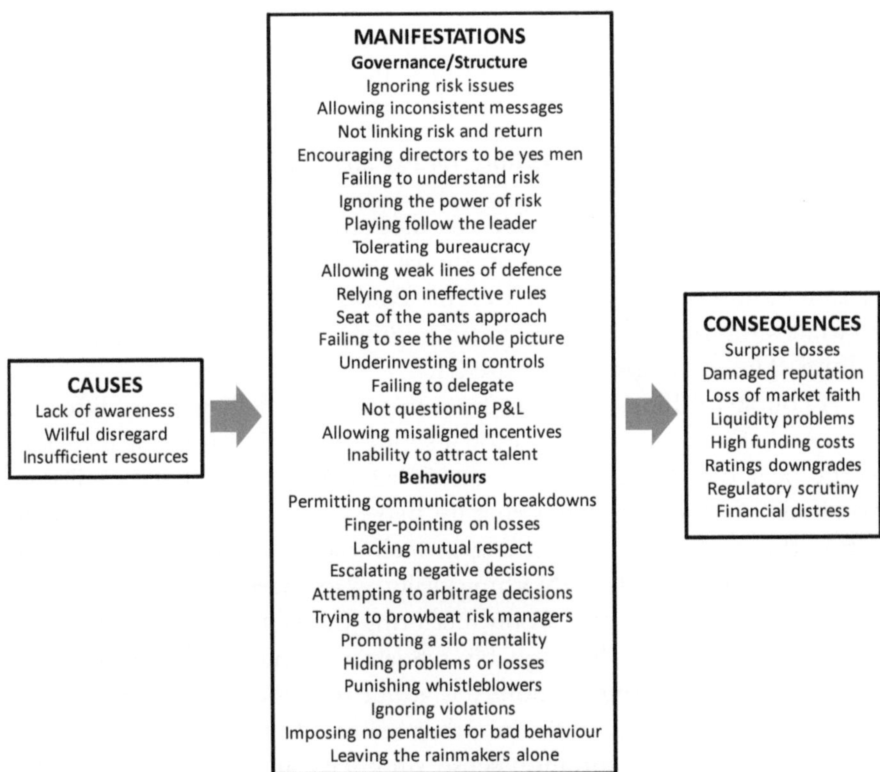

Figure 20 The causes, manifestations and consequences of a weak risk culture as identified by Banks

Structure and governance imperatives		Knowledge and behaviour imperatives	
1.	Define a common risk philosophy	8.	Establish the right tone from the top
2.	Formalise the risk appetite	9.	Ensure enough top-notch risk expertise
3.	Assign accountability	10.	Ensure proper business expertise
4.	Develop the correct incentives	11.	Reinforce the three Cs – communication, coordination, cooperation
5.	Build operational sophistication	12.	Demand common sense, simplicity and clarity
6.	Rotate personnel	13.	Build credibility
7.	Inject new blood from outside the firm	14.	Promote mutual respect
		15.	Develop a risk memory

Figure 21 Fifteen imperatives identified by Banks

I think most people would agree that these manifestations – poor behaviour as a result of poor culture in the BC model – are indicators that an organisation is in for a nasty risk event. Banks uses the structure of Figure 20 to develop fifteen imperatives for building and strengthening the risk culture. These are listed in Figure 21.

A couple of things stand out from this as potentially new or different. Firstly, what's this about operational sophistication? I think it is related to the dear old ISO 31000 principle that risk management is tailored. You have to create the right structure, make the risk function prominent, define the mandate clearly, invest in technology infrastructure and use relevant and reliable data. Nothing really to see here.

There is also an emphasis on recruiting the right people rather than training them. Again this probably reflects a financial industry perspective. Similarly building credibility is about the risk function being able to work constructively with the other teams. At first sight it's hard to object to demanding common sense, simplicity and clarity. This relates to the organisational design, rather than conversations about risk and uncertainty and how to deal with them. This is an important point as we shall discover shortly.

Overall then, Banks's account of how to improve the risk culture in the financial sector is more direct, less exploratory and easier to understand than the contents of the IRM report. On the other hand it does not add much and we can come to the same conclusions: that the emphasis on supporting the risk processes is very worthy, but the key, and underemphasised, aspect is the quality of risk awareness and the quality of risk decisions.

Another point worth considering is the organisational context. How much do you gain from a well-developed risk culture if your customers, your suppliers or your shareholders do not have a matching view of risk? Whilst you can regard credit risk (for customers) and performance risk (for suppliers) as just two more risks in the register, gaining an appreciation of these risks and managing them will require your understanding to spread into your stakeholders and, potentially, will need you to seek to influence their risk culture. This is a corollary of the approach we have taken in this book in which your organisation is part of a much bigger risk management system. We'll come back to this in the summary.

SAFETY CULTURE

There is one facet of risk where the impact of organisational culture is particularly well understood. Arguably safety culture can be regarded as a solved problem. What do we know about this?

Regulatory guidance

In fact, if you visit the website of the UK Health and Safety Executive you will have some difficulty finding the official view; you have to navigate to *Guidance/Topics/Human factors* and then *Organisational culture.* This page will inform you that the largest influences on safety culture are: management commitment and style, employee involvement, training and competence, communication, compliance with procedures and organisational learning. These are all well-rehearsed topics from the work we have reviewed already. The HSE also points you to different pages dealing with leadership, behavioural safety and learning organisations.

The link to behavioural safety is particularly interesting with its emphasis on the B part of the BC model rather than C for culture.

More detail is provided in further links, including a briefing note and an extract from the inspectors' toolkit. These documents are of unstated vintage, but it is noteworthy that most of the material with dates is at least 15 years old, supporting the assertion that safety culture is a solved problem.

The briefing note states that a healthy safety culture is one where there is:

- visible commitment to safety by management
- workforce participation and ownership of safety problems and solutions
- trust between shop floor and management
- good communications
- a competent workforce.

It provides a set of management actions which are asserted to help bring these desirable conditions about.

The inspectors' toolkit provides a definition, four key aspects and an assessment tool. The definition is similar to those we have seen already:

> *The safety culture of an organisation is the product of individual and group values, attitudes, perception, competencies, and patterns of behaviour that determine the commitment to, and the style and proficiency of an organisation's health and safety management.*

The key aspects are management commitment, visible management, good communications between all levels of employee and active employee participation. The assessment tool contains a number of questions to gauge each of management commitment, communication, employee involvement, training/information, motivation, compliance with procedures and learning organisation.

You get the picture. There is little here that we haven't already covered. You can read more of the same in an IOSH document.[6] Some of the emphasis is slightly different such as, in the safety case, an unfortunate us-and-them distinction between management and workforce (actually

---

[6] Promoting a positive culture: A guide to health and safety culture, 2015, available at www.iosh.co.uk/positiveculture.

unconducive to a good safety culture). There is also less emphasis on following the rules and more on risk awareness and being unafraid to stop work. This definitely is conducive to a good culture, as is the promotion of behavioural safety which enables both elements of BC to be addressed.

Perhaps the strongest point of the safety culture material is its simplicity. It has, of course, to be written to engage and influence a wide range of people and so we see documents, which, like the IOSH one just cited, are very easy to read, absorb and implement. This is a contrast with the wide-ranging and academic nature of the IRM report for more general risk management.

What is clear is that an emphasis on safety culture has brought about considerable improvements in safety performance, which means, in this case, reduction in risk. This is illustrated graphically in the HSE briefing note which shows a chart illustrating how

> *"over the last 60 years or so, industry first reduced accident rates by improving hardware (effective guards, safer equipment), then improved employee performance (selection and training, incentives and reward schemes) and then changed the way they manage and organise – especially by introducing safety management systems."*

Even in my own experience as a humble desk-bound consultant, there are clear and visible improvements in safety of construction sites and the like, including the visible commitment of managers. Maybe this is an illustration of the gains available for improving risk management more generally.

High reliability organisations

There are some fields of activity which are regarded as especially high risk. These include the highly complex, tightly coupled systems which are considered to lead inevitably to *normal accidents* in the terminology of Charles Perrow. Perrow's view is that such systems, difficult to understand, reacting on fast timescales and with potentially very serious consequences are inevitable accidents waiting to happen. According to

Richard Bookstaber this helps to explain the collapse of the financial system in 2008.[7]

Research shows that these systems actually have many fewer incidents than you would expect. Some of the activities which are the subject of this research include aircraft carrier operations, nuclear power stations and fire-fighting teams. You might raise your eyebrows at nuclear reactors being in this list, but this should not detract from the good practices which have been identified to deal with 'risks that emerge from the system' as the resilience engineers say. You can read Perrow's ideas about the alternative approach of de-concentrating in his chilling book[8] on how risk has become enhanced through corporate influence on governance, especially in the US. De-concentrating, or keeping things simple, also lies at the root of Bookstaber's ideas on cockroach risk management: cockroaches have a single control in their risk management plan: turning away from draughts.

There are several sets of principles which can be applied to create HROs. The one which appeals most to me is the idea of 'mindfulness' as set out by Weick and Sutcliffe in their very readable little book.[9] This has 5 elements:

- **don't simplify** – this runs directly counter to much management wisdom (often associated with the alleged inability of managers to understand anything complicated); the devil is indeed in the detail
- **attend to operations** – pay constant attention to what is going on, realising that just because things have gone OK up to now, this doesn't mean they will continue that way, in fact recognise the potential for overconfidence and complacency
- **focus on failure** – likewise keep a careful eye out for things going off track so that risks can be recognised and controlled early
- **build resilience capability** – in terms both of investing in capacity and making sure people will make the right decisions when the time arises

---

[7] A Demon of Our Own Design: Markets, Hedge Funds, and the Perils of Financial Innovation, Richard Bookstaber, Wiley, 2007.

[8] The Next Catastrophe: Reducing Our Vulnerabilities to Natural, Industrial, and Terrorist Disasters, Charles Perrow, Princeton, 2011.

[9] Managing the unexpected: Resilient performance in an age of uncertainty, Karl E Weick and Kathleen M Sutcliffe, 2nd edition, Jossey-Bass, 2007.

- **defer to expertise** – not formal superiority; the idea that decisions can migrate through the organisation to find the person best placed to make them.

The five principles (which I have reordered and restated in a way which makes sense to me) are pretty well established as a means of improving the safety of complex systems. But do they have much to offer organisational risk management, especially at the strategy risk end?

First, it's helpful to consider the idea of mindfulness itself, very similar to risk awareness in that you are constantly alert to the possibility of risk – and opportunity, for that matter – and work to reduce it. It's very important that risk becomes something that is the daily subject of managerial conversations and not just something that sits in a register to be processed every month or whatever. Managers need to set the example, inculcating a culture of challenge and risk awareness, and bringing risk and the way it is to be dealt with up in every discussion. This is part of dealing in a natural way with risk.

Incidentally one fallacy which Weick and Sutcliffe bring out is very important. Apparently the Columbia shuttle launch was permitted because previous strikes of detached items had been survived. These near misses were interpreted as proof of the robustness of the shuttle rather than an indication of a new hazard. Humans are quite good at using survival of previous crises as evidence that we will survive the next one – look no further than climate change – but it will always be a bad argument.

Another helpful anecdote from Weick and Sutcliffe concerns the bottle of champagne Wernher von Braun had sent to the engineer who caused a rocket failure though a maintenance error but owned up. That was something that really helped the programme. A great lesson for our own NHS and its whistle-blowers.

Secondly, refusing to oversimplify (whilst not over-complicating for the sake of it) is also a good discipline. It is often quite difficult to articulate how risks will play out, but it's necessary to do this and if we are good at it we will get fewer surprises. What's more, it's clearly important to develop a culture in which assumptions are questioned.

Thirdly, the analysis reinforces the importance of investing in resilience and antifragility: giving yourself options and spare capacity. This is something to factor into your risk attitude as we'll come to shortly. The message here is just the same: you need to invest in safety; you need to invest in resilience; you need to invest in risk management.

Finally, the idea of deferring to expertise is an interesting one. I'd broaden out the concept of passing decisions round the organisation to the more general idea of communication. It's important for the risk profile to be broadly shared and understood. For example, Kaplan and Mikes[10] carried out a review of corporate risk management in a number of companies, broken down into three risk categories:

- **Preventable risks** – routine, downside, undesirable internal risks which can be managed by prevention and the usual controls
- **Strategy risks** – which you take to achieve objectives, may have upside, and manage through the usual risk management formalism
- **External risks** – which are beyond the influence and control of the organisation; for them you need to identify and mitigate impact.

Their conclusion, especially for the strategy class is that more and more open communication is needed. Their survey showed a range of methods including independent review boards, a central team of trained facilitators and embedded risk experts. One of their case studies was JP Morgan who, embarrassingly, having been held up as a role model, ran into problems. This was tentatively attributed to failure to implement an otherwise effective risk management strategy throughout the organisation. More generally, while it may be difficult for many firms to buy into the idea that sometimes it may not be primarily the managers who make the key decisions – and of course, it's important that we recognise that it's managers, not risk managers who decide how to manage risk – organisations need to be alive to the risks of ignoring expert advice, or being closed to it. Again that was a major feature of both shuttle disasters.

Kaplan and Mikes are unequivocal in recommending that risk management advice needs to be a non-embedded, separate thread, 'effective risk management is also costly, because it has to be separate from existing strategy-oriented functions.' The resilience engineering discipline would not accept this. It seems there is a fundamental disagreement on

---

[10] Managing Risks: A New Framework, Robert S Kaplan and Anette Mikes, Harvard Business Review, June 2012. Available at hbr.org/2012/06/managing-risks-a-new-framework.

whether you can embed risk management properly in enterprising organisations.

The study of resilience engineering, safety culture and HROs has generated considerably more literature than the five bullet points of mindfulness. You can see more at the Resilience Engineering Association website[11] and Ashgate[12] has published a compilation of articles in which these principles are applied to the banking crisis.

PLAYING GAMES

We have already noticed that once you introduce people into risk management you have a fundamental rule change. You are no longer dealing with a set of randomly occurring events, but instead you are faced with a rational opponent intent on achieving his objectives, at the expense of yours where necessary. You move from decision theory to game theory. This is a fact of life for security risk analysts and managers but it is not a big feature for many risk practitioners who manage to forget it as a result.

You might remember that one of the reasons I introduced the OODA loop is its explicit adoption of competitive principles. The quicker you get round it, the faster you adapt, the more opportunities you have to mess with your opponent's mind, to confuse him, to put him off, to set him going in the wrong direction.

Even within an organisation, the presence of more than one person creates a predisposition for competition. We have already discussed the tension in banks between traders and business managers on one hand and risk managers on the other. The Infrastructure UK report on risk management[13] is unusual in that it also deals explicitly with another tension: that between project managers who game the risk process to get extra funds for their projects – and an easier life – and financial managers who aim to strip projects of unnecessary money so that more projects can be

---

[11] www.resilience-engineering-association.org

[12] Governance and Control of Financial Systems, Gunilla Sundstrom and Erich Hollnagel (Eds), Ashgate, now Routledge, 2011.

[13] Managing cost risk and uncertainty in infrastructure projects: Leading practice and improvement, Report from the Infrastructure Risk Group 2013, available from the website of the Institute of Risk Management, www.theirm.org.

pursued (or cash returned to shareholders, or higher executive bonuses or whatever).

This means that an important, but understated and under-investigated element of risk culture is a proclivity to play games, with individuals and with the system.

In fact, the IUK report identified six types of possible risk gaming.

- Project sponsors will tend to adopt assumptions which favour a project, which might be gaming (also known as 'strategic misrepresentation') or might be genuine optimism.
- Financial managers will tend to exert pressure to reduce risk contingencies irrespective of actual risk levels to address more short-term financial needs.
- Project managers will tend to overstate risk so as to secure and maintain large contingencies, for example to avoid the ignominy and career impacts of overspending.
- Contractors may price unrealistically in order to win work and then use commercial means to maintain their profits.
- Project managers may resist any activity that leads to reduced contingencies. This may include mitigation activity that could lead to reduced risk levels needing less contingency.
- Financial managers may exert pressure for reporting forecasts to be smooth and budget-compliant when – by definition – they will vary with time as the project progresses.

The IUK report goes on to say that all such gaming opportunities are increased for complex projects, undermining transparency and control where the risk is already more difficult to appreciate and manage. The report also lists a number of other cultural factors which affect risk management on large infrastructure projects.

IUK recommends a greater management focus on risk mitigation to deal with these gaming opportunities. Specifically it cited London Underground which sets tough targets for risk mitigation on its project managers whilst ring-fencing the contingency funds which are allocated. This is driven partly by the organisational perception that project managers are not being as aggressive as they could in reducing risk because they are afraid their contingency comfort blanket will be taken away. It is not entirely clear how this works but the point that is brought into sharp relief is that risk management becoming a project control matter is potentially very damaging for the risk culture. The financial management paraphernalia of budgets and contingencies has its own culture. This culture is one of hitting budgets, delivering earned value and keeping to schedule. Financial mangers do not want to hear about uncertainty, how costs may exceed P50 (half the time apparently!) or that risks might have happened that were not on the register.

We know that putting business first is inimical to the safety culture, indeed to safety. We know there is some kind of trade-off between profit and safety – though many safety types would argue this is not the case. But we understand – if you want to put it this way – that the only good profit is safe profit.

The relationship between the financial culture and the risk culture is more paradoxical in that the objectives of both are aligned: the aim is profit maximisation (or whatever the organisation is trying to achieve). The difference is in the perspective and the means. The financial culture is one of fixed numbers, control environments and, "don't tell me about your problems," or, "if you can't do it I'll find someone who can." Naturally this creates gaming and a host of other undesirable behaviours and outcomes, like stress, promotion of thick-skinned idiots and so on. The risk culture is about embracing uncertainty, understanding it and creating a shared plan to deal with it. The IUK report focusses on the technical interface between financial management and risk management but there is an arguably more important cultural disjunction which needs to be resolved.

One aspect of what needs resolution is the role of the risk numbers, especially probabilities. It's clear from my caricatured descriptions in the previous paragraphs that there are culturally distinct aspirations for risk quantification. Financial managers will say, "well, if you must recognise uncertainty, at least calculate the risk accurately so that we know what to put in the contingency pot." The risk analyst understands the impossibility of that, as rehearsed at length in the rest of this book, but, of course, tries to be as accommodating as he can. We need to be realistic about what is possible.

FROM RISK CULTURE TO RISK ATTITUDE

I promised a definition. Here it is.

- **Culture** is the *information* which people have in their heads which can be *learned* by others and affects the evolution and functioning of organisations.
- This **information** includes ideas, values, beliefs, behavioural strategies, perceptual models and organisational structure.
- It can be **learned** through imitation, observations and inference, interaction, discussion or teaching.
- **Risk culture** is that part of the *information* that relates to risk and uncertainty.

This definition is heavily based on that given in Chapter 7 in connection with bounded rationality. This is quite specific in equating culture to information, albeit of different sorts. The BC model is explicit in that culture affects organisational performance, though the middleman of individual behaviour is left out, including decisions.

This definition does not explicitly mention risk attitude either, though clearly the types of information listed would encompass the individual attitudes to risk that I have described earlier in this chapter.

But what about the organisational risk attitude? This will of course be shaped as a matter of policy, as we shall come to in Chapter 5, but it must also match with the organisation's risk culture, and the preceding discussion provides plenty of indicators as to how this might happen. For example:

- risk is taken seriously by everyone in the organisation
- risk will be dealt with comprehensively
- risk management requires (or not) independent oversight
- the existence of risk should not provide opportunities for gaming.

But thinking about the risk culture, especially for safety risk, has led us to more direct clues as to how we might shape an attitude to risk. For example:

- we will aim for a mindful approach, with its five practical elements

- we will take a precautionary approach
- we will aim to be resilient
- we will aim to be antifragile.

These attitudes conflict with the idea that you model all the risks and control them in line with the costs and benefits. They are, however, relevant to the risk attitude and they are instigated by cultural concerns. This means we can see that when we come to risk attitude as part of governance in Chapter 5, we will have two inputs: the formalised and analysed plans from Chapters 2 and 4 and the cultural drivers from this chapter. Organisational risk attitude is driven in part by the organisational risk culture, as well as *vice versa*.

The mindfulness concept has just been discussed in some detail, but we have not so far described resilience or, its prodigal brother, antifragility. The descriptions that follow are quite long and quite self-contained in that they pick up and repeat many of the strands discussed elsewhere in this book. This is particularly the case for antifragility. But I think it is important to have a full grasp of the concept as it provides a valuable – essential even – perspective on how an organisation can develop its attitude to risk. An attitude which will contain a massive counterbalance to relying on risk analysis.

Resilience

For some time, it's been a theme in meetings between risk management people and business continuity people that the world's ills can be solved by being resilient. Specifically, you don't need to worry about that boring old risk profile when resilience means you can deal with anything that's thrown at you, up to and including black swans.

This was put at its starkest by Michael Power[14] who has said we must look to the business continuity community to fix the mistakes of risk managers and accountants, particularly the latter:

[14] The risk management of nothing, Michael Power, 2009. Accounting, Organizations and Society, 34 (6-7). pp. 849-855.

> *"The problem goes much deeper: no less than an accounting style of knowing and a logic of auditability are responsible for restricting the development of a risk management which might have done a better job."*

This is reinforced by World Economic Forum reports on global risk which have identified resilience as the solution for big global risks which are external to you, even if you are a nation state. But it's often difficult to get a proper debate going on the relationship between resilience and risk management which is what I want to turn to here.

Let's start with what resilience is. This discussion is based on an analysis I did some years back of WEF reporting on global risk.[15] According to the WEF resilience is:

- **for an object**, the capacity for bouncing back faster after stress, enduring greater stresses and being disturbed less by a given amount of stress (an interestingly comparative definition which raises the question 'compared with what?')
- **for a system**, maintaining system function in the event of disturbance.

Thus for adaptive systems – like nations, but, by extension, any organisation – resilience is the capability to (1) adapt to changing contexts, (2) withstand sudden shocks and (3) recover to a desired equilibrium … while preserving the continuity of its operations. The WEF (supported by PwC) carried out an assessment exercise for national resilience which was based on 5Rs which they derive from this: robustness, redundancy, resourcefulness, response and recovery.

This suggests resilience is about dealing with the consequences of things happening rather than stopping them happening. This something of a piece of received wisdom about the difference between business continuity and risk management. However, I think this is rather artificial, not least because the future is not neatly partitioned into events with causes (whose probabilities are to be reduced) and effects (to be minimised). Possible futures are sequences, or rather complex networks, of cause and effect.

---

[15] Global Risks 2013, Eighth Edition, World Economic Forum, 2013. Available from www3.weforum.org/docs/WEF_GlobalRisks_Report_2013.pdf.

For example we could aim to be resilient against climate change. As part of that we might do a risk analysis of Thames Estuary flooding and decide on some criteria for when we will need to strengthen the Thames barrier. As a result we'll reduce the probability of flooding. Or we might aim to be resilient against flooding and build on high ground or buy sandbags.

The WEF definitions, with their references to 'stress', 'disturbance' and 'context', are vague about what the risks are which are materialising and it seems to me this is another characteristic of resilience (again as opposed to risk management with its risk identification/analysis drivers), that resilience can be achieved independently of what the threat is. This was an attractive idea and worth exploring further.

However detailed analysis of the resilient responses showed that many were quite specific to the risk. This is maybe not too surprising as the account takes a risk-centred approach. More subtly you can expect that resilience actions might cover several well-defined mini-risks, but only a general risk area. As I've just argued, the uncertain future is expressed as a complex network of cause and effect which exists at multiple scales. As you zoom out the structure takes on the characteristics of 'uncertainty' rather than individual 'risks', and the same applies to the controls.

Other actions, though, such as encryption and the use of TPM chips to identify hardware items, that is, we don't just identify users, we identify the devices they use, seem quite generic at least in the field of cyber risk.

Secondly, some of the actions had the generic, vague characteristics of the control in many risk registers. "Seek holistic insights and involve a range of stakeholders." Is that a world-saving resilient response or a platitudinous good thing that we can all fill a bit of space with in the absence of anything more concrete?

It's also interesting that the basic response to *adverse demographic changes* was promoting good old-fashioned economic growth. As an example, Canada had created growth through welcoming immigrants. Nice for Canada, nice for the immigrants, but is this really international collaboration, or is it just an inequality-increasing, competitiveness-centred, fragile action at the global scale?

However one action which several risks had in common is monitoring what's going on and questioning assumptions. They sound obvious (or should do now you're this far in), but are often little done in conventional risk management implementations. They are key principles in resilience engineering.

A common action between other risks was international co-operation and collaboration. Again this is a bit motherhood, but I just mentioned how the response to demographic issues is thought to be founded in atomised, nation-based competition. By contrast, enhancing our ability to build institutions to monitor, share, coordinate, find solutions to, and achieve agreement on global issues in an adaptive way is clearly a resilient response. Scoring this against the 5Rs would be a useful complement to assessing nations. The treatment of its economically failing members by the EU might be suitable cases in point.

From my point of view, this analysis was conclusive: we should see resilient, adaptive thinking as part of risk management; it doesn't replace it. But I would say this wouldn't I?

Antifragile

What's more, maybe this thinking should be antifragile. Antifragility[16] is the topic of Nassim Nicholas Taleb's last book in his trilogy on our uncertain world and how to deal with it. As the subtitle, *how to live in a world we don't understand*, makes clear, the problem is that we do not know what is going to happen. This is not just in the sense that it might be A or it might be B, with maybe some probability to reflect our belief as to which (what Taleb calls the ludic fallacy). Instead we have to come to terms with the fundamental unknowability of what might happen: the future is populated by black swans as well as all the things on our risk register. That's a fact we have to embrace, not ignore.

This means that Taleb has many harsh words for prediction or forecasting, especially where it is dressed up as scientific, especially social scientific, especially where it is economics and specially especially where it is promoted by Nobel prize winners in economics. As the sort of risk modelling this author does (and sells!) falls into this category of potential charlatanism, this something we need to discuss.

Taleb's main theme is that our modern world has committed too far to our ability to predict and this has made us fragile. Big government

---

[16] Antifragile: How to live in a world we don't understand, Nassim Nicholas Taleb, Allen Lane, 2012.

and big corporations have grossly overestimated their ability to control things for the better. This leads them to pursue paths in which the payoff is generally a small gain but occasionally a large and fatal loss. So the fragility of modernity leads to blow-ups such as – surprise, surprise – financial crises, and the scale of these crises is such that their instigators have to be bailed out with the consequent creation of moral hazard and a generally corrupt society in which the losses are not borne by those who are responsible for them.

Another fragility theme which runs throughout the book is iatrogenics: doctors are often bad for your health. This happens because (a) they are under a perceived obligation to do something and (b) what they do may not be very good for you. Taleb argues you should only see a doctor if you are seriously ill when there is a better chance that the upside will outweigh the downside.

This contains the seeds of the antidote to fragility which has two stages. First you need to be robust or resilient. This is the idea that, whatever happens, you can ride it out. As I have just described, this is starting to rise up the risk management agenda because of the perception that this enables you to manage risk without the inconvenience of listing the risks first. The idea of the resilient organisation is a vaguely defined article of faith in the business continuity industry, for example. But without stopping to debate this, Taleb takes us to the next stage of antifragility, the idea that we can manage our affairs so that we can benefit without understanding the world (in detail).

The essence of antifragility is that we don't bother with probabilities; instead we think about outcomes and, specifically, try to put ourselves into a position where there are downsides – perhaps many of them – which don't hurt us much together with large upsides which will make us rich, happy or free. It is an investment strategy based on this which has allowed Taleb to make the money which subsidises his scholarly lifestyle.

In order to make this make this work better, you have to do two things: (a) focus on giving yourself future options which will tend to give you this desirable position and (b) make sure you subject yourself to volatility so that the options become apparent. Thus Taleb recommends a volatile approach to all aspects of life: diets with severe fasting, interval training, occasional lifting of extreme weights, and the like. This leads to the idea of tinkering or *bricolage* as he calls it, presumably a reflection that

DIY for the French is more of a journey than for us, objective-driven B&Q customers. Try things out as long as the downside stays small. Invest in research and spare capacity. Investigate and fix a few things that ain't broke.

One model for all this is life itself. Volatility causes small mutations to arise for natural selection (or selfish genes) to take over and choose from the rich mix created. Of course this has the slightly fragile consequence that, "what kills me makes others stronger." No antifragile escape from death then, and indeed, ⋆SPOILER ALERT⋆ the book concludes with the demise of Fat Tony, his ever-present Brooklyn wise guy who has an innate comprehension of antifragility and, in one of the book's many humorous moments, wins a rancorous debate with Socrates. (The point of the debate was to show that the Socratic method debased valuable notions that are hard to express: turning the unintelligible into the unintelligent. It is an important feature of Taleb's non-understood world that you cannot express all of what little you know about it.)

Indeed, as a contrast to modernity, Taleb appeals to the ancients for support. He believes that a deeper wisdom is possible than that afforded by an (over-)scientised view and an over-rationalised approach which leads us to think we can understand and control things better than we can. So he leads us through a rich cast of Mediterranean, and especially Levantine, philosophers and wiseacres. Perhaps the most praised is Seneca the Stoic; the aspiration of stoicism is to become indifferent to life's kicks. By doing that you adjust your preferences and with them your utility. At a stroke the downside is reduced and you have made yourself antifragile. A neat, and sensible, trick for an individual though it is more difficult for corporations to pull off.

This emphasises the point that antifragility will work best for small units. They will tend to have the agility which enables them to create options and to recognise the need for decisions. The small is beautiful idea runs through the book as an antidote to the tendency to corruption by an overconfident and political environment in which individuals do not suffer the downside of poor decisions, or at least a downside which is commensurate with the impact of these decisions on others. Cue, of course, state-protected bankers.

This leads to another of Taleb's core ideas: skin in the game, and it also brings us back to forecasting. His position is that you should never believe any expert, or prophet, or forecaster unless they both live by what they are preaching and will be seriously adversely affected if it turns out to be wrong. I touched on this in the previous chapter in the discussion of the outside view and Flyvbjerg's 'fools and liars'. Once again, it strikes me that the ethics of risk analysis is quite a tricky topic given its inherent weaknesses: that it cannot be comprehensive, for example black swans, and that it is subjective, hence non-unique, and therefore open to pressure and gaming.

These are severe shortcomings but not obviously to the extent that you should not have a go at it. Sketching out a view of what might happen seems to me a useful exercise, especially if you are describing possible chains of events and worst cases, and collating information about what happened to others. And trying to give some idea of the comparative likelihood of some of these chains of events seems like a good idea too, even when these numbers are really just made up and you recognise that there is the possibility of something important you haven't thought of turning up.

What's important is for these problems to be recognised and not ignored. You cannot treat the work as a scientific truth and that's a matter for both the forecaster and the forecast to. I have many examples from my own experience of what can happen when the analysis is taken too seriously. But don't consign the risk analyst to that special part of hell reserved for economists quite yet; just let her know it's there.

Leaving this on one side, what else is one to make of antifragility? Time and again I found examples of behaviours I could recognise as my own: the avoidance of big downside risks, a lack of commitment to maximising expected utility in spite of its theoretical perfection. As I write this I am – possibly unwisely – painfully seeing off a toothache without the potentially iatrogenic effects of antibiotics. Even I have a portfolio of sorts and some years ago I realised the stupidity of Markowitz-style optimisation and sacked the guy who wanted to charge me maybe 20% of the portfolio to buy and sell in line with it. As an ex-astrophysicist I remember my incredulity at the use of the diffusion equation to value options, as in Black/Scholes/Merton (the most derided inhabitants of Taleb's economist anti-pantheon). So yes, I have a little skin in Taleb-world and I'm minded to take it on board in both my personal and professional life.

What does all this mean for organisational risk management? The answer is: quite a bit, and this is just a high-level view. The thinking is developed pretty uncritically from the book.

Many of the problems I have identified with common practice risk management lead to fragility. The principal one is the belief in predictability: not as in, "I know what's going to happen," but as in, "I can list the things that might happen, take action to prevent most of them and be prepared for the rest." Whilst the second is greatly preferable to the first, our ability to do it well is clearly short of what we would like.

If we want to be antifragile we need to recognise that this kind of upfront analysis will not work, or at least be the full story, and think about what else we need to do.

Avoiding fragility

As well as being aware of the limitations of prediction, we need to identify the specific areas we are vulnerable to and aim to be resilient to those things we can identify. For example management fads like JIT are inherently risky (as is reliance on management fads generally, especially unquestioning or uncomprehending reliance). Instead you need to create redundancy, that is, have enough of everything to cover your potential needs, and not just your needs on the basis that you will manage away all the risk.

More generally you need to identify your turkey situations: those which have big downsides without a corresponding upside. Taleb would have you look out for concave curves of outcome, but I find this unhelpful mainly because it is not very memorable (is it concave up or concave down?). He asserts this is easy to spot, but personally I need a little more practice to get attuned.

Finally you should not be worrying about your reputation. It's Taleb's observation that those individuals or organisations that don't obsess over reputation are the ones that actually enjoy the best. I have been amazed that for quite a time now, ever since Tony Blair thought it would be a good idea for the British public sector to engage in a little 'best practice' risk management, that local authorities and civil servants talk endlessly and seek advice about reputational risk. This not only constitutes a misuse of public money – it's not what they're paid for – but is also palpably ineffective.

Creating options

Second, your organisation needs to have a mindset in which it creates options for itself. For example, redundancy creates options: if you don't use the additional resources you can exploit them some other way when the opportunity arises. You need to do things which are not strictly necessary: potter away at your *bricolage*, engage in practically-motivated R&D, fix things which ain't broke, try stuff which sounds interesting, network widely on matters of only tangential interest.

(Fixing what ain't broke is a personal gloss on antifragility. Taleb actually refers to this only once that I remember, as a description of the ultra-interventionism of an oversized French government. But I see it as a kind of tinkering which might also be called continuous improvement, one management fad I do approve of. It's important to recognise that you have to look out for the opportunities which come out of kicking things around.)

Investing in antifragility

It's becoming obvious that there is a cost to being antifragile. It's the antithesis of the kind of over-budgeted, cost-stripped, outsourced, centrally-controlled outfit that dominates much of Britain these days, the Harvard-Soviet model as Taleb would call it.

Returning to the British public sector, we know that these techniques have been enthusiastically applied in most areas in the last couple of decades. This has included the almost universally applied contracting out of core services. It seems this is an inappropriate response to high labour costs and there is very little opposition from any political front, apart from public sector unions of course. The result is highly fragile service delivery and a widespread perception that the public sector is pretty useless at doing anything much, apart from feeding the profits of a raft of really scummy outsourcing companies. It's a scandal no-one wants to do anything about, at least until it goes wrong – see the concluding section of this chapter.

As a counterexample which reflects some antifragile strictures, think about the Olympics. First, the opening ceremony was commissioned on essentially a personal basis with Danny Boyle. Not bad for a £27m job, but it reflects Taleb's reminder that you'd trust a mafia boss before a civil servant because the civil servant is slave to a large and amoral organisation. The best business is person-to-person. I'll describe the Olympics capital programme arrangements a bit more in Chapter 5. It's generally accepted that this was pretty expensive: it had large contingencies – 'redundant' money. But the money came in useful when the financial crisis meant no-one wanted to build the Olympic village, and again when the commercially-run organising committee ran into trouble. And to close the circle, the redundancy of (surprisingly) available armed forces personnel was useful to implement a contingency plan when one of the outsourcing profiteers blew up. Central control was a compete illusion for G4S and its hapless Chief Executive.

This raises a question as to whether your desire to be antifragile is related to your choice of industry, the business you are in. Can you be an antifragile high-street retailer or a fraudulent workfare organiser? I don't know.

The business most praised by Taleb for its antifragility is Apple, as established on the principles espoused by the blessed St Steve. It was interesting to see the short-lived career of a Dixons (now Currys) retail boss at Apple. It would be equally interesting to see how long an Apple shop executive lasted at Currys. I can only say that the 'genius' of the Apple tech geeks I have had the misfortune to trip across is completely fake, but then I'm not an Apple fan even if I can understand their antifragility. Plus I'm not sure control freakery is really antifragile.

Staying agile

There's no point creating options if you don't decide to exercise them. This means the antifragile organisation has to be constantly making timely decisions and acting on them. Timely means not too early as well as not too late. There is a clear advantage in delaying decisions – to collect more information, see which way the tide is turning – as well as being decisive when necessary. Indeed the whole redundancy idea means you need to keep alternatives running instead of committing too early, if at all, to one.

This is clearly difficult for the big organisation. The response is perhaps to delegate and to do this effectively you need to have the small downside culture: farm-betting decisions have to be outlawed as a matter of company culture.

Of course some time it may be necessary to turn the tanker on a sixpence. In this case it's clearly best to decide early and implement effectively. It's always been of interest to me that the accepted wisdom of project management is that you map out a plan before starting and then plod ahead through the plan, noting variances and the like. Process seems to run out when the project runs into trouble and needs to be recovered. It's probably here that process is most needed: all too often recovery is so complex that it too fails, creating a worse failure. I'm clear that antifragile projects should have a much better recovery capacity than is generally the case, and this should be planned in.

Organising

This brings us to the organisational and cultural issues which need to be addressed. As ever these are key to having an approach which is natural and not just an additional bit of process.

First of all there is no such thing as antifragile risk management; fragility is risk, just another name really, and if you are going to have someone dealing with it, they should be the Fragility Manager.

From the cultural viewpoint the organisation has to be risk and option aware. It has to be agile and it has to be innovating, tinkering, creating volatility. This suggests that it has to be devolved with delegated decisions. In short it should be modelling itself on life, making changes and rejecting what doesn't work. One of the clear properties of antifragility that I've not mentioned so far is the so-called *via negativa* – focussing on what not to do so as to achieve simplicity. I'm still unclear on how this fits with the large organisation. I suppose the answer is obvious: it doesn't and the organisation needs to keep splitting to as to promote self-managing sections and fractal-style growth.

How do you create these values throughout the organisation? They need to be inculcated by the everyday conversations that people have. Managers need to be asking about risks and controls, concavity and convexity. What else can we not do? What else can we tinker with? What do we need to decide now? What can we decide later?

From the process viewpoint, it is still necessary to think about risks and what to do to stop them happening and what to do if they do. You also need to do fragility (or convexity) analyses. You need to think about resilience and redundancy. You need to do all of this in ways which are more usable than the standard risk register approach. And, sadly, you can probably dispense with a lot of the probabilistic analysis unless there is no way of avoiding large downsides after all. That's where this approach started. All in all, there is quite a raft of new tools which could be developed.

To conclude, I often argue that the main characteristics that modern risk management brings to an ancient and natural process are an aspiration to comprehensiveness and visibility. Most of the rest of the principles stuff in the risk standards is motherhood, apple pie or just plain incomprehensible voodoo. Coming back to the principles of comprehensiveness and visibility, what can we now see? The idea that we can create a complete risk register is futile; you cannot predict the black swans that will turn up. But you still need to construct the possible outcomes for the fragility analysis and you will need to understand how the downside ones are limited by the measures you plan to put in place. The aspiration to completeness is still vital, I think. These issues do still need to be visible throughout those parts of the organisation which need to know them. There is plenty of scope to create smart tools which will support this.

CONCLUSIONS: FROM CULTURE TO INSTITUTIONS

What are we to do about risk culture? In some ways it's pretty clear. There is a reasonable consensus about the fundamental model of behaviours determined by attitudes, beliefs, knowledge and so on. If you know what behaviours you want, you can do things to modify various aspects of this culture. Despite the different assessment models there is a reasonable consensus about what should be included, what the key aspects are and how they can be changed.

This book starts from the view that the culture should be the starting point of risk management: the process is light touch to support a natural approach. I have formed this view because I think that common practice risk management processes are virtually unembeddable. As a result I think a rebalancing is needed from what is in the literature: away from those aspects which are focussed on compliance with the processes and towards those aspects which measure the quality of the appreciation of uncertainty and the coherence of the decisions that are made. This rebalancing is more evident in the safety culture work we have reviewed.

This is potentially quite difficult as these aspects are less amenable to a tick box approach. The assessor needs to be able to form a mature judgement on fairly technical, but subjective matters. But it's no surprise that in trying to improve risk management we are forced to grapple with the complex realities of risk and uncertainty rather than just rely on a process which is clever enough to do so. It's worth saying that the risk issues faced by organisations are much more complex than the safety issues, both technically and conceptually. It's very easy to take an approach in which nothing is done unless it's safe compared with the need to balance risk and reward for an organisation.

But if we can rise to this challenge we can design suitable assessment tools based on the material reviewed, looking at individual predispositions and knowledge and we can design programmes to effect change in these and the resulting risk-related behaviour. In doing this we can even address what the IRM report[17] refers to as *latent culture risk*, that is, the risks that arise from the organisational culture. The report asks two questions:

- Are you aware of the risk created by the way in which you manage risk?
- Do you encourage yourself and your people to raise and challenge risk-producing behaviour in order to drive your change agenda?

Analysis and mitigation of latent culture risk is important in any consideration of risk culture and how to improve it, but there is a slight difficulty in that any project aimed at achieving change will be carried out within the existing cultural environment and there are latent culture risks undermining it.

Overall then, while organisational risk culture may not, like safety culture, be a solved problem, we have a pretty well-defined way ahead, and plenty of useful tools to deploy. The next challenge is to create a culture in which our highly subjective understanding of risk is merged with our rigid business management approach.

Before talking about that in the chapters that follow, I want to dwell on two momentous events which have happened in the last year as I write this in January 2018. Both of them reveal huge holes in our safety and risk culture respectively but they also reveal some hope for what we can achieve and point the way.

---

[17] *Op cit.* Chapter 7.

In 2017 we had several serious terrorist attacks which shocked us and grabbed the headlines for a week or two. But terrorism is a fact of modern life, around for as long as I can remember and mostly well-managed by our security services. We have to accept some residual risk of very serious attacks. The truly shocking event of 2017 was the Grenfell Tower fire, not just because it killed more people, but also because it was so palpably avoidable. It represents a massive and surprising failure of safety culture.

On Sunday 13 January 2018 not many people had heard of Carillion, or at least were not particularly concerned by it. On Monday it collapsed, and in the following days the full consequences became clear in terms of the risk to tens of thousands of jobs, the viability of thousands of SMEs, the completion of numerous major projects and the delivery of many public services. There are potential political ramifications about the delivery of these services, the financing of public infrastructure and company law. Carillion had issued several profit warnings in the previous six months and its difficulties were common knowledge in the industry well before then. But few preparations had been made for the risk of collapse and all the contingent risk. It is another clear failure of risk culture.

These two events have a number of common features to go with their cultural failings:

- The true causes of the event remain unclear and it is unlikely that they will ever be revealed in a sensible way.
- A prime reason for this is that they both extend into the political sphere, not just in the sense that they are so important and disastrous that politicians will feel the need to assert their determination to take steps so that they will never happen again, but also because the circumstances around these events are highly political: the balance of responsibilities between central and local government, outsourcing of public services, the need for austerity measures, inequality and so on. There are too many political agendas to defend and promote for the truth to emerge.
- A second reason for our lack of understanding is the dreadful quality of reporting on these events. The nonsense which is put out by press and TV is truly astounding; there seems to be little commitment to investigation and the truth and, understandably given the human price of both events, emotional agendas to be pursued.

- Both events involve many organisations. If Carillion had a good risk culture, something I'll come back to in Chapter 6, it was dependent on the risk culture of thousands of supply chain organisations and the risk culture of government (which, for example, is severely lacking in the tone from the top aspect). If the safety culture of the original architects and contractors of Grenfell was good, then the residents were also dependent on the safety culture of many small contractors and design companies and project managers and materials suppliers and industry organisations and standards writers and building inspectors and umpteen types of regulator and emergency services and housing management organisations and so on. Quite a challenge.

The first point to draw from this is that no risk culture is an island. All organisations interact with other organisations and are dependent on the excellence of the risk management in these partners for the quality of their own risk management. The resulting extension of the management cycles was a key element of the model set up in Chapter 1, but we need to think about culture in these more complex systems as well, just as we noted earlier that most organisations have subcultures and hidden cultures.

Talking about complex systems means that it's also reasonable to conclude that these events were normal accidents. You can see that actually they have emerged from complex *social* systems in which no actors were in real control. Whether they were closely coupled is more questionable. Certainly the actors were linked, but with no real overriding timescales like the meltdown of a nuclear reactor or the take-off time of a jet fighter. There was plenty of time to allow Carillion to collapse in a more controlled and less costly way. What seems to have prevailed is a continuing preference for options bearing a faint hope of survival against all good sense; I've highlighted this several times in this book and it's a really bad heuristic. Maybe we need to modify the tight coupling idea to encompass failure of coherently decisive intervention.

Leaving that on one side we can add Carillion and Grenfell to the list which includes, for example, Three Mile Island, and the two Challenger incidents but the really depressing thing is that society is unlikely to learn from them. One reason for this is that culture is not operating in a vacuum: it is conditioned by institutional constraints. In Chapter 1

I mentioned the work of King and Crewe[18] on UK government blunders. Their book is a fast-paced tale of incessant disaster, predictable and hugely expensive. The blunders are committed by governments of all shades and all (recent) eras. King and Crewe identify twelve root causes for what we would call these risks materialising. Five of these they categorise as human error and seven as system failures. The 'human errors' can also be seen as culture problems.

- **Cultural disconnect** means that policies are formed, options explored and decisions taken with no real understanding of the impact of those decisions on the people affected who are completely outside the milieu inhabited by politicians.
- **Group think** is well known: policies get developed by small teams who neither welcome nor seek the advice of outsiders. Alongside this comes a bullying culture where alternative views, different ideas or dissent (such as risk identification) are crushed.
- **Prejudice and pragmatism** follows on from this. Initial prejudices, such as private sector good – unions bad, remain unchallenged as do initial assumptions. This militates against pragmatic solutions.
- **Operational disconnect** up and down the management chain. Ministers create policy without consulting the poor sods who will have to implement it, and, indeed, know it cannot work. Government projects are particularly susceptible to this as the chains are so long. What is also a key factor here, though this is not highlighted by King and Crewe, is the importance of good supervision. Assuming you can let people get on with what you have told them to do is a pervasive fallacy in all organisations.
- **Panic, symbols and spin** means doing something so as to be seen to do something (such as expelling Russian diplomats), or just to protect your reputation.

These 'errors' are familiar to us all and they are clear indicators of a malfunctioning risk culture, independently of their role in government projects. King and Crewe think their seven system failures derive from specific characteristics of the UK government which do not necessarily prevail in other countries or organisations. These issues can therefore be

---

[18] The Blunders of Our Governments, Anthony King and Ivor Crewe, Oneworld, revised and updated 2014.

regarded less as cultural phenomena and more as institutional failings. They are as follows.

- **The centre cannot hold** is a result of the weak prime ministerial control of silo-ed, often warring Whitehall departments. There is little the prime minister can do to enforce joined up thinking and action.
- **Musical chairs** refers to frequent changes of ministers and senior civil servants. It leads to poor understanding, and encourages short term thinking and lack of ownership.
- **Ministers as activists** means that they are increasingly expected to create and pursue new initiatives, and at breakneck speed. They spawn ill-defined projects and then swan off on the next round of musical chairs.
- **Accountability, lack of** derives from King and Crewe's observation that, contrary to what is popularly believed, ministers rarely pay a price for their administrative blunders. The head of a civil servant is occasionally lopped off (often unfairly) but ministers need to be warier of sexual adventures or looking fools on Question Time.
- **A peripheral parliament** simply flags parliament's very weak role in identifying initiative risks and getting them managed. It's all submerged in party political warfare and the failure of MPs to see themselves as legislators. There is very little technical scrutiny of new bills.
- **Asymmetries of expertise** arise in all purchasing situations where the supplier knows much more about the product than the buyer. Government is the victim of wideboy outsourcing or IT firms. It seems to me that agencies outsourcing their functions always forget they need to develop new contract management capabilities.
- **A deficit of deliberation** is a result of the unrealistic timescales that are set for government initiatives. The activist minister wants to see immediate progress and is unwilling to sit down, frame the problem, identify political sensitivities, develop options, assess them, and so on.

It's arguable whether these seven failings are all unique to Westminster. Asymmetric expertise is an occupational hazard for us all (and not just in purchasing situations – as King and Crewe make clear these projects were submerged under layers of know-nothing consultants like me). What's more some of these causes might also lie in the 'human error' box: you get activist managers everywhere. But King and Crewe make a very important point that culture shades into institutions so that to manage your risk culture you need to attend to firmly implanted features of your organisational arrangements, not just the people. It's clear that the cultural failings we can identify for Grenfell and Carillion were amplified through the exact same institutional failings that are listed by King and Crewe.

The authors present some suggestions for how the system could be made more robust, but apparently without any serious hope that they will be taken up. We face a major challenge in our society.

What can we say about improving our own organisation's risk culture? At the detailed level we can carry out the aspects assessment recommended by the IRM and implement a project to improve it.

In a more practical way we can develop an attitude in which we seek to be resilient, indeed antifragile. We need to tinker and we need to avoid big downsides.

Finally, we can build on the lessons of high reliability organisations. Our best hope in turn for that, at least based on what we know so far, is to practice 'mindful organising'. Quoting from Wikipedia[19]

> *"Mindful organising forms a basis for individuals to interact continuously as they develop, refine and update a shared understanding of the situation they face and their capabilities to act on that understanding. Mindful organising proactively triggers actions that forestall and contain errors and crises. Mindful organising requires that leaders and organisational members pay close attention to shaping the social and relational infrastructure of the organisation, and to establishing a set of interrelated organising processes and practices, which jointly contribute to the system's (team, unit, organisation) overall culture of safety."*

These are fine and compelling aspirations for our society, and for our organisation and its stakeholders. Let's have a look at what Weick and Sutcliffe's five characteristics of high reliability organisations might mean for broader risk management. My interpretation of this is contained in Figure 22.

---

[19] Yes, I know, and me a great mocker of management fads, but it's very well put.

Preoccupation with failure	**Preoccupation with uncertainty** What might happen? How likely is it? What can I do about it?
Reluctance to simplify interpretations	**Reluctance to simplify interpretations** But there is benefit – arguably – in seeking clear and simple explanations of the complex.
Sensitivity to operations	**Situational awareness** What's going on? Why?
Commitment to resilience	**Commitment to antifragility** Give yourself options, avoid situations with potential high losses.
Deference to expertise	**Deference to expertise**

Figure 22 What we can learn from HROs

These are essentially values or maybe attitudes, simple ones which we can use in a heartbeat way to inform our behaviours, our decisions and our communications, as we go about our work. As such they can form the basis of our individual risk culture and in aggregate create our organisational risk culture.

That's not too difficult, is it?

Chapter 4

Tools for explicit risk management

Completing the loop and making it formal

This chapter follows on from Chapter 2 which was concerned with natural risk management. There, the emphasis was on risk analysis and decision making, the technical aspects of risk if you like. That chapter concluded with a short discussion of the circumstances in which a formal, explicit approach to completing the management loop is required rather than the informal, 'in my head' approach to observing and orienting which might be suitable for small, entrepreneurial organisations. Accordingly, this chapter is about the management layer, the formal processes of measuring and reviewing performance, supplemented by the explicit steps we added to the loop of forecasting and synthesising, integrating the forecasts with the performance data.

Recognising that there are no risk management processes, just tools for facilitating the consideration of risk in management, this chapter is structured into tools for risk forecasting, for risk performance measurement, for risk synthesis and for risk review. A significant feature is that these tools will have to interface with financial management processes, something that leads to significant cultural challenges. The emotionally intelligent, imaginative and continually communicating risk manager is faced with cold-hearted accountants and project controllers for whom uncertainty is incomprehensible anathema.

As if this were not bad enough you will also need to interface with commercial processes which will focus on the treatment and transfer of risk.

There are many perspectives to management and because we now understand that risk management does not have its own processes, it is simply part of the mainstream management processes, there are many perspectives on risk as well. In this chapter I shall focus on three:

- the performance perspective
- the control perspective
- the commercial perspective.

However, there are many more takes on management and we'll have a look at some of these in Chapter 6 when we come to a recap.

TOOLS FOR RISK FORECASTING

> *"A budget is a budget, contingency is contingency and a forecast is a forecast."* Client project manager

It's hard to argue with these words of wisdom, but they do need a little elaboration. We put the forecasting short-circuit into the management loop to emphasise the point that when we reach the review stage we probably need to be comparing performance with a forecast that has been prepared previously. As I have just noted, this will bring us into the realm of financial management and control, and, specifically, budgeting. These are disciplines that have developed without reference to risk and uncertainty and one challenge is to recognise risk within these established mechanisms. To understand this better we need to spend a little time on how budgets are put together – not a topic for the faint-hearted.

Budgeting

The budget is a financial control measure providing managers with spending constraints against which their performance is judged. As such it is fair game, naturally enough, for vast amounts of gamesmanship. This causes problems for the honest, open communications you need for risk management, as we've just seen in the previous chapter. You might think that budgets are built up from reasonable forecasts but it's no surprise that there's a bit more to it than that. To see how this works in more detail it's worth looking separately at business-as-usual and project-based organisations.

Business-as-usual

Most organisations have an annual budgeting round. It is primarily a financial control exercise and the output is a set of costs, broken down by expenditure types, activities or whatever. If the unit is revenue-earning there will be sales numbers as well. The numbers will be aggregated and distributed up and down the organisation. The job of the manager is to live within these costs and revenues; if you don't, there are likely to be serious consequences.

Generally, the starting point for next year's is the current year. This is adjusted for changes in objectives and responsibilities, planned initiatives and so on. It will also be adjusted for the boss's view that all managers can live with 10% less money at any given time so there will be implicit objectives to leave people by the wayside, increase unpaid working time, create stress and so on. Sound familiar?

What is generally not present is any kind of risk-based forecast, and there is not usually a budget item called contingency, or some other euphemistic name. If something goes wrong you'd better hope something else goes right to pay for it (and even then, you probably have to cover up the shuffling between boxes). If that fails you have to try to find money from somewhere else (that is, some*one* else) with the career damage that might imply.

On the other hand, if you do manage to bring your numbers in under budget, your sole thanks will be getting it chopped off next year's. This results in the frequently-seen end of year spending splurge on nice-to-haves and just-in-cases.

So business-as-usual organisations might profess to be totally committed to best practice risk management but may not live up to that ideal in practice, especially when it comes to money.

In this environment, far from the forecast informing the budget, the forecast will be determined from the budget, at least initially. As you go through the year, and the updated forecast has to accommodate the actuals (that is, spend to date), you will adjust it, generally showing a magical return to budget at year-end for as long as plausibly possible.

Projects

Projects are different, different in two ways. First, each project is different from any other and as a result it cannot rely on last year as its initial estimate. Secondly, an annual budget can (or at least should) only be a mechanical calculation based on a full project budget. Projects have to build their budget up from scratch, based on activities, bills of quantities, programmes and the like. To do this you need a baseline forecast of these matters which can be costed in a time-dependent way, and then you need to think about risk, turning the baseline forecast into a risk-based forecast. Then you can start to think about the budget.

At this point it is worth mentioning that the forecast is not just about cost. It also covers the completion dates and intermediate delivery dates, and maybe other project features, so it is potentially a very rich description of what it is hoped will happen.

Turning the forecast into a budget presents two challenges.

- There is just as much opportunity for gaming as in business-as-usual organisations. Project managers want to squirrel away money against a rainy day; financial directors want to squeeze the cost of projects to the minimum and they want certainty, so that any spare cash can be extracted and used for something else.
- The risk-based forecast is just that: the answer is a subjective probability distribution of the cost. This is unacceptable: forecasts are by definition fixed numbers. You can argue till you're blue in the face (as I have) that forecasts are essentially probabilistic, but (like me) you will lose and have to find a way to create fixed numbers for your forecast, covering cost, time and whatever else is important.

A further complication is that projects are mostly carried out in a commercial environment and this throws in another concept alongside forecasts and budgets: price. This is also subject to gaming. For example a company might need to win work at all costs to service their debts and as a result tender too low for their projects, perhaps hoping to make it up with claims. Sound familiar?

What you then cannot do is start the project with a forecast, still less a budget, which indicates an overspend against the price or even a dent in some required margin. The project commercial environment is endemically set up for gaming around contract terms and conditions, including how they relate to risk, and yet again this is not conducive to good risk management.

These machinations mean that the project world is suffused with confusion about the distinctions between price, budget, forecast, contingency, risk provision and so on. This explains the outburst quoted at the start of this section and I was sorry my colleague did not extend her philosophical elucidations to 'price', so that we had a complete set.

A final challenge in project budgeting is the probable need in big organisations – and especially government – to consider annual budgets as well as those for projects. Projects are generally part of a higher-level business-as-usual organisation and the resulting requirement can drive perverse behaviour in the subsidiary projects as well in the marketing department or wherever else.

Building the forecast and budget

With this introduction to budgeting, it is easy to see what needs to be done. Ideally you will start with a baseline plan. This will comprise a set of costs and a programme. You go on to carry out a risk analysis and decide on your risk control measures, adapting the plan accordingly, all using the tools from Chapter 2. You then use the resulting risk model to create a forecast, and the forecast is used to develop the budget. The difference between the baseline and the forecast is often called 'risk' and the difference between the baseline and the budget is called 'contingency'. This means that contingency is budgeted funds to cover risk materialising, that is, anything that is not in the baseline. Contingency is a recognition that unanticipated matters will arise and that some financial provision will be required to deal with them. So far, it's simple.

Whilst budgets are generally set for a whole project or a year and not altered, forecasts might be updated every month in the light of emerging performance (also known as actuals) as we shall cover in the next section.

Budgets are generally imposed or agreed with a management style, for example 'stretch', and, as we have seen, are not necessarily based on a best estimate of how the future will unfold. Traditionally, the contingency might be set at 5%, 10% or whatever, based on experience, say. The debate around optimism bias and reference class forecasting was discussed in Chapter 2 and, again, these are methods to get to risk-aware budgets without detailed risk-based forecasts.

Risk modelling aspires to provide a much better basis for this. The risk model is essentially a probabilistic forecast. However, your average financial or project controller is not sympathetic to this and generally insists on something deterministic to support single number budgets and contingencies. Weather forecasters will tell you there is a 20% chance of rain (though they do not generally describe their sample space in enough detail for you to understand what they mean by this). I have not so far met a client who is satisfied with a forecast that says there is a 20% chance of an overspend, such as would in principle be the case if budgeting were at P80.

Therefore, we will adopt the convention that a forecast is a single picture of the future which needs to recognise risk in some way. Figure 23 gives an overview of the similarities and difference between a forecast and a budget.

Property	**Forecast**	**Budget**
Covers	Cost, duration, output	Cost
Updated	Periodically, for example, monthly in light of performance	Rarely, on re-baselining or at start of year
Purpose	Show what the future holds	Hold management to account
Nature	Single representation of the future	Single number, summed over various items
Recognition of uncertainty	Based on risk model but cannot present ranges for variations from the forecast	Contains contingency for uncertainties crystallising
Scenario	Typical, recognising uncertainty, so might be P50 or expected value	Depends on management approach: stretching, should be achievable or whatever, so might be P20 or P80

Figure 23 Forecasts and budgets

There are some slightly difficult technical issues to develop the representations and scenarios this table refers to. Looking more closely at how to build a contingency it's helpful to consider cost and time separately.

Cost forecast and contingency

One difficulty arises because, although you can use the risk model to identify the expected cost and P20, P50 or P80 costs, there are no unique future scenarios which have the corresponding properties. By this I mean that you can build your risk model, carry out a Monte Carlo calculation, get the cumulative probability distribution of outturn cost, and identify the P80, say. You can then use the difference between this cost and the baseline cost as contingency, that is, part of the budget. But no specific Monte Carlo simulation corresponds to either the expected value forecast or the more extreme P80 used to develop the budget.

To understand this better, consider an extreme case (where what I have just said is to some extent not true!). The example shown in Figure 16 in Chapter 2 (page 74) charts the S-curve for 4 risks. The P50 is 10, corresponding to Risk 1 happening and no others. The P80 is 13 which occurs when Risk 1 and Risk 4 happen but not the other two. (The risks are listed in the box on page 75.) In this case you can identify the scenarios leading to P50 and P80 but:

- this is possible only because these risks have crisply defined impacts (2-point quantification); if the impacts were uncertain (for example, 4-point quantification) the impacts would overlap
- there would be little point in looking at these scenarios to the exclusion of others in which the excluded risks materialise
- the mean of 9.4 does not correspond to any identifiable scenario.

This reinforces the point that you should not seek to break down the contingency into different sources. Contingency should remain unallocated because it is derived from the aggregation of many different risks, some of which may happen and many hopefully not. There is often pressure from financial controllers to separate contingency into its different risks or causes, or cost breakdown structure elements or in some other way. This needs to be resisted as it is not rational, for the reasons just mentioned. However, there *is* an element of contingency that could, in principle be allocated.

This arises from the need to create a forecast *scenario*, not just a cost number. There is a reasonably straightforward way of doing this. It is to use the expected value of each contributing cost. As total cost is the sum of the costs and the expected value of a sum of random variables is the sum of the expected value of each (whether or not they are independent) we can break down a forecast which is expected value into components which are also expected values. These components might be a cost breakdown structure, the costs of individual activities, or whatever.

We noted in Chapter 2 that risk models dealt with both ranges and systematic increases due to the prevalence of downside risk or uncertainty. This means the expected costs are generally higher that the baseline costs, both for individual items and as a whole. You can allocate that part of the contingency which is an increase in the expected value to the relevant activity, with only the rest remaining unallocated. By definition this is the difference between the forecast and the contingency.

In summary, if you want a scenario-based cost forecast I think the only way to do it is to work with expected values. You will be left with unallocated contingency, representing the difference between the budget and the forecast. You will also have a budget which is different from the forecast cost. This is natural and sensible: forecast and budget have different purposes. Astonishingly though, there are some benighted projects where the budget must not only equally the forecast but also, at least initially, the *price*.

If (like many projects) you wanted to use a P50 you (like many projects) would get into a host of technical difficulties, though the materiality of these is likely to be small, as generally P50s are close to expected values. In these situations the difference between the P50 budget and the baseline can be regarded as contingency and is best left unallocated, although in principle most of it could be.

Time forecast and contingency

Time and programme are different. Apart from the technical matters I'm coming to, we do not usually talk about the time budget of a project. The terminology is usually time risk allowances and float. The technical issues arise because you cannot add contributing durations to get the total duration of the programme.[1] You can adopt the expected duration as the forecast programme duration but this does not give a scenario. I believe the key requirement is to have a forecast programme which is consistent with the forecast cost and this means that the duration of each element must be such that its cost is the expected cost of that element. Most of the time this is simple, but there is no guarantee that complications will not arise in situations where the cost and duration are not simply related.

The risk-aware programme you create in this way will be consistent with the cost forecast and you will be able to allocate float to each activity as the difference between the forecast duration and the baseline duration. But it will not necessarily have a duration equal to the expected value of duration, nor any other statistical properties.

If now you select the P80 as your time contingency, there is also no unique corresponding scenario. The difference between the P80 and the duration of the forecast is the unallocated contingency which can also be called terminal float.

This situation is quite complicated and not generally well understood. It is made worse by commercial considerations. The complexity can be exploited by smart commercial managers in the hope of gaining advantage. If each risk is allocated to either of two stakeholders, client or contractor say, then it is not in principle possible to apportion any delay between these stakeholders. To get round this it is necessary to consider the order in which the sources of delay arise. This is considered in more detailed later in this chapter.

A further complication is that it is traditional for planners to introduce *time risk allowance* (TRA) as an extension of the duration of individual activities. Normally TRA represents day-to-day inefficiencies which are not part of the risk model. However, this needs to be checked, and it is certainly confusing to have a programme which contains three types of risk: TRA, contractor risk and client risk, all with corresponding

---

[1] One potential solution to explore is where the programme is represented by growth in earned value (discussed later in this chapter). Component earned values do add up and therefore you can think about a programme forecast as expected value of earned value (EV^2). This is automatically consistent with the cost forecast but I shall not pursue this further here.

float or contingency. This can get unnecessarily complicated in commercial discussions.

In summary, there are many ways to create forecasts and budgets. One way is to:

1. Set up a plan of activities. Call this the baseline and cost it.
2. Create a risk model to identify how it might lead to costs and milestone dates that are different from baseline.
3. Identify a cost forecast as the expected value of all the contributing costs.
4. Identify a budget as the cost of the baseline and additional contingency either to bring the budget up to the expected value of cost, or some other amount depending on management style. If you choose the expected value, the forecast is equal to the budget.
5. If you chose the expected value or similar (for example P50), it should be recognised that this is not a reasonable worse case and that additional contingency may need to be drawn down, for example, from programme level contingency.
6. You could create the programme forecast from the expected value of the durations. Alternatively you construct it so that the costs are the expected costs. These are not necessarily the same. Only in the latter case is cost of the time forecast equal to the cost forecast.
7. Programme contingency can then be added on as terminal float to bring the project duration up to P80, again depending on management style.

Activity	Uncertainty	Duration	Cost
Planning permission	Duration uncertainty	Triangular (6,8,12) weeks	£3k per week
Site clearance	Workforce: uniform (10,20)	150 worker-weeks / workforce	See text
Construction	Duration uncertainty	Triangular (10,10,12) weeks	£20k per week

Figure 24 Activities and uncertainties in the simple project risk model

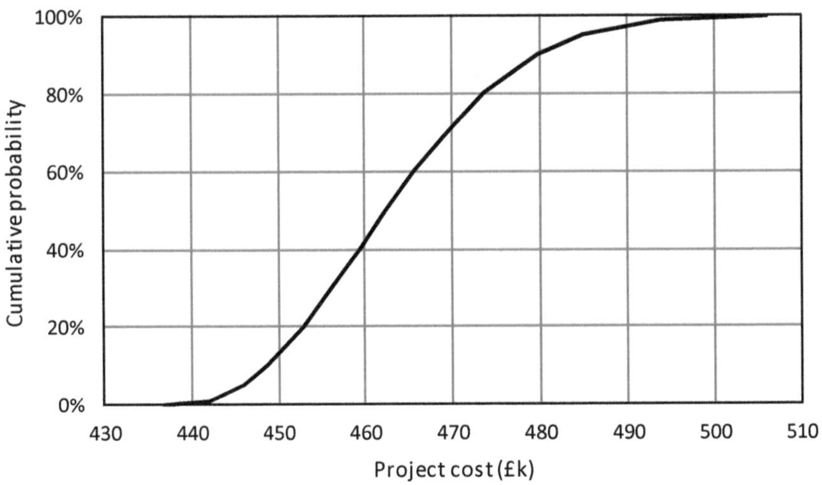

Figure 25 S-curve of project cost

To help explain this further, here is a worked example which is an adaptation of a simple case study in my previous book.[2] You may find it helpful to recreate the example. A construction project has three activities: obtaining planning permission, site clearance and construction itself. Construction cannot begin until the other two activities are complete. Figure 24 shows the data for the duration and risk of each activity.

The site clearance activity has a slightly complicated cost: there is £5k per week for a project office and £1k per worker-week with an additional cost of up to 20% for larger teams to reflect recruitment difficulties.[3] With these numbers, the calculated S-curves for cost and duration are shown in Figures 25 and 26.

The forecast cost is set at the expected value of £463.9k and the budget is generously put at P80, £474.3k. Compared with the baseline of £435.5k there is therefore £38.8k contingency, of which £28.4k could be allocated if you wished. The relevant numbers are summarised in Figure 27.

---

[2] Estimating Risk: A Management Approach, Andy Garlick, Gower, 2007, p203.

[3] This example has been selected to illustrate specific points, not necessarily to be realistic. For the avoidance of doubt, the cost of the clearance in £k is $3D+150(1+W/100)$ where D is the duration in weeks, $D=150/W$, and W is the workforce size, taken as uniformly distributed between 10 and 20.

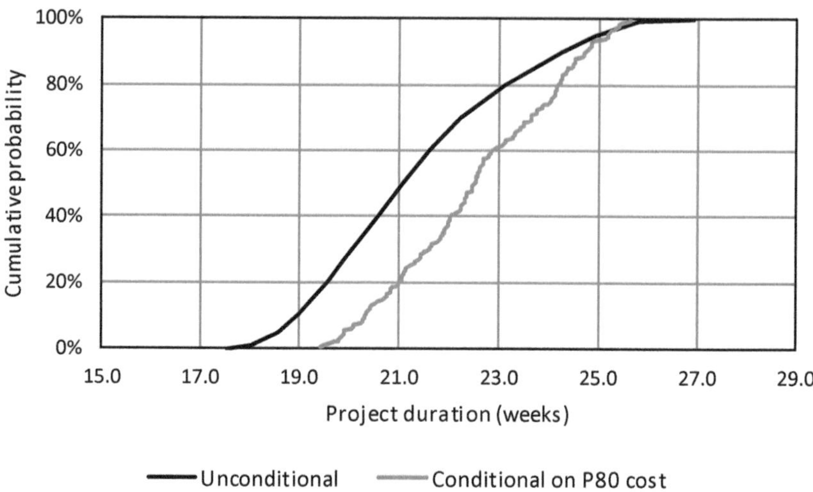

Figure 26 S-curves of project duration

The corresponding programme in which each task has its average duration would have an overall duration of 21.1 weeks, although the average duration is 21.4 weeks. However, the forecast used is such as to recreate the forecast cost and actually has a duration of 21.4 weeks, close to (but not exactly the same as) the average duration. The complication arises in the clearance task where the cost is a complicated function of the uncertain workforce size. The average workforce size is 15, the average duration arises when the workforce is 14.4 and the average cost when it is 14.0, which is what is in the forecast. Obviously, I've designed this to illustrate the complexities and real life is generally simpler.

	Duration (wk)	**Cost (£k)**
Baseline	17.5	435.5
Forecast (EV cost)	21.3	463.5
Budget (P80)	23.1	473.7
Contingency	5.6	38.2
Allocatable	*3.8*	*28.90*
Unallocatable	*1.8*	*10.2*

Figure 27 Forecast, budget and contingency numbers

The P80 duration is 23.2 weeks so there is terminal float of 1.8 weeks in addition to the float or contingency on each activity. There is no P80 scenario for the budget: the difference between the forecast and the budget is not allocated even though it arises from the risk model.

You can of course use the Monte Carlo results to explore the scenarios which result in P80 costs and durations. The S-curve duration chart, Figure 26, has marked on it the S-curve for the duration of simulations in which the cost outturn is close to the P80 cost. You might be surprised to see how much variation it has. (Why?) You can then look at the subset of these scenarios which are also close to P80 programme, but it is hard to see that this has much practical value.

Figure 27 clarifies that you can break down the cost contingency into allocated contingency (part of the forecast) and unallocated. I would question the usefulness of this: it's just a financial management matter where too much allocation complicates the future task of management. What I think is more useful is the time equivalent, the allocation of float. It is clearly useful to know where your float lies on the key tasks and what terminal float you have. This makes sense where the overall contingencies are set at P80. A more stringent management style might insist on expected value budgets in which case all the contingency is in the forecast, emphasising the pointlessness of cost contingency allocation and destroying the terminal float. An even more stringent style leaves the project manager searching for additional savings or plucking up courage to go to the programme manager.

As the quotation which introduces this section makes clear, the concepts of forecasting and budgeting are not difficult. However, if you want to base them on a risk model there are some technical problems. These issues can be overcome, but the solutions are often not widely understood or applied.

TOOLS FOR MEASURING RISK PERFORMANCE

One of the principles on which this book is based is that we deal with risk in a way that is broadly adaptive. That means, among many other things, that instead of formulating a plan, complete with a comprehensive set of risk control measures, and then plodding though it, we continually monitor how we are doing on risk and make adjustments to suit. Adaptation – as circumstances dictate – is the norm.

This reinforces the importance of measuring and understanding your risk performance – how you are doing with regard to uncertainty. If risk management is about promoting preferred futures at the expense of less preferred, then you need to check that this is what is happening. Risk performance measurement has not received the attention it deserves in previous formulations of risk management and this section aims to address this. It's concerned with understanding how you have done to date: what risks have materialised, which have not, which risks you hadn't thought of, and so on.

As noted at the start of this chapter, we can take a performance perspective, a control perspective or a commercial perspective. We look at each successively.

Performance perspective

I'm using the term *performance perspective* for that view of management which typically announces itself with truisms about measuring and managing, is concerned with performance indicators (and strategic objectives, etc) and, more than likely, runs a balanced scorecard. This is a philosophy which favours 'the effect of uncertainty on objectives' view of risk.

Risk can be fitted into this perspective though a concept called key risk indicators.

The idea of KRIs is that they are measures that will provide a heads up that a risk is becoming more likely. Put technically, the probability of the risk event, conditional on the KRI reaching a trigger level, is very much greater than its unconditional probability, though this is not a definition you will find anywhere else. The concept is that you can measure your risk performance by comparing the actual value of the KRIs with some target value.

KRIs have been a feature of operational risk management in financial institutions for some time. For example, Figure 28[4] shows a typical set of KRIs which might be defined at a strategic level across the range of risks which a bank might be subject to.

[4] Based on a presentation by Steve Townsend of Tesco Bank at an IRM North West meeting in July 2012.

Financial risk	Profit margin Capital ratios Liquidity
Reputational risk	Debt rating Customer retention Complaints Regulatory engagement
Operations and people risk	Change Staff attrition IT availability Systems integrity Outsourcing/supplier performance

Figure 28 KRIs for a bank

The definition of a suitable set of KRIs for a given risk profile is not necessarily straightforward. In particular it is possible to get bogged down in distinguishing between KRIs and KPIs. COSO has provided some guidance on this.[5] The tenor of the guidance is that anything that is a KPI is not a KRI. This means that the KRIs given as examples are all external measures. For example, the risk of bad debt has KRIs of customer financial results and industry 'collection challenges'. A chain of grocery stores has 13 KRIs, only one of which is internal. This relates to the performance of its construction arm in opening new stores on time, which again is external to operations. The COSO picture is one in which trigger levels are set for the KRIs to provide a stimulus for review and potential change of plan.

I think this emphasis on external KRIs is misplaced. It is helpful in terms of getting people to think outside the constraints of the performance of their own organisation. However it is clear that internal measures provide warnings that risk is increasing. In fact this is a manifestation of the simple point that the quantification of risk can be carried out using historical data: the past may not be a complete guide to the future, but it certainly tells you some interesting and useful things, especially the recent past.

[5] Developing KRIs to Strengthen ERM, Mark S Beasley, Bruce C Branson, Bonnie V Hancock, COSO, December 2010, available from coso.org.

As a simple example, the number of near misses is a clear indicator of the risk of a more serious accident in the safety context. Using the 'risk triangle', the frequency of lost time incidents is a measure of the risk of a fatal accident. This is a core performance indicator in many safety management systems.

A more sophisticated example is the study of precursors in a hazardous industrial plant. If an accident sequence is modelled by an event tree, the occurrence of events along the branches of a tree provide an indication of which endpoints are becoming more likely. And if these endpoints have higher impact the risk is clearly increasing. The Accident Sequence Precursor Study of US nuclear reactors[6] enabled risk models to be validated and/or updated.

In practice the changes in most risk profiles can be tracked through a set of internal trends and external measures. For some reason this has not received as much attention as some aspects of risk management but good practice should clearly aim to collect information about the development of significant risks and issues, and act on it.

Some people distinguish KRIs from KPIs on the basis that the KRIs are forward-looking. However, KPIs should be too as there is little point, at least once the historical information has been recorded, in looking anywhere than to the future. The consulting firm PwC has published a guide[7] on forward-looking information which includes seven pillars for effective communication of the future.

1. Explain the resources available to your company that help to attain your objectives and how they are managed.
   - *Yes, a focus on your resources bears on resilience, and, specifically, you might want to mention the risk culture. So a KRI might be anything that affects your resources and their capability.*
2. Describe the principal risks and uncertainties that may affect your company's long-term value or prospects.
   - *Great idea, should have thought of that!*

---

[6] See for example http://www.nrc.gov/reading-rm/doc-collections/commission/secys/2011/2011-0138scy.pdf.

[7] Guide to forward-looking information. Don't fear the future: communicating with confidence, https://www.pwc.com/gx/en/audit-services/corporate-reporting/assets/pdfs/860-global-forward-looking-guide.pdf

3. Clarify the significant relationships with stakeholders that are likely to influence the performance of your company and its value.
   - *So stakeholders are a risk and anything which changes your relationship with them might trigger a KRI.*
4. Provide quantified data relating to trends and factors likely to affect your company's future prospects.
   - *The point that most KRIs are externally focussed.*
5. Spell out any uncertainties underpinning forward-looking information.
   - *Not sure what this adds.*
6. Communicate targets relating to those key performance indicators (KPIs) used to manage your business.
   - *Another great idea for managers to think about.*
7. Demonstrate the linkage of other content areas within your reporting to your longer-term objectives and the strategies to achieve those objectives.
   - *I think this underlines my point that management is risk management.*

I don't want to dismiss the idea of KRIs. Any thinking about what signs there might be that the future might not develop as anticipated is clearly valuable. But I don't find the thinking around KRIs is very compelling in terms of, for example, developing a complete set or having something distinctively different from KPIs. I also think there is a danger that pursuing a scorecard of KRIs too hard can distract you from keeping in mind the broad set of risks and uncertainties you have developed, and the even broader number of ways you might see that things are potentially going pear-shaped.

I have often tried to derive a set of KRIs for a project or organisation but have never felt they told me much more than I could see wearing a generalised scouting hat.

Control perspective

Whilst the performance perspective on risk measurement is focussed on developing a bespoke set of risk indicators, the starting point for the control perspective is the budget and also the risk model which supported the forecasting and budget process. I'm taking for granted that, whether the environment is business-as-usual or projects, there is a process of periodically comparing the actuals to the forecast, and that the variances which are observed will be explained in some kind of narrative.

The obvious approach is to identify what risk events have occurred over the period since the previous measurement, which ones have not, and whether there have been any events that had not previously been considered.

Strictly speaking this is nothing to do with risk; it is just performance measurement *per se*, another example of where 'risk' management is a superfluous concept. However, the discipline of matching events up with the risk profile is a valuable one.

One rigorous approach is to formally attribute every change in forecast revenue, cost, time or quality to a specific risk having materialised. This sounds ambitious and, indeed, it is difficult to persuade management to do it. However, in an environment where these forecasts are being produced and reviewed each month, it is not too difficult to carry out an analysis of the variations. Any trivial changes can easily be set against an estimating error risk, or similar, which you just need to keep an eye to ensure it does not become material.

One interesting event which always sparks debate is where risks happen which were not part of the profile. First there is a debate about whether it was in fact in. You can often find risks which represent pretty much the same thing, though pedants will invite you to read the precise wording of the risk register entry. In any case, it is not clear what difference this makes other than triggering the need to make sure it is explicitly recognised in the future risk profile. Some will argue that events of this sort show the weakness of the risk activities that are being carried out, though it's fairly unrealistic to expect that a risk register capable of being managed by the risk advisor, let alone one which is limited by a management request to limit the number of items on grounds of team manageability, will cover everything that eventuates.

Others may consider that the contingency is there only to deal with the risks that have been thought of, and that other risks should be taken as an immediate hit on profit. This seems rather contrived and in my opinion is (a) unnecessary and (b) could only be suggested by people who take risk profiling work more literally than makes sense. Contingency is there for all deviations from forecasts, however caused.

Which brings us to the vexed topic of how to deal with black swans, as described in Chapter 2. They are sometimes described as low probability, high impact events. This is nonsense by definition, as if they could have been foreseen in advance they were not in your sample space and therefore certainly could not have had a probability (even zero). This is not to say that there are not plenty of these low probability, severe events which may occasionally turn up and exhaust your contingency. If it's only occasional, that's life, if it happens all the time then you need to take the hint that there may be something wrong in your risk profiling.

The genuine black swan is relatively rare as post-facto rationalisation is virtually a truism which makes it hard to justify that it could not have been foreseen. I guess it's a matter of judgement and, once you're dead, the issue of whether you were killed by:

- a low probability event
- an unknown unknown
- a perfect storm (whatever that is)
- a black swan,

is probably just yet another useless categorisation exercise, similar to others mentioned in this book, though maybe there is progressively less dishonour in the manner of your demise.

Taking a different tack, I mentioned in Chapter 2 (Figure 17 and page 78) that a useful alternative to activity-based risk analysis for programmes and timescales is to measure physical progress. Independently of the actual detail of the tasks completed you can follow whether or not the work is being crunched, and, on the basis of this, develop a view of when the work will be complete.

A common, or maybe the only approach to this is so-called earned value analysis (EVA). The key to this is that physical progress is measured in terms of the forecast or budgeted cost of activities completed – not of course the actual cost. So your initial plan can be plotted out as a graph of earned value against time: if at any time your actual cost exceeds the earned value you are running over budget, and if your earned value is less than what is planned you are behind schedule. This description is oversimplified, and the technique suffers from the obvious shortcoming that, for example, getting a planning consent is cheap, hence low value, compared with building a railway tunnel, but one is worthless without the other. Nonetheless, in matters of risks which hold up production and actions which maintain production, but not necessarily the production which was planned, earned value risk analysis and performance measurement is a useful tool.

However the measurement is made, a periodic report which rationalises actual performance against the identified risks and uncertainties is the single most effective tool for measuring risk performance.

Commercial perspective

So far, I have not elaborated much on how risk is treated within commercial contracts. It is of course a truism that risk is transferred by contracts and, like many truisms, it is not actually true. There are few risks you own which you can genuinely get rid of without retaining some sort of reputational impact, excess, incident management cost, or whatever. As well as trying to assign responsibility for different types of risk, some contracts also aim to specify the risk management processes between the parties to the contract.

Foremost among these in the UK is the New Engineering Contract which in its most recent form (NEC3), contains provisions for both client and contractor to identify risks before the contract starts and put them on the contractual Risk Register (where, of course they will be dealt with in accordance with the terms of the contract if they materialise) and also provides a process for risks that emerge. The requirement is for one or other party to issue an Early Warning Notice to formally notify each other of any matter which could:

- increase the Prices
- delay Completion
- delay meeting a Key Date or
- impair the performance of the works in use.

These EWNs have to be placed on the Risk Register and the parties have to meet in Risk Reduction Meetings to discuss and agree what is going to be done about the issue raised.

You can see that if you took this literally with an event-based definition for risk you would issue an EWN for every risk you thought of. It would just be a way of building your risk register. In practice, though, EWNs are only issued if something material happens, the precursor to a risk if you like, which you might also refer to a KRI being triggered or, potentially a new risk emerging.

In theory you do not need a EWN for events that have happened. Other contractual processes deal with that. The upshot of all of this is that the operation of EWNs and the attendant processes under NEC3 is confusing and varied, and NEC itself is frustratingly vague about the relationship between the contractual Risk Register and the sort of common practice, day-to-day risk management with large risk registers that takes place on many projects.

One of the root causes of this is the failure to recognise that risks are chains of events and there is no specification of what sort of event should be in risk register, what sort of event merits the creation of EWNs and what sort of potential event the EWN should be giving notice of.

None of this would be hard to sort out and I have been in projects worth billions of pounds where no-one has bothered to do so, in spite of the popular boast that the EWN is the jewel in the NEC crown.

Conclusion

The performance perspective, the control perspective and the commercial perspective are all concerned with two simple concepts.

- What uncertainty has crystallised or, as you might put it more crudely, what risks have happened?
- What has changed in the prospects for future uncertainty, or what risks might happen, what are the precursors of this?

You can structure your thinking about these concepts in advance by creating a risk model and defining KRIs. You can also take the view that you are scouting for the risks and uncertainties that may affect you, and raise EWNs so that everyone knows. However you structure your thinking, you need to be able to articulate it clearly and comprehensively, ready for the next stage. You need to avoid traps like:

- KRIs with too narrow a focus
- ignoring risks that were not on the register
- commercial wrangling over early warnings.

You need a risk performance report that clearly identifies what has changed since the last one and why. The control perspective provides a good recipe for his.

TOOLS FOR RISK SYNTHESIS

We inserted synthesis into the OODeming loop in order to provide a point where the forecasts meet actuals (using the control language) prior to the *Review/orient* stage. In many ways this activity is trivial or has been covered already: the narrative of actuals versus forecast just described provides a rationalisation (or synthesis) of risk performance. However we have not covered the risk profile going forward, or more accurately our updated view of the risk profile in the light of what we now know. Or, to put it yet another way, tested the validity of the risk model.

Updating your risk profile

There are two circumstances in which you might want to update your characterisation of the risk exposure:

- proactively, as a result of routine measurement such as that described in the previous section
- reactively, as a result of a trigger event occurring.

When we come to updating our risk profile there are several things to consider:

- dropping issues which are no longer relevant – those risks which have passed
- adding more detail on those issues which are coming into focus – maybe the commissioning programme for a new building, or the construction stage following a project feasibility study
- updating those issues for which we have gained some experience, but which have the potential to deteriorate further or to materialise in the future as well.

The first item in this list is straightforward and the second one has essentially been dealt with already in Chapter 2. It is the third, updating, task which is more novel and which I am going to focus on here. However, it is the first two items which generally require most of the work and a key message is that refreshing these areas is the important element of an adaptive approach. Note that we have not at this stage discussed changing the risk profile to reflect changes in the risk control measures. That is covered in the next section.

If a risk materialises we don't know if that means we should increase the future probability, reduce it or make no change. For example, in a construction project we may have the following situations.

- If the risk of bad ground where a hole needs to be excavated materialises, the risk of that happening in the future, for that particular hole, has disappeared. It can be taken off the register.
- If the risk of heavy snow preventing site access materialises, the risk of that happening again in the future is perhaps unchanged on the basis that an event which was expected has occurred and the model says another one could as well.
- If the risk of a slip, trip or fall on the worksite materialises, the risk of that happening again is probably larger than previously thought as a weakness in the safety management system is potentially emerging.

So you need to think though each case on its merits. I'm mentioning this in such detail as the control types think that where a risk happens, you draw down the contingency against it, so there's none left, so it can't happen again. Put that way, it's not hard to spot the logical flaw. I noted earlier that the controllers like to allocate contingency to a specific risk and that this is fundamentally wrong. In fact the contingency drawn down for a specific item probably exceeds the contribution to the contingency that the item made – if this is identifiable. The even more serious point from the controllers' point of view is that, even where the forecast and contingency match initially, there is no reason why they should not diverge in the light of events. New risks emerging and old risks materialising can both act to increase the forecast. That's why the budget (including contingency) may be the budget (including contingency) but over time the budget (including contingency) and the forecast may part company quite seriously (and generally not in a good way!).

This is quite informal and most of the time an informal approach to updating the risk model may be adequate, but there are mathematical techniques you can deploy to make an apparently more objective job of the update. The reason is that this is essentially a statistical inference task, and, correspondingly, there are two methods to consider. As the word 'updating' suggests, the first possibility is to use a Bayesian approach. The second, by contrast, could be called 'classical statistical'; these are the two great schools of statistical inference.

Bayesian updating

> *How often have I said to you that when you have eliminated the impossible, whatever remains, however improbable, must be the truth?* Sherlock Holmes

Bayesian updating is a conceptually straightforward method where the information gained to date is used to update the model. As the quotation of the great detective indicates, you need some kind of belief about the various hypotheses being considered and use the data to tell you what your new beliefs are. Needless to say, you express your degree of belief using subjective probabilities[8] and to the extent your data falsifies some of the hypotheses, you increase your belief in the others. The Bayes approach uses the probability of getting your observations conditional on each hypothesis to formalise this. It's a very powerful technique.

The simplest example is probably a Poisson process. Suppose concrete quality failures (or safety incidents, or industrial action, etc) are assumed to occur with a return period of T, and your probability distribution of T at the start of the project was $p_0(T)$ – some distribution obtained from the data available at project start. Suppose also the relevant activity has been running for time, t, and that N occurrences of quality failures (or safety incidents, strikes) have been experienced. The updated probability distribution of the return period is:

$$p_1(T) = Kp_0(T)\, e^{-t/T}T^{-N}$$

where K is a suitable normalisation constant. Typically you would use a non-informative prior such as $p_0(T) = 1/T$ and get to an expected value of T or work out the number of quality failures to be expected during the remainder of the project.

Whilst conceptually straightforward, this approach may be very difficult to apply due to the complicated formulas involved. What's more, it is only valid for situations where a Bayesian approach has been used to construct the risk model. The rarity of this means that the method is

---

[8] This is hugely important philosophically: you are using subjective probabilities not just for a physical event now, but for the event that a hypothesis is correct.

unlikely to have universal practical value though it may be of use for individual risks.

Classical statistical updating

Here, instead of adjusting everything to reflect the information gathered, we instead scan the information for clear evidence that something needs to be changed. For example, staying with the Poisson process, if the assumed probability of an event during the time t was 20% (T=5t) and the event occurred twice there is clear evidence that the return period is too long. I would propose reducing in line with the observed rate, T=t/2. Equally if on average the expected value of the number of events is three (T=t/3), and in fact none have been experienced, this suggests lengthening the return period to reflect the data, in this case T=2t, say (not zero!).

As an operational rule I would recommend that if the chance of the observation is 10% or less, the parameter should be changed so that it is 50%. The values given above are only approximately in line with this (for example in the last example we would have set T=1.44t) but the differences are not material. For the record, I should say that what I propose here is a cheap and cheerful approach to classical statistical confidence bounds; it may be crude, but it is good enough, and is within the range of what is achievable with the data available.

For other uncertainties, such as inflation, the update will be more a matter of establishing what has happened to date and then making an assumption about the future. For example, if the painting subcontractor is consistently exceeding the initial estimates, this will have to be built into the remaining tasks. If quality inspections are consistently under resourced and consistently take longer than expected to rectify, then this too will need to be built into the model going forward. What's more, the hold-ups in the quality function may lead you to increase the assumed timescales for handover to the client: you will have identified a clear systemic dependency.

This leads us into lessons learned, another important feature of the adaptive approach. Clearly at every stage of risk performance measurement and updating we have to make sure we update the risk profile to reflect what we have learned:

- on the project, through performance measurement

- elsewhere in the organisation
- elsewhere in the industry
- in the environment generally.

We record the lessons we have learned since the last update so as to ensure these can be acted on by other projects.

Reporting

These findings on risk performance, the updated risk model, emerging risks and lessons learned have to be combined into a report. This report goes in two directions:

- to the review process
- to the synthesis process of the governing unit.

The second of these is discussed in the next chapter, but now we come to the review process of the basic management layer.

TOOLS FOR RISK REVIEW

The risk review is the key stage in our management loop. It is where we open up our risk analysis to challenge by stakeholders and we consider the options for changing what we are planning to do. By having effective reviews we can adapt quickly to changing circumstances. Note that we are returning to this for the second time as we kicked off risk analysis in Chapter 2 with the initial review which we termed establishing the context. As we go through the loop time and again we are updating our view of risk and changing our plans. This is the adaptation which is a key attribute of risk management in this book; by doing it quickly we can fill in the gaps and address the shortcomings in the previous trips round the loop. This reduces the impact of the quick and dirty assumptions made to get going.

This is also the stage in which our loop model receives direction from the governing unit. This will need to be built into the review process as and when it changes, which we come to in Chapter 5.

The *Review/orient* stage of the OODeming loop follows *Synthesise* and is followed by *Plan/decide*. The boundaries between these stages are very fluid. The rationalisation of what has actually happened might well take place in the review; and the review might well take decisions about new risk control measures. But the chief characteristic of the review is that we take a broader view of risk than the purely analytic. It is an opportunity for risk geeks to take a back seat and for managers to intervene, to display situational awareness and emotional intelligence, as is their special skill.

This might seem at odds with the philosophy of this book which is to place responsibility for risk management *at all times* with managers. But the reality is that activities such as risk analysis and the preparation of progress reports is carried out by specialists, quite often in a formulaic way. The review stage of the management loop is our opportunity to get away from the formulas and take a view that is informed by the opportunities and pressures of the 'real' world managers inhabit.

At this stage it's worth discussing the fuller picture[9] of the OODA loop, originally prepared by John Boyd the creator of the concept, see Figure 29. Boyd said:

> *"The second O, orientation—as the repository of our genetic heritage, cultural tradition, and previous experiences—is the most important part of the O-O-D-A loop since it shapes the way we observe, the way we decide, the way we act."*

This underpins the key role review plays in risk management as well.

It's interesting how the simple OODA concept has become so messy in this representation. "Implicit guidance and control," what I have called direction, seems to impact everywhere, but especially on *Orient* as in the Chapter 1 governance model. Equally most possible feedback arrows have been added (I chopped them down a bit in redrawing the diagram). The orienting core is broken down into five impacting factors which is in fact the interplay between analysis and synthesis and:

- previous experience – current risk model.
- new information – emerging risks and lessons learnt
- cultural traditions – risk culture
- genetic heritage.

---

[9] Figure 29 is redrawn from the diagram by Patrick Edwin Moran - Own work, CC BY 3.0, https://commons.wikimedia.org/w/index.php?curid=3904554

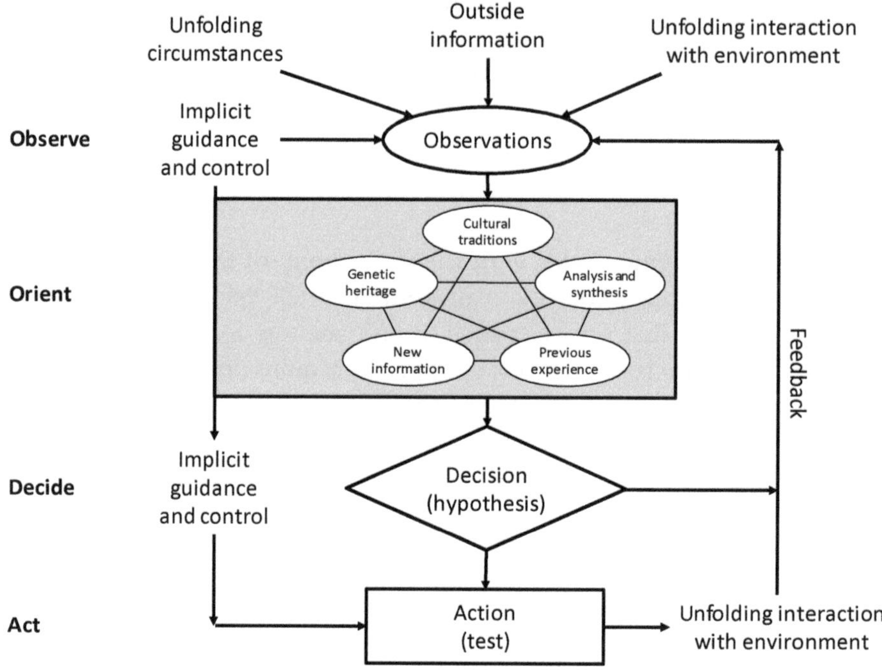

Figure 29 John Boyd's OODA loop

With a bit of imagination we can turn the genetic heritage of the individual fighter pilot into the inherited institutional framework of the organisation to reinforce the picture of culture shading into institutional drivers that I developed at the end of Chapter 3, and which I find very compelling. The OODA loop provides most of what we need for risk management and, in particular, inspires the mission of the review.

Note too, that the final decision may not perhaps be part of the review. It is ultimately taken by responsible managers, not a committee, and this is why it is a separate stage both in OODA and here (though not in Deming which is, perhaps, ambivalent).

Coming to the review itself, I'm taking for granted that this is a face-to-face meeting of some sort. We need to decide who should be involved and what the agenda is. I envisage that this is a largely internal meeting, but it's worth noting that Kaplan and Mikes in their paper,[10] discussed in the previous chapter, mentioned that JPL have a system of independent risk reviews by independent advisors. These reviews are very challenging and confrontational, albeit they are also underpinned by an ultimately constructive purpose. They are said to get the local experts to look outside their immediate environment, "lift their noses from the grindstone." This is worth thinking about, though in my opinion there should always be an element of challenge in the all-pervading conversations about risk I think are necessary, and when the challenge spills into confrontation it stops being constructive. There's a fine line between adult conversation and bullying and it's part of the culture that needs extreme caution for everyone to contribute their best.

Logistics

Everyone who has something to contribute should be invited – within reason. This will include managers, suppliers, customers, risk experts, safety and environmental types, planners, financial and project controllers, and so on. You just have to ensure it does not become too unwieldy.

With regard to how often, it might generally fit into a monthly reporting cycle, though it's not all that clear why we ordain our affairs in alignment with astronomical coincidences. As we are emphasising that risk management is an aspect of management-as-usual, it follows that risk will be discussed as part of routine reporting or, at least, on the same cycle.

However, reviewing risk is best done little and often with the emphasis on often. For example, the NEC contract requires that Risk Reduction Meetings should happen within seven days of an Early Warning Notice being given. That is, everyone should get together within a week of any material issue coming to light to wrangle over whose fault it is. Oh, sorry, I mean "co-operate in:

- "making and considering proposals for how the effect of the registered risks can be avoided or reduced

---

[10] Managing Risks: A New Framework, Robert S Kaplan and Anette Mikes, Harvard Business Review, June 2012. Available at hbr.org/2012/06/managing-risks-a-new-framework.

- "seeking solutions that will bring advantage to all those who will be affected
- "deciding on the actions which will be taken and who, in accordance with this contract, will take them and
- "deciding which risks have now been avoided or have passed and can be removed from the Risk Register."

What follows from this is that each review may be a relatively small scope exercise in terms of the activities covered. This is necessary to get the required detail of coverage of essential matters. Risk is generally a complex business and prone to debate which is too superficial. You will also need to have higher level discussions as well, which bring together the outputs of the detailed reviews. What's more, meetings that last longer than an hour are a pain.

Agenda

It is tacitly assumed in many organisations that the agenda for the risk review is the risk register. The review becomes a risk register review, which has several potential problems:

- the output is an updated risk register, nothing actually changes
- emerging risks are not discussed or introduced into the analysis
- you get bogged down in wording and pedantic debates about whether an issue is actually covered by the risk
- given the size of many registers, they go on and on
- there is no formal record apart from the updated register.

A key element of explicit risk management is the proper recording of risk reviews. So there should be a standard agenda along the lines of:

- review of actions from the previous meeting
- direction from the governing unit and any changes in it
- changes in the risk context, as recorded in the context document described in Chapter 2, including a review of key assumptions to avoid assumption neglect
- deviations from planned performance and reasons (that is, risks materialising, both recorded and unforeseen)
- emerging risks, whether from early warnings, changes of objectives, other projects, lessons learned, or whatever

- potential changes of plan, including more, different or fewer risk controls
- potential risk process and culture improvements which would normally happen less frequently than reviews of the risk profile itself
- potential updates to the risk management plan
- other business.

The key document supporting all this is a risk report from the synthesis stage which provides a performance commentary identifying the risks materialising, significant changes from last time – closed risks, emerging risks and updated risks – risk management actions and planned new ones, risk process points and so on. The risk report needs to provide the groundwork for discussions on options for changing the risk management actions, potential additional opportunities and so on.

It's worth saying explicitly that these reports should be closely based on the routine management reports to the extent they are available. The management reports should compare actual performance with planned/forecast performance and also provide an explanation (sometimes called a commentary or narrative) of any variances. The risk angle is to interpret these explanations as the materialisation of risk, whether previously identified or not. As we have noted, any variance can be interpreted this way which provides a direct link to the risk model.

With this preparation it should be possible to have an open and informed debate on matters of risk and uncertainty.

Needless to say the session should be properly written up and the relevant changes made to the risk model (updates to the risk register, for example) and the recommended action plans. To the extent the plans are not agreed in the meeting, there will be actions on managers to make the necessary decisions and ensure they are implemented. It can be argued that the risk review meeting records are what encapsulate our knowledge and understanding of risk rather than the risk model itself. This is another reason why the common practice emphasis on risk register reviews is misplaced.

It is apparent that the risk review, if properly actioned, can replace the formulaic assignment of responsibilities which is characteristic of many common practice risk management frameworks. The unit manager is responsible for risk and they decide how it is to be dealt with. They place actions on the relevant people to implement this and they check up that whatever has been decided is happening. This gets rid of explicit requirements for risk owners, risk action owners, risk coordinators, and so on which grace the pages of many a risk management plan. Nonetheless a document which states how risk and uncertainty are to be taken on board in management processes is undoubtedly a necessary part of explicit risk management and we come to the risk management plan shortly.

Change

The whole purpose of review is to identify if there is a need to do something different, a need to change the plan. The driver for this may be something happening on the outside: a new regulation, incipient trade barriers, competitor entry, bankruptcy of a supplier, a disastrous project elsewhere in the organisation and so on. Or maybe there is a need to respond to performance in your own area, a fabrication facility breaking down, the resignation of the chief executive, an idea for how disruptive IT can improve efficiency or a contamination incident.

Such changes can sometimes be decided on and implemented informally, but in an environment with budgetary disciplines and other controls, there is a generally a rigid change process.

This process, quite rightly, assumes that the need for change does not come out of the blue. So part of the change process is the identification of trends, matters that might affect costs, delivery times, product quality or any other objective. Logically you can expect that such issues will have been recorded as risks and that, as they become more and more likely, they will be recorded as early warnings, incipient ('unsubstantiated') trends and full blown ('acknowledged') trends. Projects often have a dedicated nomenclature to reflect this, with associated registers and processes. Perhaps inevitably, this gets a bit more complicated than it needs to be, and the risk of double counting grows in parallel.

In principle, though, it's pretty simple. You can maintain a risk model which is adjusted to reflect what is observed. Probabilities can be increased towards one as the inevitable is approached and the risk profile and forecast can be adjusted to fit. The forecast outturn cost is often called the AFC, anticipated final cost, and as it changes, the formal change process can be invoked to draw down contingency. This means that the contingency element of the budget is reduced and other appropriate line items in the budget are increased accordingly. Sometimes it may even happen that budget lines release cash to contingency.

Of course the time may come when the contingency is exhausted. At that point a more formal change process is required to increase the budget, essentially drawing down contingency from somewhere else. That's one possible change. Alternatively you may decide to do something different, which often involves cutting back on scope, and that leads to another type of change. A specially convened change review will look at all the options, including the attendant risks, before reaching a decision and then updating cost and time plans appropriately. Pressure from a remote FD may mean that contingency has to be released to spend elsewhere. A good description of an effective project change process is given as a case study in the Infrastructure Risk Group report[11] on the London Olympics. You can find more detail online[12].

The risk perspective offers a reasonably straightforward perspective on change. Naturally I think project controllers and others would be well advised to adopt it instead of their own, often contrived and overcomplicated, recipes.

The risk management plan

There needs to be a statement of how management intend to deal with risk and this document is typically termed a risk management plan. Its contents would include:

- recognition of the direction received from the governing unit (see next chapter)
- inclusion of, or reference to the risk context document (see Chapter 2)
- overarching risk management principles, including adherence to natural risk management
- roles and responsibilities

---

[11] Managing Cost Risk and Uncertainty in Infrastructure Projects: Leading Practice and Improvement, Report from the Infrastructure Risk Group, 2013. Case study 4, page 58.

[12] Browse learninglegacy.independent.gov.uk, for example the notes on AFC and baseline control, and contingency management.

- schedule of activities, including the pace of progress around the OODeming loop
- risk analysis techniques and tools as appropriate
- risk forecasting practices and formats
- risk reporting formats
- risk review formats.

As just noted, the responsibilities section should be minimal, and probably only needs to confirm the role of the manager and, if needed, the risk facilitator.

Tools and techniques may be extensive to deal with the risk profile identified in the context document in line with the direction provided and local policies. This book is not primarily about the IT support which is available to carry out Monte Carlo calculations, including QSRAs, evaluate fault and event trees, build Bayesian networks, record HAZOP sessions, draw decision trees and so on. And it particularly does not dwell on those behemoths of common practice risk management, the risk database.

This is deliberate, and partly because the risk database – a tool for recording risk lists – has proved spectacularly ineffective in providing an environment for agile, adaptive and natural risk management. They are cluttered up with extraneous tables and fields and are focussed on easy solutions like the colourful risk matrix at the expense of something useful. What's worse, the vendors of these systems have a track record of encouraging clients to introduce explicit risk management through the expedient of starting with implementation of the system: buy first, think later. Sadly, the buyer's regret is suffered not by those responsible, but the poor old risk facilitator and her risk analyst.

Yes, dear reader, I have a lot to get off my chest, but having done so, I have to admit that I am short on better ideas as I have detailed in Chapter 2. A fortune awaits someone who develops a tool which elegantly supports natural risk management.

The risk management plan is updated, as required, as a result of review.

SUMMARY

In some sense this chapter comes to the heart of what it means to assert there are no risk processes, just tools to help managers take risk and uncertainty on board in their business-as-usual and project management processes. Different organisations do things different ways and there are potentially many risk tools to support these processes in the appropriate way.

Seen this way, this chapter can only scratch the surface of the possibilities, yet, whatever the context, the tasks have a series of common functions:

- forecast the impact of risk and uncertainty (as in Chapter 2)
- create a management environment which accommodates this risk-based forecast in a sensible way
- monitor performance against the forecast and explain variances
- update your forecast in the light of circumstances
- decide what to do about it.

The challenge is obvious. We all have our own views about the likelihood and impact of risk and uncertainty and as a result, (a) we cannot be confident we are doing the right thing and (b) we can exploit this to play games in negotiating our budget or our price to meet ends which are not necessarily aligned with those of the other players.

There's no magic bullet to deal with this problematic truth. We can only rely on the culture we discussed in Chapter 3 to make our assessments and discussions as honest and open as possible, and to try to align objectives as far as we can.

From this managerial challenge we move on to the governance challenge of making it work throughout a large organisation.

Chapter 5

Tools for risk governance

Aligning the organisation for effective risk management

The previous chapters have first discussed natural risk management and then added a management layer to provide the necessary formality. This creates an organisation which is comfortable and competent in dealing with uncertainty. We now come to adding what I call the governance layer, which focusses on directing that competence coherently across the organisation as a whole.

The context for risk governance was set in Chapter 1 where I emphasised that this coherent approach is a serious matter for senior organisational management. That is why I used the term 'governance'. This is where the various corporate governance guidance reports which have accumulated over the years – Cadbury, Turnbull, Combined Code, Sarbanes Oxley, and so on – are applied. It is also frames the scope of what is popularly known as ERM, enterprise risk management, in that it concerns what happens in the organisation as a whole, though the picture in this book is one which does not restrict itself to the organisation itself, but aims to influence how risk and uncertainty are dealt with throughout the stakeholder network.

The management loop model proposed for this in Chapter 1 is the same as that used to describe the management layer activity of Chapter 4 with two important generalisations.

- Instead of a single loop there is a hierarchy of loops extending to different levels and functions of the organisation and even outside it to the supply chain, customers and other stakeholders.
- In this hierarchy there is generally a governing-governed relationship as shown in Figure 7 (Chapter 1, page 37) in which the governing unit:
  - provides direction to the governed unit (as part of *Act/do* in its own management loop)
  - audits the governed unit (as part of *Observe/measure*)
  - receives reports from the governed unit (as part of *Synthesise*).

Each of these is discussed here in a structure that mirrors that of Chapters 2 and 4 where relevant. Throughout this section I shall use the terms governing and governed units. They are not the most felicitous – and I considered others – but have the advantage of being clear.

It can be expected that direction is largely given at the point where the new management unit is spawned whilst the auditing and reporting functions are much more part of routine looping, so we start with a governing organisation setting up a new loop.

An interesting question is where in the management loop of the governing unit this begins to be an issue. The routine review is likely to identify the possibilities for a new business unit, product or project, so this is where we will start. We then go on through the whole OODeming loop with *Decide/plan/forecast* being focussed on setting up new governed units, *Act/do* being concerned with providing direction to the governed units, *Observe/measure* being about audit, *Synthesise* looking at the issues of bringing together reports from what might be several governed units and finally back to routine *Orient/review* with the governed units in place.

Some of these sections are relatively short in that there is not much to add to the corresponding activities in the previous chapters from the governance perspective.

TOOLS FOR DEVELOPING THE STRUCTURAL OPTIONS

In the course of routine, risk-aware management review it will become apparent that there are opportunities, or the necessity, to set up new business units, to kick off new projects, enter into new strategic contracts, develop new products or markets or whatever else. Alternatively, maybe you are considering outsourcing a key function with all the opportunities and risks this step might bring. These potential new activities may merit their own management organisation and management cycle.

This is, of course, a key point. Most likely the seeds of these activities or ideas will have been growing under the auspices of the existing unit. The possibility of setting such activities free to swim on their own is what is now on the table. What we are really considering here is an appraisal of strategic options which might result in a new management entity with its own management loop supported by its own risk management tools. This is a preliminary to actually deciding to make the structural change, and figuring out how to effect the necessary governance changes, discussed next.

It's important to remember that we might also be considering the winding up a structural element. Projects reach their end and deliver an asset for use in business-as-usual. A product may become obsolete or a market may be unprofitable and need to be closed down. Maybe the outsourcing organisation has gone bust. The same principles apply in this situation and the governing unit's context documentation, risk management plan and risks analysis will need to change accordingly.

As ever then, we are bringing our collective experience, our background and cultural knowledge to bear on our appreciation of the risk profile now, and with the potentially changed structure. However, it is important that these decisions, often with long-term commitments and high stakes, are analysed as thoroughly as possible, and this is covered in the next section.

The preliminary to this is that a complete set of choices is taken into account. So far, I have described the potential decision in terms of binary choices – make or buy, carry on or demerge – but it is important that the full range of options is considered, and these options are likely to have distinctive risk profiles. If you keep your security in house you can respond to a new threat; if you outsource it, you may have problems both in day-to-day contract management – a new skill you need – and you may be tied into the old way of doing things or maybe just the cheapest way. Or maybe you can benefit from innovation. It is surprising how many organisational changes such as this go ahead with no real appreciation of the changed risk profile which will be faced as a result.

What is needed for this are high-level versions of the risk context tools discussed in Chapter 2. The way to create these is to take the current risk context document, part of the risk management plan as we identified at the end of the previous chapter, extract what is relevant to the proposed change and expand it for the options under consideration.

The checklist from the relevant part of Chapter 2 (pages 44-45) provides a guide here for the matters in your risk analysis context document which might need to be developed further. You might record this in mini risk context documents. Perhaps the most important element of this is to check that the proposed change in structure is compliant with the regulations and guidance which are relevant to your entity. In other words, are you potentially setting up something which is inconsistent with the risk direction, and other constraints, which have been passed down to you?

Clearly, too, implementation plans for the change under consideration will have to be sketched out, including high-level activities and controls, such as recruiting new managers and maintaining the risk culture, and alterations in the stakeholder map. All of this will then enable potential changes in the risk profile to be mapped out alongside the baseline costs and benefits of each option.

TOOLS FOR RISK GOVERNANCE DECISIONS AND PLANNING

Working from the mini risk context documents, you now have to reach a decision on the change in structure and sort out the relevant plans and forecasts. Many structural changes are relatively routine. For example, a project may move from its development stage to implementation. This would generally be reflected in a different management structure and disciplines, and a handover process, including risk information. Many organisations have a routine 'gates' process to facilitate the transition and check that the project will be successful, including taking risk on board.

More complex changes may need you to understand the risk profiles better and you may need to set up risk workshops and the like to explore it. You will need to adapt your risk analysis to reflect the changed structures under consideration. In doing this it's important to take a balanced view, comparing like with like: your current risk model is probably very detailed, but at this stage you have only a coarsely-grained view of the changed scenario. Again, this underlines the importance of focussing on the main sources of uncertainty – for both scenarios.

The key to this should be doing just enough to support the decision. In principle the detailed risk work will be done in the new management entity: at the higher level the key issues have to be analysed to make sure they contain no significant issues for which there is unlikely to be a suitable management approach.

Once a decision has been made it is time to start on implementation, described in the next section, and planning and forecasting. In general, the plans and forecasts for the governing unit will be developed in the governed unit, reported back and adjusted in line with the loop iterations. However, before this is up and running, it may be necessary to create outline plans and these may well be derived from what exists, industry benchmarks, the outside view, and so on. It is essential that the plans allow for the implementation of the risk control measures which have been appealed to so as to allow the decision to be made. Sounds obvious, but it doesn't always happen.

TOOLS FOR RISK GOVERNANCE DIRECTION

This is the key element of the management loop for risk governance. This is the stage at which, having decided to set up a new element of the organisation which is to have its own management cycle, you need to ensure its risk taking is aligned with your organisational needs and objectives.

The literature contains several approaches to this:

- risk management policy – which generally contains brave statements about how important it all is and how you are going to do it with registers and matrices and so on; the risk management policy does not generally reflect on the nature of the risk
- risk appetite – as discussed in Chapter 4 – which comes much closer to thinking about the specific risk profile, but which is based on a rather unfortunate metaphor that there is an amount of risk that it is good to eat; this may also be implemented through coloured risk matrices
- risk attitude – based on the concept of individual risk attitude discussed in Chapter 3 and scaled up for the organisation.

It seems that the best points of all these should be combined in something we could call risk governance direction, recognising that some parts of it will be formal instructions and others may be more in the nature of guidance. It is essential that the governed unit has the opportunity to develop its own most appropriate tools and techniques for its specific circumstances.

This brings us to an important aspect of the governance model: at some point it has to stop. We are used to seeing fractal-style structures which continue up and down in scale indefinitely, but for the organisation there is a top, and at this point the organisation has to set its own direction. This particular loop must be self-governing as well as self-managing. So in describing the tools for risk direction we shall take the time to describe any specific aspects for the centre of the organisation.

Topics to consider for risk direction

An approach to this favoured by some organisations is simply to issue the risk management plan: the governed unit is directed to comply! However, a more nuanced approach would consider each aspect and tailor the contents of the risk management plan to meet the specific needs of the unit being set up. This section provides some indicators for this, albeit based on the description of the risk management plan in Chapter 4.

As with most things in risk, the directions will contain process points and content points. The process points will be concerned with how risk management is carried out and will to some extent depend on the nature of the risk and uncertainty – the content. Thus, the process aspects should follow the description of the risk, though often the approach is the other way round, seeking to impose corporate systems whatever the specific circumstances and risk profile.

The emphasis should be on the interfaces – the nature of the constraints the organisation wants to place on risk taking and how risk is reported – rather than interfering with the precise details of how risk is analysed internally. But if the organisation works on risk lists and matrices, then risk will have to be reported in lists and matrices independently of what methods are used to create this data.

Typically the directions would cover the following points:

- unit objectives
- significant risks and uncertainties – outline risk profile
- guidelines on how the objectives are to be met – key opportunities and risk control measures
- management policies – risk management policy
- risk attitude and decision making
- culture – risk culture
- management processes – as they relate to risk
  - responsibilities
  - risk analysis
- budget – contingency.

Note that two of these bulleted items are exclusive to risk and uncertainty – the risk profile and the risk attitude; the others are parts of broader aspects of the directions. Each is now discussed in turn.

Outline risk profile

This first essential component of a risk attitude statement is the risk profile which contains the current understanding about the uncertainties the organisation faces *and which it is likely to face in the foreseeable future.*

This is a particular concern at the top level as the publication of the risk profile is now recognised as good corporate governance. The FRC UK Corporate Governance Code[1] requires:

---

[1] The UK Corporate Governance Code, Financial Reporting Council, April 2016.

> *"C.2.1. The directors should confirm in the annual report that they have carried out a robust assessment of the principal risks facing the company, including those that would threaten its business model, future performance, solvency or liquidity. The directors should describe those risks and explain how they are being managed or mitigated."*

This guidance is developed through a series of other reports on corporate governance which have been presented over the years. Specifically, it follows on from the well-known Turnbull report on internal control which has now been superseded by the FRC's detailed guidance on risk management.[2]

The question of current versus future risk profile is an interesting one. The Code just quoted refers to the risks the company faces at the time. However it seems to me that shareholders would have an interest in possible new risks emerging as a result of decisions the directors might take such as betting the farm on a new market, and it is only reasonable that a picture of the uncertainties facing the company such include such matters. A case in point was the founder of EasyJet's very public concern, in his role as a shareholder, about the risk of expanding the airline's fleet too quickly. This is a refreshing change from the more normal shareholder role of pressing for ever higher profit and dividends, pushing directors into taking more and more risks to satisfy these expectations. When we discuss the risk attitudes of company agents, we must also think about those of shareholders, and other stakeholders as well.

The detail and degree of quantification of the risk profile will increase as the organisation becomes more mature in risk management, but at any point in time the organisation should be able to produce a description of the main types of uncertainty, the impact they could have, and how likely that impact is to materialise in the light of the organisational plans to deal with them. This has been discussed in Chapter 2.

Maybe it is worth a word about the types of risk to profile. One definition of risk is 'the effect of uncertainty on objectives' and one approach is to think about your objectives one-by-one and see how that prompts your risk thinking. This is useful, though somewhat overdone, and organisations with trendy balanced scorecards can use those to think

---

[2] Guidance on Risk Management, Internal Control and Related Financial and Business Reporting, Financial Reporting Council, September 2014.

about important uncertainties. For firms, the main objective is creating shareholder wealth (under the Anglo-Saxon model) and this makes for a conceptually very simple approach to risk profiling. Other organisations may have different objectives with a greater emphasis on delivery of services or the quality of those services. Few organisations do not have financial objectives and almost all are driven by a desire to grow and, most of all, its obverse, to survive.

As well as these strategic uncertainties, most organisations have day-to-day risks to avoid: fraud, loss of data, service unavailability, and, pre-eminently, doing it all safely. These all need to be covered, albeit briefly in some cases, as our risk attitude statement will also take these types of risk on board.

Moving away from the top level, the work on the risk context recommended in the previous section is relevant, especially the mini risk context documents which should have been prepared as part of decision making for setting up the governed unit.

Thus, the statement of the risk profile itself just needs to reflect the work that has already been done, through the risk reviews of the governing unit and feeding into the decisions about structuring. Typically it would be set out by risk type in a comprehensive way. The descriptions would be largely verbal, though the current level of qualitative or quantitative profiling could be added. In many cases there may be a reasonably comprehensive risk model, for example in the case of a project moving from development into implementation.

However, the aim is to present a clear, non-technical picture of the significant risks and uncertainties the governed unit faces and a detailed risk register may not be the best way to communicate this. It almost never is.

Opportunities and risk control measures

The aim here is similar and it may well be decided to combine the description of the risks with the outline measures needed to deal with them. Of course what is done about risk and uncertainty is essentially a matter for the management of the governed unit so this section may be rather short.

However, this is the opportunity to provide corporate direction on the way things should be managed: we transfer all construction risk to contractors; we outsource data security to Capita and so on. The governed unit will have to recognise that the directed control measures may not be 100% effective and of course such controls have a cost associated with them.

It is also an opportunity to indicate what lessons have been learned from previous experience, whether within the organisation or outside. A formal lessons learned process is very useful and drawing attention to the controls that are likely to be required should be beneficial to the governed unit.

Risk management policy

This is likely to be a repeat of the policy of the organisation, potentially with nothing to add, though some governing units may expand on the specific details which are relevant for their activities, with perhaps further expansion for the governed units.

At the top level, the policy is likely to comprise statements of intent that risk is considered comprehensively, that compliance with certain legal, regulatory and safety matters is required, and that the organisation has systems for implementing the management and governance layers. It will say what the benefits of this are expected to be, that the management are totally committed to it and that they engender an effective risk culture. Line management is, of course, totally responsible for risk management. It may also cover the other risk management principles that may form part of the risk management plan.

From the perspective of this book, this is all pretty much obvious and the need for a risk management policy in addition to the other material is quite questionable.

Risk decision making

Our risk attitude prefigures how we are going to take decisions where risk and uncertainty are important. This is central to risk management and Chapter 7 goes into this in some detail, aiming to present a coherent view of several threads of risk decision theory on the basis that risk managers need to be familiar with the issues even if they don't often use the techniques. The formulation of the risk attitude is also central to risk governance of the organisation starting from the top. For both these reasons we first go into some detail about decision making, summarising some of the material in Chapter 7, before coming to the risk attitude itself.

We know that risk decisions are generally going to involve tradeoffs between different objectives and different types of risk. We also know already that we are only going to take risk because we have to: it is the best course in the circumstances. We are not going to take a risk, or face uncertainty, because we want to; we are not going to do so because of some risk appetite.

It is also worth saying that no organisation should be content to leave its risk decision making to undefined personal risk attitudes which result in the behaviours observed by researchers and described in Chapter 7. The attitude of every organisation to risk should be that all material decisions are reached by a systematic approach which involves identification of the options for action (or inaction) and analysis of the implications of each of these options. This exercise may be carried out from first principles for major strategic decisions; or it might result in a set of decision rules for day to day decisions such as whether to offer a client a mortgage.

The next point is the decision itself. With the adoption of the systematic approach I can assume that you have identified the need for a decision, you have identified the uncertainties, you have identified the options you want to decide between and you have identified what happens under each option and outcome: you have set up a payoff matrix. Obviously doing all this is a major task, but it also makes sense to see first of all what the implications of the decisions are.

The important point here is to recognise the difference between modelling what people do and providing guidance on what they should do. The narrative in Chapter 7 moves steadily from the prescriptive to the descriptive. We can assume that the organisation will be concerned only with what it should do at this stage. Of course we also need to discuss the effect of people doing what they are actually inclined to do, and what the organisation should do about it.

The first important point about all systematic decision theory is that its central preoccupation is the tradeoff between the impact of risk and the likelihood of the impact occurring. The highly mathematical theories of Chapter 7 differ in the nature of the assumptions they make about this tradeoff. I have mentioned already that risks decisions are also about the tradeoff between different types of impact. I described in Chapter 2 about how years ago we agonised over the risk of steam explosions in nuclear reactors. We knew the tradeoffs were there – between the intolerable consequences of an accident and the economic benefits of electricity, between the intolerable consequences of an accident and the very low likelihood that it would happen based on the evidence available – but couldn't be sure how to make them.

Decision theory forces you to articulate your preferences. What's more, it forces you to articulate them in a specific tradeoff form, or else you appear to be irrational. And when you have accepted this, you have to (a) express your assessments of the likelihood of events as subjective probabilities and (b) choose whichever option maximises the expected value of your utility, that is, an integrated measure of the desirability of different impacts. Your utility, a subjective concept too, represents your tradeoff between different types of impact. This optimising approach is subject to the criticisms that it is impossibly time consuming, and that, as an optimisation, the benefits are very marginal anyway.

The only alternative is to adopt various heuristics which often work well, but bring with them the risk that they are inappropriate for the particular decision-making situation. What to do? I think the answer is clear. You have to adopt the systematic approach of analysing risks and options, otherwise what you are doing lacks transparency. But you should not overwork it. You should be able to recognise situations where one option is clearly superior to another, but is only marginally better than a third, if at all. Choosing either the first or third is OK in these circumstances. Either way the solution is good enough.

But there is a practical problem with this, one that gets exaggerated in many applications, and which leads to risk appetites and the like, but an important problem nonetheless. It arises because one of the essential assumptions in decision theory is invalid, at least in the eyes of many people. This assumption is continuity, that is, small changes in impacts lead to small changes in preferences. On the face of it, it sounds reasonable, but what if some of the options result in someone being killed in some versions of the future? We may regard this is as qualitatively different and it will violate the continuity requirement. If this is the case, our preferences suggest we need to consider the management of risks to human life separately to other risks and this is exactly what we do. Organisations develop their plans on the assumption that only 'safe' options are considered. Thus safety management is considered separately and safety management does not form part of organisational risk management. This is entirely appropriate: the comprehensiveness and attention to detail of safety risk analysis and management is, or should be, much higher than what is needed for ordinary business risk management.[3] We should not be too surprised if the philosophies and techniques differ between the two disciplines. This truth is not always recognised and has led to the inappropriate adoption of some methods and unwise attempted integration.

The attentive reader will see that I have now contradicted myself. Perhaps you were uncomfortable when I blithely said that decisions about nuclear reactor accidents were a tradeoff between likelihood, safety impacts and economic impacts. But now I am saying you need to stay safe, and comply with your safety management system, before all else. You can have your own views on this, and you can distract yourself with the thought that reducing one safety risk often causes another to bob up elsewhere. It's widely reported that in the aftermath of the attack on the World Trade Center in 2001, there was an excess of people killed in road accidents which was around 50% of the number killed in the attack itself, and *six* times the number killed in aeroplanes on 9/11.[4] This was due to people choosing to go by road because of the risk of further attacks using airplanes. This behaviour has been widely ridiculed, though the argument is silly: the fact that no such attacks actually took place is no evidence that the subjectively assessed risk of going by air was irrational. Leaving this distraction to one side, we probably have to face up to the reality that everything is a tradeoff, even the lives of people. We know we cannot reduce the risk of death from a terrorist attack, for example, to zero. But for day-to-day purposes building and complying with an exacting safety management system is a practical way to reflect the high utility implicit in both your health and safety preferences, and those of society. Safety management is rather an effective and desirable heuristic.

This raises the question of what else. Potentially many issues could be the subject of overriding ethical considerations like human safety. Environment is an obvious one, and, more mundanely, many risks seem to

[3] With the flipside thought that maybe we spend too much time on business risk analysis.

[4] Risk Savvy, Gert Gigerenzer, Penguin, 2015. Page 8.

derive their importance from their role in job preservation. On the whole it is not practicable to make special cases of everything and even in the matter of human life the fact is we have to, and we do, make tradeoffs.

With this exception then, we need to maximise expected utility and we should expect the organisation to develop its subjective probabilities. In my experience organisations generally have little difficulty in doing this to their satisfaction, at least as far as making the decision goes. (Though to be accurate, they generally fool themselves into pretending the probabilities are real.)

The utility concept has two aspects. Firstly you are using a common scale for different types of outcome. Secondly you can express preferences about risk itself, perhaps assigning a very high disutility to scenarios in which you approach bankruptcy, or articulating a preference for diversified portfolios over non-diversified ones. Utility is a mechanism for expressing risk aversion.

Risk aversion is in turn a rationalisation of the existence of risk premiums in commercial deals. I'm defining the risk premium to be the price of transferring risk which is additional to its expected value. Typically a firm, an insurance company say, will charge a risk premium to take on risk, and most of us recognise the validity of such pricing. A construction company which charges a price based on the P80 of cost is striking a reasonable deal. Often this deal will contain a tacit probability of eroding its profit or even its contribution to overheads. There's a model of this in Chapter 7.

Diversifying risks is a common objective of managers, but a questionable one. In the economy of firms and investors it is actually for investors to diversify their risks through their portfolio holdings. It is an understandable agency effect that managers will try to diversify since it reduces risk and protects their jobs, and probably their reputation. But it is, at first sight, suboptimal for the market as a whole.

What, then, about survival? Should firms adopt a utility function which greatly reduces their propensity to take farm-losing risks? At first sight, again the answer should be 'no'. A market in which firms are avoiding big uncertainties will be suboptimal for investors. However, this needs to be balanced against the excess costs of bankruptcy.

The financial costs are perhaps not as much as you might think. Most of the activities will continue in a different organisational structure. The employees will move to where the activity is resumed. Some may be inspired to branch out in innovative ways and increase productivity. Others may be prompted into overdue retirement. But leaving the economic stuff on one side, the human cost is high. Some people do lose their jobs permanently. Most employees go through a period of high stress and reduced income. Many suppliers suffer bad debts and cash flow crises and may themselves be pushed into administration. In practical terms survival of the firm must be a major preoccupation of risk management.

Returning to the point about the organisation as serial decision taker, we take it for granted that many decisions are taken every day by people in different parts of the organisation and that these decisions differ in nature as well as strategic impact, ranging from routine operational decisions – a bus driver executing a manoeuvre or a trader rebalancing their portfolio – to strategic decisions about new products or markets. Chapter 7 makes clear that multiple decisions are a recurring theme in the discussion of decision theory; many aspects of the theories do not deal well with this. For example, repeated risk averse decision making *where the probabilities are known* is irrational; you *know* you will do better in the long term if you maximise expected value rather than (risk averse) utility.

However, one aspect of the theory which resonates a lot more in the context of a risk attitude is the idea of expressing preferences over a whole range of real and hypothetical propositions. If the organisation is to have an attitude to risk, and for this attitude to guide its individual decision makers in the course of their work, it must be able to deal with all the risk issues which will arise and the options that will be considered, and the discipline necessary to take a systematic approach supports this.

With this preamble, how can we best formalise a statement of the attitude to risk for our organisation?

Risk attitude

The organisational risk attitude will flow from the risk profile in the light of the organisation's overall approach to decision making. The starting point should be an indication of the risk profile that the organisation is subject to. This could be as little as a list of the types of risk in play, or it may go further to provide some kind of preliminary analysis of causes, impacts and, maybe, likelihood. Either way, there needs to be a policy statement that these risks should be analysed further as required.

For each type of risk you can identify three potential attitudes: compliance, toleration or optimisation.

Compliance

Certain types of risk can be managed in line with external requirements which have to be complied with. This will include health and safety, fraud, regulatory breaches and so on.

This is sometimes referred to as no appetite or zero tolerance. What it means is not that the relevant risks are reduced to zero, but that there is an accepted system of controls to maintain a very low level of risk. This could be the safety management system or the financial controls and delegations. These control systems can be designed on the basis of established good practice and the risk attitude statement may set out the standards or guidance which need to be implemented. Essentially the existence and operation of these systems removes a segment of risk from the mainstream of organisational risk management and its decision making.

The organisational attitude is, "comply."

Optimisation

Other uncertainties can be managed in line with the principles of decision theory. This was explained at some length in the previous section and the key message is that most of the time you need to try to maximise expected utility. What this means is that we identify the possible ways the future might turn out, assign subjective probabilities to these futures and subjective scores as to their attractiveness – utility – and do what gives us the best probability weighted mean score. In other words we look at the upsides and downsides and take risks because we think the potential upside is worth it.

As I have outlined, both in this chapter and Chapter 7, there are many theoretical concerns about the practicability and suitability of this approach, this attitude. However in practice it seems to work pretty well. It is usually possible to facilitate a group of managers into giving a view as to the probabilities of different outcomes and to identify the consequences. Valuing the non-financial consequences can be problematic. For example some organisations express zero appetite for reputational risk but are a standing joke for the way their projects always overspend and come in late.

For this attitude the organisation needs to specify its utility in some way, and in most cases this will be financial value. Essentially we do a risk-aware cost-benefit analysis. The reason for this is that risk-averse utility rarely adequately represents our organisational preferences. This is shown in Chapter 7, for example in the modelling of a portfolio of shares, and also in my previous book.[5] As another example, the UK government guidance on investment (the 'Green Book') contains a formulation for risk aversion which is of no practical value. The practical solution is to limit the probabilities of adverse events such as making a loss or bankruptcy and the risk attitude statement may cover the organisation's convention for this, for example, bid at P80.

The organisational risk attitude is, "take the risk if it's worth it."

Toleration

Reputational risk is a good example of an impact which is hard to quantify and which we know we are going to have to bear. This brings us to our third attitude, toleration.

The idea of tolerating risk was first put forward by Frank Layfield who was inspector at the public inquiry for the Sizewell 'B' nuclear power plant in the 1980s. He challenged the HSE to develop risk criteria based on the idea that society only tolerates risks to health and safety; it does not accept them (the word that had previously been used). The HSE responded[6] by setting levels of individual risk which would represent the limit of tolerability (a neologism at that time). These limits were genuine risk levels, phrased in terms of the probability of death. Specifically the limit set on the risk of death of a member of the public was one in ten thousand per year. The report also set an achievable benchmark ten times lower, and regarded a level ten times lower than that, one in a million per year, as a level beyond which, "it would not be reasonable to seek further improvements to standards if these involved a cost." There was a similar, but higher, set of numbers for members of the workforce.

---

[5] Estimating Risk: A Management Approach, Andy Garlick, Gower, 2007. Chapter 7, page 141.

[6] The Tolerability of Risk from Nuclear Power Stations, HMSO, 1988. The document that launched a thousand carrot diagrams.

The legal requirement for safety is that risks should be reduced as low as reasonably practicable (ALARP) which was interpreted as requiring any improvements in safety which did not entail a grossly disproportionate cost. As described in Chapter 2, this is essentially an optimisation with a 'grossly' inflated disutility. The risk tolerance levels did something different: it required that the risk should not be unfairly imposed on specific individuals. It was an ethical criterion which went beyond maximising expected utility.

Since then, however, the tolerance concept has been widely and inconsistently abused in other contexts, and especially when people start talking about 'risk appetite'.

A better example might be a limit on the nature or volume of subprime mortgages a bank imposes in its lending department. This might comprise risk-based lending criteria and monitoring the total amount lent. However, I think this can be seen as a control measure for the bank's total exposure due to the lending unit. For the bank itself, there could be a risk attitude of limiting exposure to loans to what is covered by reserves. This raises the question of what the exposure actually is – for example the default rate if there is a change in the economic climate. In practice banks do not really have that attitude. They calculate the risk and assess, rightly or wrongly, that the risk of exceeding reserves is small. I imagine they would not survive if they did not do this.

The point I am trying make here is that tolerating risk does not go much beyond accepting the inevitable. The natural attitudes to risk are either to comply or optimise. There may be ethical considerations to limiting risk, but we have already consigned safety to the comply box. Other tolerated levels are simply what can be achieved with risk control measures. This leaves us, for example, with the reputational risks we noted as difficult to optimise. I think the issue of reputational risk is rather overstated, but, whatever the truth of that, we know it's hard to measure and that any public undertaking will be subject to the risk of reputational damage. We know the controls are prevention and dealing with risks that materialise in the right way. Our attitude is to recognise it and deal with it. The best we might do in the analysis might be a flaky qualitative risk matrix, but that will not stop us putting controls and actions in place to reduce the likelihood and plan for the worst. We may also want KRIs to act as alarm bells.

The organisational risk attitude is, "tolerate and manage."

Attitudes not to have

This all seems quite simple; surely there's something missing? Well, of course it is simple, but some things are missing because I think they're a bad idea.

I have probably said enough about risk appetite. We don't have the attitude that we need to eat enough risk to stay alive.

We also do not have unreasonable attitudes. "Our appetite for project risks is such that all projects must achieve their objectives and not exceed their cost/time parameters set out in delegations and protocols." To be fair, I think this means that you have to get the delegations and protocols changed before the cost/time parameters are exceeded, but we should be able to do something more realistic than this.

We also should avoid meaningless guff. The attitude I've just quoted was prefaced with the remark, "our approach to the appetite for risk management occurs at three levels." It's a good indicator of the poverty of common practice risk management that people feel compelled to write risk management plans filled with such nonsense.

Risk culture

It is important to bear in mind that decisions are actually made by people, maybe working alone, maybe working in groups.

It's clear from Chapter 3 and also Chapter 7 that – if you didn't know it already – people can have a major impact on performance which is not necessarily in line with what the organisation wants. People are humans, and indeed, mostly *Humans* as identified by the psychological researchers, which means they have wide range of biases and heuristics; they have their own objectives and agendas, they are driven by their emotions and as a result have their own attitudes to risk. Working in groups induces its own dynamic and tension and this leads to a group risk attitude, which may be harder to define. The relationship between individual risk attitudes and those of groups is well described by Murray-Webster and Hillson.[7] This shows that working in groups alone is not sufficient to ensure that individual attitudes to risk are overridden by the stated organisational attitude. Instead group dynamics may lead to the

---

[7] Managing Group Risk Attitude, Ruth Murray-Webster and David Hillson, Gower, 2008.

prejudices and attitudes of dominant people carrying the day. Murray-Webster and Hillson provide some techniques to support optimal decision taking, but it is clear that working on a shared culture is the best way to achieve what is needed.

To put this another way, we can see that there is a potential problem with natural risk management which is that *by nature* we take bad decisions in the face of risk. We need to be alert to this and train ourselves to ring alarms when it is happening. As I note in Chapter 7, we are not very good at this, but organisations can help, both by providing a formal framework – the management level – but also by providing mutual help to ring the necessary alarms – the natural risk management level. This needs to be part of the culture.

To grow the right culture it is important for the organisation first to define its own risk attitude, and then to take steps to ensure that people behave in line with that risk attitude rather their own, or their team's. This means avoiding so-called agency effects. Chapter 3 provided a summary of what we know about risk culture: how to ensure natural risk management works as well as possible in your organisation. There are several assessment tools, for example the IRM cultural aspects model, and the risk governance direction may specify desirable targets for the results of the assessments as well as more general statements about what risk culture the organisation aspires to.

The risk attitude section of the governance directions may set an organisational style for the culture, in terms of the solidarity-sociability axes for example, but, looking at the eight IRM aspects, the aspiration must be to do well in all of them. More practically the organisation may set a trajectory to achieve mindful organising, with its five characteristics listed at the end of Chapter 3.

Process requirements for risk

Responsibilities

It is customary for this part of the guidance to go into considerable detail about roles and responsibilities: who's ultimately responsible, who should be risk manager, risk owners, action owners, and so on. As already noted in Chapter 4, this seems a bit superfluous. The manager is responsible for everything, including dealing with uncertainty, and it is up to the manager how this responsibility is discharged, including through delegations. To the extent that risk management is a natural activity it should not be necessary to have lengthy prescriptions for how the manager should do their job.

Risk analysis

Organisations like to specify what risk analysis techniques should be used up and down the organisation. They like to publish risk management plans which look very like other risk management plans. They like to set out qualitative assessment schemes with pretty colours to be used at each level of the organisation. They like to require that QSRAs are done on all project programmes regardless of whether these programmes are in a fit state to be QSRAed, whether any useful information or insights will result and whether there is something better that can be done.

Having said all this, it is obviously necessary that the results of the risk analysis that is carried out by the governed unit, and reported back to the governing unit, are capable of being synthesised in a reasonably easy way and this leads to a minimal requirement for risk analysis.

The section on risk governance synthesis deals with this and there is little more to say here.

Budgets and contingency

In Chapter 4 we treated forecasting and budgeting as part of the management layer. This is appropriate, but we cannot ignore the fact that budgets are often downward imposed, or at least that budgets generally have to be approved at higher levels. This includes that part of budgets that relates to risk, what we have called contingency.

This would not be part of the main direction document which we have been discussing in this section up to now, but it is reasonable to think that budgets would, for example, emerge from the governed unit's planning process, be integrated into the report that is sent upstairs from *Synthesise*, integrated into the governing unit's report for review and then, approved or modified, sent back down as an element of the direction.

As part of this, contingency would be subject to certain rules, especially as it would have to integrate with the contingency management process of the governing unit. In my previous book[8] I described how you may maintain contingency funds at different levels, for example, project, programme and portfolio, and then allocate these funds as events dictate. This is a very efficient means to handle the finance, mainly because there is (in principle at least) much less volatility in portfolio costs than those of projects. What's more there is considerable flexibility to change requirements, swap resources around and accelerate and delay work in a multi-project compared with a single activity.

To make this work, of course, you need to be very tight with the allocation of funds at the lowest level, projects, say. This means that the budget might be set at a very low level such that the chance of the project being delivered within budget is quite small. This will lead to a culture of project managers focussing on cutting costs and also applying for additional funds. The efficiency is bought at a cultural price.

This concludes the discussion of the risk management direction which a governing unit may issue. The final point to remember is that the direction may be subject to periodic updating in the light of new circumstances. This might include a substantial change in the risk profile, for example a new risk emerging, or a revised approach to inculcating an appropriate culture.

TOOLS FOR RISK AUDIT

The Chapter 1 governance model assumes that instead of (or as well as) measuring performance, you are auditing what the governed business unit (or project, or contractor, etc) is doing.

The principle of internal audit is well understood and indeed is often well integrated with risk management. In fact, we have noted the popular three layers of defence model for assurance of performance in which operational management is the first layer, risk management the second layer and audit (internal and external) the final layer. This model does not align with the view of this book that operational management look after risk and uncertainty as one of their main responsibilities. They may be helped by risk experts, but the geeks are not there to provide a separate line of reporting, and they are not part of the audit function. I'm not

[8] *Op cit.* Page 123 *et seq.*

dogmatic about this though, as it could be an additional responsibility which is certainly built into many organisations, especially in the financial sector.

Risk-based audit schedules are now commonplace and all that needs to be said here is that audits can enquire into all aspects of risk management to ensure that the unit is being managed in line with the guidance and to provide some assurance that performance will be in line with targets and forecasts. Typical areas of enquiry could include the following.

- Does the risk context document exist? Is it accurate? Does it reflect the organisational guidance provided?
- Have the risks and uncertainties been explored? Are all material risks recognised?
- Has a risk model been constructed? Does it reflect the material risks? Has a justification been provided for the quantification? Is the justification reasonable? Have obvious dependences been incorporated in the model?
- Does the management action plan recognise the material risks? Is it fit for purpose?
- Is the management action plan being implemented? In a timely way?
- Are forecasts being produced? Is financial management aligned with them, including the provision of contingencies?
- Are regular risk reports being produced? Are variances against forecasts being explained? Are the explanations plausible? Is performance consistent with the risk model? Is it reconciled with the risk model?
- Are regular risk reviews being carried out? Are they minuted? Are actions discharged? Do they take a broad view of emerging issues, including those raised by the risk report, but also taking an outside viewpoint? Are lessons being learned and acted on? Are options considered to address issues arising? Are opportunities to do better being sought? Is it possible to improve adaptability and agility?
- Are risk culture assessments being carried out? Is there a plan to improve the risk culture? Are the identified shortcomings being monitored and corrected in some way?

At all stages this should focus on the most significant risks and uncertainties in the opinion of the auditors, those that have the potential to seriously affect the attainment of the unit's objectives.

This all comes together into an audit report which is synthesised with the risk reports at the next stage.

TOOLS FOR RISK GOVERNANCE SYNTHESIS

Synthesis in the governance layer requires the integration of:

- the risk reports from the governed units
- the audit reports from these units
- the risk measurements of the governing unit itself.

As a preliminary to this discussion we consider how risk analysis works up and down the organisation.

Risk analysis in the organisational hierarchy

It's obvious I suppose, that, in the kind of hierarchical structure we are trying to understand here, there will be a corresponding hierarchy in the way risk and uncertainty are addressed. However the specifics are not so simple and it's worth examining this in a little more detail.

For example in organisations which use risk registers and risk matrices there is often a concept of escalation. This means that the lower level unit formally identifies specific risks that are to be brought to the attention of management at the next level for consideration. Generally these will be risks that hit some level of concern on the risk matrices, though it is not entirely obvious that this is a good criterion. The risk may be perfectly well managed at the lower level and just reported a serious issue as part of the risk review. Alternatively the lower level risk registers might be scanned to identify generic issues which can then be entered as a significant risk at the higher level. And in turn these may be communicated to other governed units.

This approach makes sense though it does require a lot attention to detail and the usual problems of deciding the best approach to populating your risk registers at each level.

More problematic is the definition of the risk matrices. It is not obvious that you need a different scoring scheme at different levels of the organisation, but some managers feel the need for this. A smaller project will have an impact scale that is reduced compared with larger ones, or the programme to which it belongs. This reflects two fallacies:

- smaller projects have smaller risks
- you have to have a decent sprinkling of red risks.

Maybe it's seen as detrimental to a project manager's virility if they don't have some apparently juicy issues to deal with. In any case a perceived need to divide the impact category boundaries by three or ten to make it useful at the next level down just underlines the weaknesses in the qualitative analysis concept which I rehearsed in Chapter 2.

Using quantified risk models does not necessarily make the problem go away. Imagine you have a programme of projects, each one with its own QSRA. Your programme schedule may be an aggregation of the individual projects, or it may be a collection of key milestones from the projects linked in a suitable way to provide a forecast of when the programme will achieve its objectives. Either way you can create a programme-level QSRA, but you will find there are technical issues; in the first case you will have a large number of disparate risks to handle across a large number of activities and in the second case you will have to extract high level 'risks', quantified as probability distributions, from the lower level analyses. In the first case you will have to do a lot of work to recognise the dependences which exist between the different projects and their risks, and in the second case the opportunity to do so has gone because they exist only at a lower level.

These issues are not unique to hierarchies. Or, to put it more accurately, since hierarchies are always a feature of risk analysis this is a pervasive problem. However it is best exemplified in this particular context. The issue is that, although we prefer to look at things from a high-level perspective, what actually happens depends on the low-level detail. In point of fact it is very hard to roll up a detailed project schedule to create a high-level programme for QSRA which has the right logic so that it responds in the right way to the risk perturbations. A cost programme is more easily rolled up against a specific cost breakdown structure (function, for example), but falls apart when a different cost breakdown structure (location, for example) is required. Similarly, it's useful to rationalise your risk profile using a risk breakdown structure, but this can be misleading in terms of the detailed interactions, and again falls apart when project control types come along and want to see the risk analysed by their cost breakdown structure of programme activities. Not only is it meaningless – always a welcome message! – but also very difficult, though generally you'll think of some formulation to humour them, if not keep them happy.

As I mentioned in Chapter 2, I know of no general solution to this problem. What does help is to follow the guidance of quantifying a relatively small number of sources of uncertainty. This reduces the scale of the problem. However, as also mentioned in Chapter 2, you need to make some kind of adjustment for the cumulative effect of minor things systematically going wrong against a baseline of everything going right.

This idea is difficult to maintain in the face of that other characteristic of 'enterprise risk management', the risk database. I described this in Chapter 4, but these databases are heavily sold on the idea that they can provide risk profiles throughout the organisation, and also take on board the issues just discussed with escalation, local scoring schemes and so on. This tends to create a culture in which if it is not in the risk database it doesn't exist. After all we've paid a lot of money for it. It may be hard for a more nuanced picture based on the main sources of uncertainty to get the hearing it deserves.

However, until a better idea comes along I think we have to regard risk databases as a necessary evil. Part of the evil comes from the point that some organisations initiate risk management by buying the software, something that is sadly a key element of some vendor strategies. More effort needs to be directed at modelling the hierarchy in which individual risks are integrated coherently into issues. For example, you can develop a strategic risk database which takes a feed from the individual items on the risk list. The key point is that the description of the issues will be much richer than that of the items. This is the point at which the risk databases fall over with their simplistic escalation perspectives.

But this may be something of a digression: if an organisation runs a risk database then it will direct its units to use it. It may also direct its suppliers to do the same.

Synthesis

Compared with the bottom level units, synthesis at the governance level includes two additional considerations:

- there may be several governed units to be brought together
- the audit reports will need to be included in the material prepared for risk governance review.

Integrating units

The higher-level risk model may or may not be a straight aggregation of the lower level models as we have just discussed. On the assumption that the governing unit works on an extract of the detail of the lower level units, it is necessary to map the risk reports onto the high-level model. Remembering that the specification of the risk reports forms part of the direction, this should have been designed to be relatively straightforward.

A relatively simple environment might be a company with a portfolio of construction projects. They might vary in size, location, type, contract form and so on, but bringing them together into a coherent report, with an integrated risk profile is not difficult in principle. Common risks like an overheating supply market can be identified for management.

At the other extreme the governance of disparate units is more difficult. A software company may have a significant uncertainty about future sales of its existing product which is becoming obsolete and is in any case affected by customers awaiting its replacement. Meanwhile the new product, paid for by sales of the existing product is affected by development problems. There is an option to accelerate development and launch, but this brings further risks: the launch version may be buggy or unattractive to customers. Evidently the integration of these risks is likely to require a custom model, focussing on overall profit levels and cash flow as well as reputation.

Integrating audit

The risk reports received from the operating units will contain performance against budgets and forecasts and also provide a commentary on any significant variances. This commentary should rationalise the materialisation of risks, whether or not previously identified, and provide updated forecasts and risk models in the light of this. The synthesis team will form a view as to how credible this all is.

Audit reports provide important validating (or not) information. Most likely the audit cycle will be on a longer timescale – possibly much longer – than the business-as-usual review cycle. But when an audit report is available it provides an opportunity to look for areas where the risk profile may be insufficiently appreciated or where the processes are weak. You can then explore what the implications of these insights are.

It's not necessarily straightforward to do this, especially bearing in mind the point I laboured earlier that risk estimates are inherently subjective, especially with regard to likelihood. Teams generally do not find it hard to reach some kind of consensus about what probabilities should be used for decision making, but an independent team, such as that conducting an audit, may have significantly different ideas. The team's assessment may lie within the range that the audited team considers reasonable or it may not.

In cases of serious disagreement you need to turn to evidence. If an auditor says another production plant has issues with a process because it did not behave as expected, then they should be listened to. If the auditor says a process might cause problems with no example drawn from elsewhere, then it's just an opinion. There is a tendency to just go along with the conclusions of audit reports because they are seen in some sense as being a higher authority. That may be the case, but they are not necessarily a more informed authority so it's important to be clear about evidence versus opinion before incorporating audit findings into the risk report for review. Recall Chapter 3, where we learned from the safety culture of high reliability organisations that it's important to listen to the experts.

Manoeuvring yourself into the situation where it's the auditor's fault is not a good management stance.

TOOLS FOR RISK GOVERNANCE REVIEW

Now we are back to *Orient/review* where a structural change has been initiated and is in place. It's likely you will want to give more attention to checking that the new structure is running as planned and that no major further adjustments are needed. Apart from this, and remembering the discussions will be more strategic than at the lower levels, there is nothing to add to the discussion in Chapter 4. This the part of the management loop that is most remote from the governed units. This is not to say they are ignored, just that the reviews routinely deal with these issues as described in Chapter 4.

SUMMARY

This concludes our survey of risk governance. We have seen there is not much to it which differs from the natural and management layers. The most significant issue is how the organisation sets its policies with regard to risk attitude and risk analysis. But even here I think things are simpler than the literature on risk appetite, risk processes and risk attitude would have you believe. We should not be surprised by this: we are not tackling a fundamentally different problem here, just looking from a slightly different perspective.

It also concludes the survey of tools for risk management which was set up by the structuring in the second half of Chapter 1. I now come back to consolidating this picture, before going on to the essentials of decision theory as it relates to risk.

Chapter 6

New directions

How to achieve 'Better Futures'

The previous four chapters form the bulk of this textbook. They build on the axioms and structures put forward in Chapter 1 and cover a considerable amount of ground in doing so. Without, I hope, being over-critical, I have tried to show the potential for better ways to deal with an uncertain future than the common practice risk management we see all around us. The aim of this chapter is both to consolidate what has been proposed and to indicate what steps we can take to put it to use. To do this I shall:

- start by expanding our horizons to a top-down governance perspective on risk
- reiterate the key elements of the approach to risk management contained in Chapters 1 to 5
- conclude unfinished business with the more technical ISO 31000 methods
- look at how the ideas might be applied in one risky industry – construction.

CORPORATE GOVERNANCE AND RISK

The growth of the risk management fad in the UK has had several, apparently positive, consequences. For example, safety regulation in the workplace has become totally risk-based, with even quite small employers being required to prepare risk assessments. When you take your kids to the Easter Egg hunt in your local park, you rest easy in the knowledge that the organisers will have prepared a risk assessment which may even have been pored over by the local authority. Since the Piper Alpha disaster in the North Sea in 1988, many industries have been subject to a safety case regime where risk arguments are used to justify the operation of hazardous installations. This includes railways where many a consultant's fortunes were bolstered by the preparation of railway safety cases.

Has it done any good? I can well remember one of Her Majesty's Inspectors of Railways bemoaning the lack of maturity in the risk assessments, which I think meant that, although it makes sense to take a comprehensive and systematic look at what can go wrong, what happens as a result and what you can do about it, this prescription does not of itself solve the problem. Indeed it may obscure the key factors of a more informal approach based on experience and judgement.

To take another example, the company failures and abuses of the last century have led to a series of reports on corporate governance which increasingly emphasis risk techniques as a panacea. Again this makes sense if you believe that firms are subject to uncertain events which need to be systematically and visibly tackled.

I have quoted the UK Corporate Governance Code a couple of times already in this book (including the first page of Chapter 1) with its emphasis on the board determining the principal risks the company is willing to take and maintaining sound risk management and internal control systems. If you want to be listed on the London Stock Exchange you have to comply with the Code. It's clearly a matter of some gravity.

The Code is supported by guidance[1] which goes into more detail. It's worth reviewing this to identify any important differences in approach which might accompany this higher-level perspective. It should be emphasised that the guidance is mainly focussed on board responsibilities and not how these might eventually get translated into working level activities. There are a number of requirements.

- **Long term viability** The board should make a robust assessment of the principal risks to the company's business model and ability to

[1] Guidance on Risk Management, Internal Control and Related Financial and Business Reporting, Financial Reporting Council, September 2014.

deliver its strategy, including solvency and liquidity risks. The emphasis is on viability and survival. The board itself should do this assessment and decide on the company's response.

- **Adapting** This should not just be an annual exercise, but an ongoing process which can respond rapidly to emerging issues. The same applies to monitoring the risk management systems which need to be embedded, not treated just as a compliance tick box.
- **Culture** There is an emphasis on culture and the board's responsibility for defining what it should be and ensuring it is achieved. For example, the guidance places some emphasis on leadership style and reward systems, as well as whistle-blowing.
- **Risk appetite** The board must determine its willingness to take on risks, especially those which the organisation is willing to take to achieve its strategic objectives.
- **Risk management systems** The guidance has little new to say, compared with ISO 31000 for example, on the specific details about process and embedment. However the board is required to assess the impact of the values and culture of the company on the effectiveness of the systems.
- **Skills, knowledge and experience** The board need to assess and address their own.
- **Statements in annual report** This report needs to contain statements of the principal risks referred to earlier, how they are being managed, that risk management and internal control systems are in place and that their effectiveness has been assessed. The board is also required to give its opinion on whether the company is a going concern and whether it will remain so over a future period. This is broader scope than the going concern elements of the financial statements. This is only one of the communications responsibilities assigned to the board: it must take responsibility for external communication on risk management.

These responsibilities are clearly quite serious and comprehensive. You, as an investor, might think that the performance of any company that takes them seriously should be assured. What's more, these requirements are testable. Shareholders and anyone else can consult the annual reports of these companies to see what their principal risks are, what they are doing about them and how good their risk management system is.

So let's have a look and, yes I know it's a cheap shot, let's have a look at Carillion. Their annual report for 2016 does indeed contain the principal risks and statements about risk management. Even its title, "making tomorrow a better place," not only mirrors this book's, but is a reflection of Carillion's view of its own viability. The period reported on ends six months before the first profit warning and a year before the company collapsed. It reports on a period during which nods and winks about Carillion's performance were commonplace in the construction industry.

The Strategic Report contains eight pages on risk which turn out to be one of the most egregious examples of common practice risk management you can imagine. There are a couple of pages of formulaic description of the 'rigorous' risk management system followed by, I can hardly believe it, a 3x3 risk matrix with the Top 10 risks, scored before something and after ('gross' and 'net'). The blobs are artfully scattered, but you know they are just (Medium, Medium) scorings or the like. The next five pages describe the Top 10, again in formulaic terms. To be fair, the top four risks do hint at the seeds of disaster:

1. **Work winning** – yes, they needed to win work at all costs to maintain some cashflow to support the ever-growing debt
2. **Contract management** – yes, to deal with 1. they needed to be competitive which then puts pressure on profit
3. **Pension liabilities** – yes, we know that, probably exacerbated by 4.
4. **Brexit** – yes, of course, and the potential loss of a cheap labour supply affects 2.

The Strategic Report also contains the required statements that the board has looked at this stuff, is happy with it and, taking on board the business plan, has a reasonable expectation that the company will be able to continue in operation and meet its liabilities as they fall due over the three-year period of their assessment. The Audit Committee twice reported to the Board on the effectiveness of the Group's internal control and risk management systems.

Of course the rest of the report, and especially the financial statements, the audit committee report and, indeed, the auditor's report deal with risk: it's informative to do a word search on 'risk' throughout this 156-page document. This adds a number of financial or treasury risks to the Top 10. There is a lot of focus on the pension deficit, but otherwise nothing significantly out of the ordinary.

Before reaching any conclusions on this, it's worth looking at more successful companies. This is risky in itself; the pages of risk textbooks are littered with paragons who shortly afterwards turn out to be fallen angels. So I just took the company with the largest market capitalisation, Shell, and the first company with a market capitalisation over £1bn on the day I looked, which would make it similar to Carillion during its long decline in share price from 2014. This turned out to be John Laing Group, also in the construction field, but an investor in infrastructure projects.

Shell's discussion of risk covers 24 'risk factors'. Each is carefully described and discussed in narrative form, and further detail is referenced elsewhere in the 228-page report. Shell's market capitalisation is nearly 200 times that of Carillion/Laing which means describing its risk exposure is qualitatively more difficult – which is not to say it is easy for the smaller companies hovering around the lower reaches of the FTSE 250. Laing too, opts for a more narrative approach, picking out 13 principal risks and taking its time over describing them where necessary. For example 'Valuation' (of the projects in its portfolio) occupies a whole page. Both companies provide the required wording about viability and assessing the effectiveness of risk management systems. For Shell it is significantly more complicated as they are subject to different jurisdictions.

What are we to make of these reports which are intended to increase the transparency of the corporate world and provide shareholders with useful information? First, they are not brilliant at communication. They are very long, yet even so, print much of their detailed material in a very small typeface. There is far too much information to absorb.

Secondly, the statements about viability over the next few years and the effectiveness of the risk management systems are, I think, worthless. This is not to say these activities have no value, or that they are not done. But these statements are now routine. All companies will say they have done the necessary assessments and you have no measure of how well. Carillion says they scenario tested their three-year business plan. They cannot have tested it very vigorously. That's not to say it was dishonest; bankruptcy is a cliff edge phenomenon. The management believed until the last minute that they could survive with a bit of help for cashflow over a short period until restructuring took effect. Their stakeholders declined to offer that help. But equally that's hardly an unforeseeable scenario. In the same way we know that, when the time arrives, all the stress testing, and the other resilience measures, that banks have carried out will not help avert the next financial crisis.

Something that would provide more meaningful information is for the results of the effectiveness assessment to be disclosed, which is in any case effectively done for the principal risks, and, particularly, any specific issues or weaknesses that were identified or addressed. What might also be helpful would be for companies to set out a few scenarios which they could not survive, however unlikely they consider them.

What about culture? Shell has little to say, apart from in the remuneration section (and also safety culture). It seems not to have cottoned on to its importance for risk management. John Laing Group is the most straightforward and is the only company to link culture directly to effective risk management, specifically mentioning openness of communication up and down the management chain and also citing a strong control and compliance culture. Carillion is the firm that mentions culture the most, but mainly in asserting vaguely that has a values-based culture. The values are: we care, we achieve together, we improve, we deliver.

Which brings us to the statement of principal risks. I think I have made clear my dim view of a Top 10 risk matrix. The statements by Shell and Laing are much more in line with what I would regard as good practice. They are narrative commentaries, such as I have recommended a couple of times already in this book. They take time and space to describe the issues and their implications properly and to set out how they are dealt with. As you go higher up the organisation, the less a risk list is appropriate to describe your risk exposure. A few thousand well-chosen words to explain how uncertainty works for you is, in principle, far more valuable than yards of corporate boilerplate, auditor's back-covering or microscopic notes to the balance sheet.

They key issue is how to judge. I finished Chapter 3 with the idea that the best way to assess the risk culture of an organisation is to consider the quality of its risk conversations. We have the same issue here. It has to be a subjective view, based on experience, logic and rigour, about how the story hangs together, how credible it is, how it could all go wrong and so on.

It's tempting to say that any company naïve enough to represent its strategic risk position on a 3x3 risk matrix deserves to fail. That's probably a bit strong, but it does provide a stark indication of the pitfalls of common practice risk management and the scope to improve.

Let's go back to the starting premise of this section, that a risk-based approach to assessing or guiding or regulating performance is superior to something more prescriptive. It is a beguiling idea, but right now, after a couple of decades or more, I think it has still to demonstrate its full value. To do that we need to do it better, the aim of this book is to make some suggestions as to how.

At this point I feel a tap on my shoulder from my virtual mentor Nassim Nicholas Taleb asking about my skin in this particular game. So I'm off to buy some John Laing Group shares for my pension fund. Wish me luck.

CONSOLIDATION

Having set out a high-level perspective on risk management, I want to come back to the key ideas of this book. I want to emphasise their essential simplicity, in spite of the many words I have devoted to filling in some of the detail.

At the core of the story is the management loop concept developed both in its OODA form to emphasise agility and adaptation, and its more traditional Deming or plan-do-review form. I have adopted the slightly ugly term OODeming loop. This loop has been augmented with forecasting and synthesis activities to emphasise performance management aspects. Of course, the management loop is part of most descriptions of systematic risk management, the key issue is how best to use it.

The loop is first iterated in its intuitive form to bring out the characteristics of natural risk management: how we do it without all the process stuff. Natural risk management is enhanced by a focus on risk culture and getting round the loop quickly so as to adapt to emerging circumstances by changing the plan. Only then do I introduce the management layer to provide some formality, especially with regard to performance, and finally a governance layer to make it work not just throughout the organisation but also out into its stakeholder environment.

In the course of this story I have tried to minimise the amount of specialist terminology and one consolidation activity is to collect it all into a glossary here. I hope the summary which follows speaks for itself. It contains the following sections:

- axioms – our foundations
- management structure
- risk glossary
- probability glossary
- tools.

I have also tried to build on – but inevitably away from – the ISO 31000 standard. The framework and process aspects of the standard were comprehensively covered in Chapter 1, but in the section which follows this one I want to come back to the principles which are intended to be the basis on which the framework and processes are built. The aim is to see how our revised approach deals with the issues they raise.

Axioms

Uncertainty axiom

The future is uncertain.

Risk management axiom

The performance of your organisation will be improved if it is governed with the explicit recognition that the future is uncertain.

No risk process axiom

There are no risk management processes, just management processes that recognise and accommodate uncertainty.

Management loop axiom

The commonly accepted iterative approaches to management and governance such as the OODA loop or the Deming cycle form a suitable basis for the definition and description of good practice management and governance processes which accommodate uncertainty.

Management structure

- **OODA loop** – a variant of the management loop – observe, orient, decide act
- **Deming loop** – a variant of the management loop – plan, do, measure, review
- **OODeming loop** – words used in this book to emphasise a combination of the *OODA* and *Deming loops* with the following correspondences: review/orient, plan/decide, do/act, measure/observe.
- **Forecast** – a prediction of outturn (cost, attainment of milestones, etc), part of the plan/decide segment of the *OODeming loop* considered separately in this book, a point value sometimes derived from a *risk profile*.
- **Budget** – a financial constraint on managers, sometimes derived from the *forecast*.
- **Synthesise** – bring measurements together and compare them with the forecast, part of the measure/observe segment of the *OODeming loop*, but considered separately in this book.
- **Direct** – provide instruction and guidance to a unit as an element of governance, part of the do/act segment of the *OODeming loop* for a governing unit.
- **Audit** – inspect the operations of a unit as an element of governance, part of the measure/observe segment of the *OODeming loop* for a governing unit.
- **Report** – return management information to a governing unit to be received by the synthesise segment of its *OODeming loop*.

Risk glossary

- **Risk** – the implications of uncertainty for a specific organisation – see the *uncertainty axiom*. A specific aspect of this might be called a *risk* or a source of uncertainty.

- **Uncertain event** – a defined event which may or may not happen related to the occurrence of a *risk* or source of uncertainty. (Mathematically, a subset of the sample space.)
- **Risk management** – those aspects of the policy, actions and affairs of the organisation which are specifically related to the explicit recognition of future uncertainty – see the *risk management axiom.*
- **Risk culture** – **culture** is the *information* which people have in their heads which can be *learned* by others and affects the evolution and functioning of organisations.
  - This **information** includes ideas, values, beliefs, behavioural strategies, perceptual models and organisational structure.
  - It can be **learned** through imitation, observations and inference, interaction, discussion or teaching.
  - **Risk culture** is that part of the *information* that relates to risk and uncertainty.
- **Risk context** – the relevant factors to be accounted for in defining the approach to *risk management.*
- **Risk management plan** – a document setting out the intentions of a unit with regard to *risk management* based on the *risk context*, the *risk direction* and the outcomes of reviews.
- **Risk direction** – instruction and guidance on *risk management* provided to a governed unit.
- **Risk attitude** – the policy and approach of a unit to each class of *risk* and uncertainty, included in the *risk direction document* and informing the *risk management plan.*
- **Risk analysis** – an exercise to understand risk and to estimate the significance of *risk* in terms of *likelihood* or *probability.*
- **Risk model** – a quantitative *risk analysis*, usually based on *probabilities*, in which assumptions about risk and uncertainty are used to calculate the *probability distributions* of certain *random variables.*
- **Risk profile** – the output of a *risk model.*
- **Risk-aware forecast** – a forecast based on a *risk profile.*

- **Contingency** – part of budget explicitly assigned to accommodate *risk* and uncertainty.

Probability glossary

(common items only, in everyday risk management use)

- **Likelihood** – a qualitative expression of a person's, or a group's, degree of belief that an *uncertain event* will occur.
- **Probability** – a quantitative expression of a person's, or a group's, degree of belief that an *uncertain event* will occur, which, with other probabilities, is processed in accordance with the mathematical theory of probability.
- **Risk (or probability-impact) matrix** – a matrix in which uncertain events are located according to their *likelihood* or *probability* and impact on categorised scales.
- **Random variable** – an uncertain quantitative representation of the effect of risk, typically the outturn cost or the time when a milestone is achieved. (Mathematically, a real function on the sample space.)
- **Expected value or mean** – the *probability* weighted average of a *random variable.*
- **Cumulative probability distribution** – the *probability* that a *random variable* is less than a specified value.
- **S-curve** – a graph of the *cumulative probability distribution.*
- **P*n*** and **median** – a specific point on the *S-curve* so that, for example, P80 is the value of the random variable for which the probability of non-exceedance is 80%. There is a probability of 20% that the random variable will be more than P80. The median is P50.

Tools

The tools we have discussed in this book are perhaps not what you might have expected. They are not a collection of checklists or software. Really, they are just lists of things to think about at each stage of the loops. You will need to figure out for yourself how they work for you and your organisation. But to the extent there are specific documents and techniques, I have listed them in Figure 30 for reference.

Tool	Comment
Risk context definition	Derived on entry to the *Review/observe* stage and recorded in the risk context document
Risk management plan	Refined by successive reviews
Risk workshop	Output is identified issues and controls, and specifically the detailed risk hotspots
Qualitative risk analysis	Produces risk matrices
Risk modelling (various kinds, including cost, QSRA, EVA, more general)	Creates the risk model and, as output, the risk profile
Outside view (reference class forecasting, Bayesian updating, statistical confidence bounds, consistency testing…)	Updated risk model, see risk performance report
Intelligent risk register	A narrative on key issues including interdependences, controls and hotspots
Individual risk attitude assessment: • risk predisposition • ethical and moral disposition • social predisposition	
Double-S assessment	Organisation location on sociability-solidarity axes
IRM cultural aspects assessment	Supplemented by Banks's assessment framework as appropriate
Culture improvement project: requirements definition	Based on culture assessment and Bank's imperatives as required
Culture improvement project: implementation plan	As suggested by IRM and others
Mindful organising	As practiced in high reliability organisations
Antifragile (and resilient) mindset	Beware black swans!
Risk-aware forecasts	Based on risk modelling, leading to AFC

Tool	Comment
Budgeted contingencies	
Key risk indicators	
Risk-based rationalisation of actuals	Recorded in risk performance report and leading to updated risk model (see outside view above)
NEC3 arrangements (contract risk register, early warning notices, risk reduction meetings, ...)	A practical implementation solution, once rationalised
Lesson learnt system	
Strategic options analysis	Create mini risk context documents
Risk attitude definition	Part of risk direction document which will also include policy, tools, etc
Risk-based audit	Now a standard approach
Risk model synthesis	Making sure the risk information can be communicated seamlessly up and down the organisation
Risk-lean thinking	For example, lean construction, see later in this chapter
Principal risk statement	As FRC requirements – adult antidote to risk registers – example of intelligent risk register, see above

Figure 30 Tools for risk management

ISO 31000 REVISITED

Although Chapter 1 covered the framework and process aspects of ISO 31000 in some detail, we did not discuss the principles from which the framework and process are supposedly derived. It makes sense to review them here to see how relevant they may be for the approach summarised in the previous section.

The principles

The eleven principles are as follows.

Risk management creates and protects value

It is axiomatic for us that explicitly attending to uncertainty improves performance. From there, it's a short step to value. So yes, this is a foundation for what we do.

In its discussion of this principle the standard asserts that risk management contributes to the *demonstrable* achievement of objectives and improvement of performance. This demonstration is actually quite hard and often impossible as we discussed in Chapter 4, in the section on risk performance measurement. That's why I prefer the axiomatic approach which embeds this principle.

Risk management is an integral part of all organisational processes

Yes, it is axiomatic that we should attend in an appropriate way to uncertainty in everything we do. But this principle is really about embedding – avoiding having standalone risk activities. The approach I have set out in this book is aimed at just that and, in my opinion, is much more successful in doing so than approaches based more closely on the standard which have resulted in the embedding difficulties typical of common practice risk management. However, perhaps I should reiterate that what I have described is closely based on the standard; it is not dramatically new, it just reflects a change in emphasis. Again, our axioms (the no risk process axiom) embed this principle.

Risk management is part of decision making

As stated, it's unclear what this means. You could just as well (or better) say that decision making is part of risk management. It is inevitable that if you are attending to uncertainty – see next principle – you will be taking it on board in your decisions – where else? I don't think this principle adds anything.

Risk management explicitly addresses uncertainty

From our perspective this is just a statement of what risk management is. It's not a principle for doing it. Some people may see uncertainty differently. For example, those who see it as distinct from event risk may need encouragement to put it on the risk register.

Risk management is systematic, structured and timely

Yup, it's up there with motherhood and apple pie. But we need to ask whether you can have too much of these good things, or, to put it another way, can they conflict. It's a plausible argument that too much system and structure detract from timeliness. We saw from the company annual reports that too much boilerplate guff detracts from insight and understanding. And I have argued that a critical success factor in dealing with uncertainty is to get round your management loop quickly. So I think that only *appropriate* system, structure and timeliness are required, and you need to determine this specifically within your organisation. This is not helpful as a principle.

Risk management is based on the best available information

We discussed sources of data in the section on risk analysis and the idea that there is such a thing as "the best" is very elusive, and not based on simple principles. This one does not help except at the very simplistic level it is pitched at.

Risk management is tailored

I guess this makes explicit the point that each organisation needs to develop its own approach to risk culture and decision making, and set up a process framework to match. There's no such thing as a standard approach which will work for all organisations and all business units. What's more it should be tailored for each part of the organisation. This is a useful principle to make us wary of too much standardisation.

Risk management takes human and cultural factors into account

I think this principle is too weak. Actually we should start with human and cultural factors and go on from there, adding more stuff with great care. That's why I start from natural risk management. Put that way, it's clearly a useful principle.

Risk management is transparent and inclusive

'Transparent' means you can't see it, but I think the intention of this principle is to say that the way risks are dealt with should be visible to all who need to know. In fact I think this principle adds nothing. As requirements emerge to communicate about risk, up and down the management chain, and with other stakeholders, the approach to risk governance will emerge to suit. Inevitably there are limits on the visibility and inclusivity of the risk management activities and information.

Risk management is dynamic, iterative and responsive to change

This sounds good, but I think it is a rather tautologous way of saying that management needs to monitor and review what it is up to. Uncertainty is no exception to this – it couldn't be – so this is bound to emerge as we develop our approach. We know these are good things anyway so there's no additional principle to emerge for risk management. You could see this as validating the point that you need to be adaptive and get round your feedback loop quickly.

Risk management facilitates continual improvement of the organisation

This extends the monitor and review principle to process as well as content. However a point that does emerge is that thinking about how uncertainty has played out in the past is a useful discipline within risk management. You could argue that this makes an organisation's risk governance a uniquely effective platform for learning lessons and continual improvement. Maybe this should be the principle: learning lessons and continual improvement should be part of risk governance.

In summary …

These principles are all correct statements and perhaps they help to provide some perspective into the scope and methods of risk management. But it is hard to get excited about them as fundamental principles.

If you start from the risk management axiom –

> *The performance of your organisation will be improved if it is governed with the explicit recognition that the future is uncertain.*

– everything else will come out in the wash. One way to see this is to consider the reverse of any of them, and to realise that would not be a position you could reach. In effect, these are not foundational principles, but indicators of good practice risk management. They are useful to review after the fact, but they do not drive the thinking.

ISO 31000:2018

With perfect timing, just as this book was going to press, a new edition of ISO 31000[2] was issued. According to ISO[3] this is a

> *"clearer, shorter and more concise guide that will help organizations use risk management principles to improve planning and make better decisions. [The] following are the main changes since the previous edition:*
>
> - *"review of the principles of risk management, which are the key criteria for its success*
> - *"focus on leadership by top management who should ensure that risk management is integrated into all organizational activities, starting with the governance of the organization*
> - *"greater emphasis on the iterative nature of risk management, drawing on new experiences, knowledge and analysis for the revision of process elements, actions and controls at each stage of the process*
> - *"streamlining of the content with greater focus on sustaining an open systems model that regularly exchanges feedback with its external environment to fit multiple needs and contexts."*

It's certainly true that the new standard is more streamlined. There are now only eight defined terms (risk, risk management, stakeholder, risk source, event, consequence, likelihood, control) compared with 29 before. There are now only eight principles compared with eleven before: two of the more anodyne ones above have gone and value creation and protection becomes an overarching theme. The text is shorter, by maybe 20% ignoring the definitions and the informative annex of the 2009 version.

---

[2] ISO 31000:2018: Risk management – Guidelines, ISO, February 2018.

[3] www.iso.org/news/ref2263.html

The main structural changes are that there is a new diagram for the risk framework, the purpose of which is to assist the organisation in integrating risk management into significant activities and functions. I think that explains better what it's for; in Chapter 1, I mentioned that this was puzzling. There is a new stage, 'integration', extracted from the previous 'design' stage, which emphasises the governance aspect and is, I think, reinforcing the need for embedment. The other main change is that 'establishing the risk management policy' is now 'articulating risk management commitment'. This might reflect my scepticism about risk management policies recorded in Chapter 5. 'Implementing the risk management process', always an odd one in the framework, has gone, and a new stage of 'adapting' has been added to 'improvement'. Here the adaptation concerns changing the framework and is not directly related to adaptability in responding to emerging risk challenges.

There are no real changes in the process section. The wording is undoubtedly improved, for example at the higher level 'establishing the context' is now 'scope, context, criteria'. At the working level the concepts have been fine-tuned and are set out more clearly.

Overall the new edition is disappointing in not taking the opportunity to enhance the role of risk culture. In fact, the one reference to this as part of continual improvement has been removed. It has not emphasised adaptability or quick response at the process level, in spite of the third improvement point above and it provides no new insights about governance in spite of the second. I think the new edition has struggled to part company in a significant way from the previous one.

If you think this is too cynical you should read ISO's verdict:

> *"The resulting standard is not just a new version of ISO 31000. Reaching beyond a simple revision, it gives new meaning to the way we will manage risk tomorrow."*

In spite of these exciting words, I have not changed anything elsewhere in this book which continues to be based on the 2009 edition. Do we need a new standard? Not yet. First we need a clear consensus on the benefits of moving from common practice based on the current one.

HOW IT MIGHT HELP CONSTRUCTION

This textbook has been written largely from a theoretical point of view. Although much of the development has been guided by my own experience of risk management over several decades, my starting point has been the ISO 31000 standard and the ambiguities and false starts it contains. As a result, the book is not full of case studies or practical examples. I hold the truths it contains to be self-evident. Indeed, although I have presented it as a toolbox, this is to emphasise the point that there are no risk management processes; I have not given lots of specific details on the tools, I have described them in outline and left them for you to join the dots as best suits you and your organisation.

I have also tried to write the book without making assumptions about the type of organisation which is managing risk. It should apply to train operators, aid charities, government ministries, schools and, ahem, banks alike, though I know next-to-nothing of many of these sectors.

So I thought it might be useful to look in more detail at one sector – construction – which I have been lucky enough to be involved with more than some others, and consider how risk management there could change and improve. But before coming to that I want to mention another management fad that is intended to promote better futures and make some risk-based comments on that.

Lean and risk

Everyone knows that Toyota grew from a small textile company to a massive global automotive manufacturer by deploying a philosophy and tools which we now call 'lean'. There are many perspectives on what it means to be lean, but they mainly focus on eliminating waste of all kinds, things that don't add customer value, things that make the work harder and, most important for Toyota, things that introduce unevenness into the work flow. Overall this amounts to a customer-pull approach where everything is focussed on giving the customer what he wants (and not what he doesn't want) when he wants it (and not before – as well, obviously, as not after). This in turn results in adopting a just-in-time strategy with no stocks sitting around anywhere in the supply chain, which is, of course, very long in the automotive industry.

To implement this, it is important to have a philosophy of continuous improvement with a focus on identifying the sources of waste and rooting them out. Being lean means being adaptive. It also means having an organisation which is respectful of people, working in teams and helping others reach their objectives. Expanding this concept, it becomes important for everyone in the customer-led supply chain to work together, so another characteristic of lean manufacturing is long-term relationships with preferred suppliers.

As well as different perspectives there are a multiplicity of tools which are deployed in the pursuit of lean. This has the inevitable result – the fate of all management fads – that it's the tools that become important. In fact the tools were just put together by Toyota to solve specific problems. They don't necessarily all work together and they may have the wrong effect when used inappropriately; managers need the experience to know what works for what, and not just blindly apply six-sigma, JIT or whatever and call it lean. That's an important lesson for any toolkit, including the tools for risk management I've described in this book.

Obviously the lean approach has common objectives with risk management. At the simplistic level they are both about better futures. In some ways they are counteracting: having stocks of material ready at hand for when you run out or the supply chain is disrupted is a classic risk control measure on every construction project, in direct contradiction of JIT and very wasteful. In fact this is characteristic of classic risk management which often makes the assumption that it will cost you money to implement control measures. I believe this is wrong thinking.

Look more closely and you can see more common features. Eliminating variability, at least in a manufacturing environment, is more or less synonymous with risk management. You attack the causes of variability ('risks') and eliminate them. The focus on this and the willingness – imperative even – to adapt and improve is a feature of risk management as outlined in this book. The same is true of the emphasis on teamwork, getting the culture right and deferring to expertise as I discussed in Chapter 3.

Of course the wheels came off lean a bit when Toyota products suffered safety-related failings leading to widespread product recalls. This caused Toyota to re-examine its supply chain philosophy as the cause appeared to be difficulties in maintaining lean and JIT in an extended, outsourced supply chain. More diversity in the supply chain was apparently selected as an appropriate response. In other words a bit of waste in the supply chain is now accepted as a way of reducing the chance of massive waste through recall. Maybe there's not such a gulf between lean and risk management as you might think.

It seems as though lean is a good philosophy, with a good culture, but could be improved with a more encompassing risk approach to start to deal with other risks than keeping the production line going smoothly.

But all of this is just a preliminary to discussing construction.

The state of construction

I have spent many happy hours and months in the construction industry working with some of the nicest, hardest-working, most committed, enthusiastic, team players you could find anywhere. In spite of this, construction is a terrible industry. You may not agree with everything (or anything) I have to say in this book, but it is, I think, a truth universally acknowledged that construction projects overrun dramatically in cost and time. Not all of course, but many more than should do given we've had quite a lot of experience of building things over thousands of years. What's more, this is not for want of formal risk management; the disciplines of common practice risk management have been in place now for quite some time in most big construction firms and projects.

The reasons are not hard to find. Construction firms operate in a competitive environment. They respond to tender documents which vie with each other to be the silliest yet. They have to navigate between the rocks of pricing sensibly – including the pricing of risk – and potentially getting no work, and under-pricing and being unable to deliver – essentially Carillion's top two risks. Construction firms do not naturally have strong balance sheets and are generally financially much weaker than their customers. But there are big risks in construction and it is almost inevitable that this combination of circumstances will lead to them going bankrupt at some point, as is modelled in Chapter 7.

Before they do, they are likely to have a portfolio of under-priced projects from which their only hope of making money is to create successful claims for more money and more time. As a result, the industry survives on inventive, game-playing commercial managers who can do this successfully whilst managing the flow of bad news back into their corporate centres where accountants are burbling about 'margin dilution' and the like. Of course these accountants – even in construction firms – live in the cosy world of business-as-usual, with strong regular, predictable cash flows to bolster balance sheets. It is almost impossible to formulate an effective plan to survive the lumpiness of project work. One obvious idea is to diversify into more regular work, take on PFIs or other outsourcing. But the comfort cushion the maintenance phase of a PFI offers promptly gets refinanced offshore into the pockets of hedge funds. And outsourcing contracts didn't do Carillion much good, partly because they too, have to be under-priced in the current competitive market, it seems.[4]

Construction projects also constitute quite complex systems. For a start, they are one-offs, not only technically, but also in terms of the network of stakeholders a large project needs. You have to put together a supply chain of subcontractors, some specialist, others the source of the bulk of the workforce. You might be deciding the details of what you're going to build as you go along, so you need a firm of undisciplined, artistic designers. Because all this is risky you are probably best huddling together in numbers and creating a project-specific JV. The different attitudes to risk between the partners in such JVs is always entertaining to observe. As well as attitudes, you can see the pot contains a mix of cultures. And that's just the construction phase; PFIs and other design, build, operate, finance projects are more complex still in principle. Companies like Carillion and Laing face a heady mix of issues

Meanwhile 'risk management' becomes a branch of project control, there to manage contingencies, not to promote an open discussion of what the future might hold and what to do about it. So there's no chance the contingencies will be exceeded or that they have been fiddled to fit an agreed price! There is an endemic denial of what things are really going to cost and this probably results in them costing even more.

---

[4] Actually I think the only way to navigate between under-priced work or none is the classic market response of innovation, improved productivity, excellence, or whatever. But mention this in the average construction meeting and you might as well hail from Mars.

Of course this is a slightly cynical viewpoint. Some projects go well. One which seems to me to be a beacon is the 2012 London Olympics works. This was a case study in the Infrastructure UK report I referred to earlier in the book.[5] I think its success was due to a killer combination: attention to cultural issues like investing in the best people and constant, open adult conversations between all parties; effective systems for forecasting, budgeting and contingency management which escalated potential changes into trends; and realistic, generous even, contingencies. It was also asserted, slightly counterintuitively, that a drop-dead delivery date helped control risk. Reasonable expectations about risk and uncertainty help promote success, it seems.

Lean construction

Another perspective on the state of construction is that the idea of plodding through a project plan – inevitably optimistic – is a failed paradigm. This was the starting point of something called *lean construction* which sought to apply some of the philosophy of lean production to the construction world.

This is an idea that needs to be developed carefully as the tools used in the production arena have a history of being misunderstood and misapplied as a result, as I noted earlier. However, the idea that you can add a production dimension to the project planning discipline is a useful one, as is the focus on doing only what adds customer value. This has meant that the philosophy of lean construction has grown and is gaining traction, though again with the issue that it might be mistaken for misapplied lean production and an overemphasis on the tools rather than the philosophy of the approach.

Perhaps the best-known technique from lean construction is the Last Planner[6] concept, so called because it puts the emphasis for work planning on the front-line teams, the last link in the chain. It you can keep the production teams occupied delivering customer value the rest of the project will follow.

[5] Managing Cost Risk and Uncertainty in Infrastructure Projects: Leading Practice and Improvement, Report from the Infrastructure Risk Group, 2013. Case study 4, page 58.

[6] Registered trademark of the Lean Construction Institute.

Collaborative planning meetings help to identify and resolve all issues which are going to hold up the day's or the week's production. This creates a focus on resources, materials, access and consents which is generally absent from the normal planning approach, however detailed. A common project control response to recognising the benefits of this is to insist on plans which are far too detailed and become very difficult to handle. In contrast the Last Planner thinking is supported by simple paper tools involving Post-Its and the like. By emphasising the last link in the chain, the team foreman, the Last Planner concept distributes responsibility more widely and increases transparency.

Compared with lean production, lean construction recognises explicitly that the aspiration of lean production to have a repeatable and repeated production sequence is unattainable in construction: all construction projects are a one-off and more comparable to prototype production. I think this leads to a more explicit recognition of risk in construction. We can aim to make production go smoothly, but there will always be variation and we must always be ready to manage it. As a result, we will accept the waste of maintaining more resilience in the supply chain to gain the benefit of fewer production interruptions.

Lean construction also places great importance on adaptation. You aim to create a bow wave of work for the production teams so that whatever the circumstances they can respond and keep the value flowing. As I have noted in number of places in this book, the planning paradigm tends to fall apart when stressed.

Finally lean construction, like lean production, places an emphasis on long term supply chain relationships with joint, reliable, smooth working, potentially at the expense of increased costs (but reduced tendering waste!). Tendering is a stunningly ineffectual process for the complexities of big construction projects and there has to be a better way, albeit this will not please people who seek proof of value for money.

Which brings us to the obvious point of this section, the parallels between lean construction and the natural risk management approach of this book:

- avoidance of heavy and distracting and unnatural process
- focus on adapting to circumstances as a natural part of management instead of waiting for a crisis

- focus on production, see for example the earned value basis for schedule risk modelling described in Chapter 2 rather than the common practice QSRAs
- lean construction places considerable importance on root cause analysis, learning and continual improvement
- emphasis on distributed decision-making responsibility and the transparency that goes with it.

In summary I see many parallels between the challenge which lean construction makes to the project planning paradigm and the challenge to common practice risk management processes of this book. Maybe natural risk management can form an integral part of lean construction, and, by extension, be part of the solution to other problems with existing management regimes, aimed at improving their efficiency and effectiveness.

Chapter 7

A taste of decision theory

A more developed discussion of the nature of probability in the risk management context and how people and organisations should and do take decisions in the presence of uncertainty

At the core of risk management is taking decisions in the face of uncertainty. The rest of it is in some sense just decoration: we should not find it difficult to do what we decide to do; we should be working comprehensively and we should be open and honest in our decisions. Accordingly, at the centre of organisational risk management must be some form of approach to decision making which recognises uncertainty. We have called this the risk attitude.

Risk decision making is a topic which has been intensively studied by economists, mathematicians, psychologists and philosophers, and our understanding is still developing. Surprisingly though, this work is little recognised in the way that organisations formulate their risk attitude and there are some good reasons for this which I am going to address in this chapter. To begin with I will provide a summary of what is known and then go on to put it in context and draw conclusions which can help the organisation understand better what it should be aiming to achieve and how it can do so. Many of the results have been used in the previous chapters; here you get the context and detail.

One of the reasons for the neglect of this body of knowledge by risk managers is that it is rather complex, quite mathematical, very hard to understand and reasonably controversial. It's tempting to turn a blind eye. I think that would be a mistake, and it's a mistake which leads to some pretty misleading ideas which have gained a certain currency. So in my account of risk decisions I am not going to shy away from the difficult complexities, but I am going to try to describe them as informally as I can. What's more, I am going to plot a course through the controversy so that we know what to do at the end. You may want to do your own research and think about it for yourself, and I have listed a few books which I have found very helpful and which may help you too.

HOW WE OUGHT TO MAKE DECISIONS – DEFINITELY MAYBE

Let's start with an idealised formulation of a risk decision problem which we shall develop extensively. Much of the narrative throughout this chapter is heavily based on that given in Wakker[1] and we now use his vendor example.

You are a street vendor and have to select your (perishable) merchandise for tomorrow which may be sunny, dull or rainy. Thus there are three *states of nature* which represent the uncertainty you face.

You have a choice of taking ice creams (on which you will make money if it is sunny), hot dogs (on which you will make money if it is raining), neither or both. Thus you have four *options* available.

	Sunny	Dull	Rainy
Ices	£400	£100	-£400
Hot dogs	-£400	£100	£500
Neither	0	0	0
Both	0	£200	£100

Figure 31 Payoff matrix for street vendor

[1] *Prospect Theory*, Peter P Wakker, Cambridge, 2010.

For every option you assume you know what the *outcome* will be for each state of nature in terms of money made. Thus there is an outcome table, sometimes called the *pay-off matrix*, which is shown in Figure 31. The decision problem is to decide which of the four options to select. Just to be clear, this chapter is about individual choice in the face of uncertainty, and that individual is you, the reader.

It's important to remember that, despite its generality, this formulation makes some important idealisations. There are technical difficulties in setting up the states of nature in the right way; a single decision cannot be considered in isolation – life is a series of risk decisions; and uncertainty gains a whole new level of complexity if you think of it not just as ignorance of the correct states of nature but recognise that what happens may be influenced by a thinking opponent (or ally, or employee, maybe) making their own decisions with their own information and their own view of what's important. The idealisations or assumptions are easily forgotten; *assumption neglect* is an important cause of poor decisions. We shall have to return to these complications.

One approach to this decision problem would be to choose that option which contains the best outcome. This assumes you know which outcome you prefer most, or more generally, that you have an order of preference for outcomes. That's easy here as the pay-off matrix contains outcomes that are monetised, and I assume you prefer more money to less. It's worth remembering that this, in contrast with the idealisation assumptions, is a really bad assumption in general. There are lots of things we care about beside money – saving the planet, beauty, happiness, including the happiness of others, freedom from uncertainty – and the trade-off between them is often quite difficult. We mustn't forget that in thinking about the easy solutions which follow.

So one approach is pick the option, the row of the payoff matrix, which contains the highest sum of money. To do this would reflect a rather optimistic view of nature on your part since to obtain that sum would mean that the true state of nature is whichever column gives that payoff. In the case of the vendor you would choose *Hot dogs* and hope that it is *Rainy*. You would be a maxi-maximiser: someone who selects the option which maximises the maximum gain in that option. A more cautious approach, one to choose if you are of a pessimistic frame of mind, would be that of a mini-maximiser: you prefer the option which has the highest *minimum* payoff. A mini-maximising vendor will take

Both[2] but might be considered a fool, or at least lacking in entrepreneurial spirit, if it is July and there has been a week of hot days with no sign of a break in the weather and is therefore almost certain to take a big loss on his hot dogs. Being a mini-maximiser seems like a bad idea, but anyone who wants to take a cautious – 'precautionary' – approach in the absence of clear information might want to go that way.

Neither the maxi-maximiser nor the mini-maximiser forms any view of what the true state of nature is. This suggests a more successful approach is likely to be that of a prophet. This is someone who assumes they know the true state of nature – they pick a column of the payoff matrix – and select that option which has the maximum outcome in that column. This seems like a good idea, especially when you realise there are ways to improve your powers of prophecy: you can listen to the weather forecast, you can consult the form of horses, you can slaughter a lamb, disembowel it and observe the entrails, you can compile a database of the cost of similar projects, you can phone a friend, you can appoint a management consultant. In short there are many oracles you can consult, many of whom are quite convincing (or at least reassuringly expensive) so it's no surprise that many people – and organisations – work this way.

But of course you're putting all your eggs in one basket. You're assuming you know what is going to happen when the whole point about decisions under uncertainty is that you don't. Surely you should not just be taking a punt on guessing what is going to happen, but you should be recognising the possibility that the true state of nature may be one of the other columns. Put this way, the next step seems logical. Why not set up a scoring scheme in which you assign a decision weight to each state of nature? You can then multiply the payoffs by the decision weights and select the option that gives you the highest score.

At first sight this does not seem like such a great idea. We all know that similar scoring schemes are often used for decision support, for example during procurement to deal with all the aspects that are not reflected in price. But when you've been around as long as I have you'll realise that they aren't very satisfactory. All the parameters tend to get middle of the road scores that add up to provide little differentiation between the options. And generally you are forced to decide based on

[2] Strictly speaking you could also choose *Neither*, but in the two non-decisive states of nature the payoff is higher with *Both* – see the discussion of 'monotonicity' later.

some overriding characteristic which you could have identified up front. In my opinion such schemes add little to an informal reflection on the available information apart from adding an appearance of science/system/objectivity.

Notwithstanding these reservations I now have to report something surprising: with a set of assumptions about your preferences which many people find pretty reasonable, this is the *only* way to make the decision. In other words any other approach to making decisions would violate one or more of these 'pretty reasonable' assumptions. To summarise, we attach a decision weight to each state of nature and for each option we take the sum-product of the weights with the outcomes under each state. We choose the option which maximises the result.

Objective and subjective probability

The topic of subjective probability is both difficult and controversial. There is a school of thought that all probabilities are inherently and fundamentally subjective. Any statement of a probability must be accompanied by a statement of whose probability it is. You only think the probability of throwing a 6 is 1/6 because you assume the dice is fair. You can see an explanation of this in Lindley's book,[3] for example. Lindley flags up an interesting question: how the concepts of subjective probability for individuals can be extended to groups or organisations. He believes that solving this question will be a major scientific and philosophical breakthrough.

Economists and decision theorists prefer a clean distinction between decisions under risk – known probabilities – and decisions under uncertainty – subjective probabilities. The mathematics is quite different; risk is about random processes, and uncertainty about lack of knowledge. Note this use of the terms 'risk' and 'uncertainty' is not the same as how they are used in the rest of this book.

Although I am bought into the universally subjective concept, I recognise that there are some physical circumstances in which it is reasonable to assume the behaviour is random with known probabilities and I shall refer to objective and subjective probabilities, whilst emphasising that for most risk management purposes the probabilities are subjective, representing degrees of belief.

[3] Understanding Uncertainty, Dennis V Lindley, Wiley 2006.

Presumably we assign higher decision weights to those states of nature we think are more likely to be the true one. In cases where the true state of nature is determined by coin tosses, dice throws, drawing coloured balls from urns, radioactive decays of nuclei with known half-lives and other situations which we think are well modelled by random processes governed by known probabilities (and everyone agrees with us), we can show that you would be pretty foolish if your decision weights (once adjusted so they add up to one) differed much from the known and agreed probabilities. This means that the decision weight you assign to each state of nature is also called your *subjective probability* that this is the true state. Subjective probability is discussed further in the box on the previous page.

Since the weighted sum of the outcomes now contains 'probabilities', it actually takes the form of an expected value, the specialist term used in probability theory to define the probability weighted value of a random variable[4] as already discussed in Chapter 2. Accordingly this means of taking decisions is known as expected value or EV.

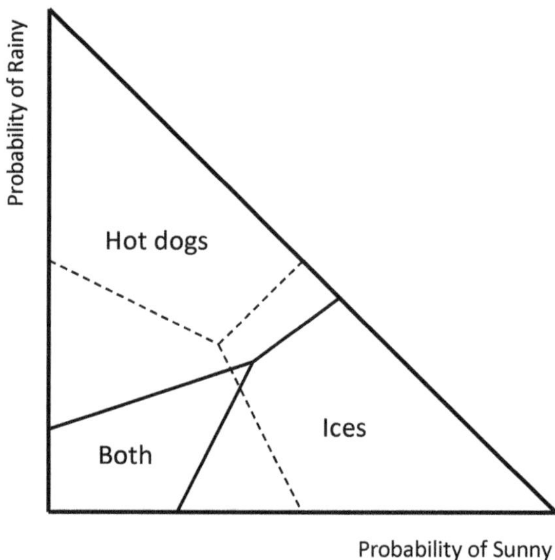

Figure 32 Vendor decision map based on probabilities

[4] Also called the mean value or average.

Figure 32 shows that the decision is based on the probability of the *Sunny* and *Rainy* states of nature. (The probability of *Dull* is the complement of the sum of these two which can never exceed one, hence the triangular shape.) Unsurprisingly high probabilities of good weather favour *Ices* whilst the reverse favours *Hot dogs*. If the weather is likely to be *Dull*, the bottom left corner of the chart, it's best to take *Both*. I've added dotted lines to indicate when you would select each option based just on prophesy, that is, deciding what the weather is most likely to be and selecting the option which is best under those conditions. You can see that similar shapes emerge and that taking *Both* is squeezed in the probabilistic treatment due to the small payoffs in that case whilst *Hot dogs* expands because of its higher best-case payoff. The difference between the two sets of lines is caused by the optimisation of expected value using probabilities instead of just going with what you prophesy; your tradeoffs are becoming more subtle. I leave it to you to judge the benefits of this.

Obviously the superiority of maximising the expected value – from now on called the EV decision rule – is a powerful result, but we should not accept it until we have reviewed the 'pretty reasonable' assumptions it depends on.

Expected value – the mathematics

In this section I give an overview of the assumptions under which EV holds as the decision making algorithm together with an outline proof that this is indeed the case.

There are two sets of assumptions: the structural assumptions and the preference assumptions. Normally only the preference assumptions are highlighted, but I think it's important to discuss the structural assumptions as well: as always in risk, you need to give attention to how the problem is framed.

Structural assumptions

S1 States of nature Future uncertainty can be represented by a set of states of nature, one and only one of which will materialise.[5]

[5] In decision theory you generally talk about being uncertain about the true state of nature, in risk management we think about the future – which state of nature materialises, or turns out to be the true one.

S2 Options You have a number of options for action available, one of which you will select.

S3 Payoff You know the outcome in £ for each option and each state of nature.

S4 Preferences You are prepared to express your preference between any two *propositions*. A proposition is simply the offer of a set of payoffs based on the state of nature which materialises, that is, for each state of nature there is a defined payoff. A preference is a statement that you would prefer one proposition to the other or that you are indifferent between the two.

Preference assumptions

P1 Transitivity Your preferences are such that if you prefer one proposition to another and the second to a third, then you prefer the first to the third (if A is preferred to B and B is preferred to C then A is preferred to C).

P2 Monotonicity Your preferences are such that if a proposition gives a better outcome than another proposition whatever the state of nature which materialises, then that proposition is preferred.

P3 Certainty equivalent Your preferences are such that there exists a certainty equivalent, that is, every proposition has a fixed payoff proposition (that is, the payoff is the same whatever the true state of nature) to which you are indifferent.

P4 Additivity Your preferences are such that if you prefer one proposition to another, then you prefer the proposition got by adding a third proposition to the first to the one got by adding the third proposition to the second (if A is preferred to B then you prefer $A+C$ to $B+C$ for any C).

You will see that you are now firmly on Planet Maths with some rather technical terms floating around. Try not to be put off; it's just shorthand. The important thing is to understand what these assumptions mean and then think about how reasonable each is. I'm not saying they're right, but if you accept them an interesting implication emerges.

> *With the eight assumptions just listed, your preferences can be represented by a set of* decision weights *such that the sum-product of the decision weight of each state of nature with the outcome under that state of nature*

for the proposition is a score of your preference for that proposition. The decision weights are unique if you make them add up to one.

This is a remarkable result. If you think the assumptions are unexceptionable you get to a rather simple way of expressing your preferences and a pretty straightforward way to select between the options: choose that with the highest decision weighted outcome.

On the face of it looks as though we have a solution to the issue of organisational risk attitude. The organisation decides on its subjective probabilities of the states of nature and decides to implement the option which maximises the expected value.

Needless to say it's not that simple. We need to review the assumptions, thus avoiding assumption neglect, and we need to understand how the conclusion arises from them. It is because neither of these activities is routinely undertaken that there is a lot of confusion about attitudes to risk.

S1 States of Nature

The idea that future uncertainty can be articulated as a set of possible states of nature is conceptually very simple. You have to make sure that the states of nature are those things that you cannot control, matters that can be regarded as uncertain until the true state is revealed. So, for example, if you are trying to decide whether to implement an additional risk control measure the states of nature must include something about its effectiveness if the measure is put in place.

To clarify this point, think about the payoff matrix for a civil engineering project with a risk of bad ground. You are considering implementing a site investigation. The site investigation will cost £50k, but if bad ground is found you can restructure your project so that £300k is saved compared with discovering the ground is bad after proceeding on the baseline assumption that it is good, and incurring extra cost and time.

The full payoff matrix is as shown in Figure 33 (relative to the project baseline). The point I'm drawing attention to is that the two right hand entries in the 'No investigation' row are the same – they must be – but the relevant distinct states of nature are in the model. As an exercise you might like to use expected value to work out the subjective probabilities

Ground / SI findings	Good / Any	Bad / Bad found	Bad / No bad found
No investigation	0	-£500k	-£500k
Site investigation	-£50k	-£250k	-£550k

Figure 33 Payoff matrix for civil engineering project

of bad ground and investigation effectiveness under which it is worth doing the investigation[6].

In summary the concept of states of nature is a natural one for risk modelling, albeit some care is needed, and we discussed building risk models in Chapter 2.

S2 Options

The idea of identifying the options for action is also fundamental to risk decisions and does not need further discussion here.

S3 Payoffs

The idea of a single number outcome, which I have taken to be monetary, is oversimplified. We know that risk decisions involve many outcomes – cost (and future revenue), time, quality, safety, environmental, reputational and so on. Although some of these are linked in a reasonably fixed way (the effect of time on the cost of projects, for example), many are not, and we need to bear this in mind. Thus the assumption is clearly not valid for most risk decisions because they have this multi-attribute property and we need to return to this. What's more as I explain in the discussion of Assumption P3 your preferences might reflect a preference for certain states of nature.

A more subtle issue here is the modelling of uncertainty compared to risk events. The risk decision literature is suffused with finite payoff matrices such as those above. In practice we know that the quality of

[6] In fact, it depends only on the joint probability that the ground is bad *and* that it is found (why?) and it is worth spending the £50k if this probability is more than 1/6.

the ground is continuously variable and that the chance of finding it is dependent on how bad it is. So risk analysts use continuous variables in their models. This is not a fundamental issue as clearly the continuous models can be discretised to a sufficient level to give the required degree of accuracy and the finite maths will work. I am simply going to ignore this point and real mathematicians will have to avert their eyes from the cavalier approach here. More importantly, practical risk analysts must make sure that their models can be articulated in states of nature terms.

S4 Preferences

Which brings us to the most outrageous assumption: that you are prepared to state your preference for any proposition whatsoever. Let's be clear. You have to take any *conceivable* row of the payoff matrix and compare it to any other one and say which you prefer, if either. You are not restricted to those which represent options for action, the actual rows of the payoff matrix. I have tried to use clear terminology by keeping the concept of options and propositions separate. They are both rows in the payoff matrix, but options are those things you are considering and can do; they are available propositions. The remainder are purely hypothetical constructs. In the literature both are generally referred to as *prospects* but I have not done so here, partly to draw a clear distinction between the available and the hypothetical and partly because so-called prospect theory is a specific set of concepts which we will come to later.

You can make a number of critical comments on this assumption:

1. It is impractical to actually consider and state your preferences: the number of propositions is uncountably infinite.
2. Why bother when you are only interested in the preferences between available options? These will be a very small subset of the total and if you know your preference order for them you can just pursue the best option without worrying about any of this.
3. What happens if you politely (or not) tell the person who is eliciting your preferences to get lost with their damn fool questions about hypotheticals, some of which are startlingly unrealistic? The whole edifice collapses.
4. Similarly, what if you try to do it, but can't make up your mind about certain preferences?

To deal with these comments you have to recognise that this is a conceptual structure designed to throw light on risk decisions. Assumptions S1-S4 are structural assumptions; the idea is that if you are happy with this structure when supplemented by the preference assumptions you will be happy to use EV to decide what to do. What's more this structure was originally explored in the context of the financial markets trying to decide how to price securities. In this context the wealth of propositions makes a lot more sense than it does in the context of individual risk decisions such as are met in risk management. This means that if you decide not to make decisions this way, an economist will tell you you are incoherent, which is probably the worst thing an economist could call you.

In the organisational context, it is worth thinking about the point that risk decisions are not taken in isolation. Each organisation at every level is constantly making decisions about risk. This means that the total number of propositions under consideration over time is much larger than for a single risk decision. So maybe organisational coherence will be improved if the organisation strives to define a set of states of nature and a corresponding set of probabilities which can inform all decisions. Of course this is conceptual rather than practical but it seems a plausible idea to pursue.

So here's something to think about. Will the organisation which publishes in its risk attitude documents future inflation projections to be used in all its activities and projects make better decisions than one which allows individual project managers to decide their own? Think about this as a principle; don't allow your views to be swayed by the idea that the published risk guidance is compiled by some economics geeks at HQ poring over reams of data.

So far this has not been a particularly compelling argument for the structural assumptions. We'll return to the point when we have explored the implications of the preference assumptions a little more.

P1-P2 Transitivity and monotonicity

Once the structure has been set up, these statements about preference are hard to argue with on the face of it, perhaps even incontrovertible: if *A* is preferred to *B* and *B* is preferred to *C* then *A* must be preferred to *C*, and if something is better than something else whatever the state of nature, then it too, must be preferred.

P3 Certainty equivalent

At first sight you might think – as I did – that there is always a certainty equivalent. For any proposition there must always be a certainty proposition that is less preferred and another that is more preferred. By successive interval halving you must be able to find the one to which you are indifferent compared with the proposition. But for the proof to work you need to preserve strict preference[7] and this assumption is needed to do so. If you always prefer an extra £1 if it is sunny to £1m if it is dull, then there is no certainty equivalent and EV does not work.[8]

This assumption is a continuity requirement, that is, if the proposition doesn't change much, the degree of preference will also not change much. The certainty equivalent assumption is one specific way of achieving this;[9] but there are others.

P4 Additivity

This is a little harder to understand than Assumptions P1 and P2, but it also seems completely logical: adding the same set of numbers to two rows of the payoff matrix should not change the preference between the rows.

We now investigate this a little more to understand how such a powerful result is obtained from these apparently innocuous assumptions. The box which starts on the next page contains a reasonably complete outline proof. But to see what drives things it's helpful to consider what the trade-off is between states of nature.

Take any proposition. Make it better by adding £1 to the outcome if some state of nature is realised. Now consider how much you need to add to the outcome under some other state of nature so that you have an equally desirable proposition.

---

[7] In the discussion I have been particularly cavalier in not distinguishing between weak and strict preference. These are analogous to the distinction between 'less than or equal to' (weak inequality) and 'less than' (strict inequality). The results are correct (I hope) but I have not dwelt on this to avoid slowing the discussion. The proof of EV in the box requires the more rigorous approach.

[8] I am grateful to Peter Wakker for taking the time to point this out to me.

[9] By mapping propositions to the real numbers which have the necessary continuity property.

Proof of Expected Value

This box is a bit more formal than the narrative in the main text, though it falls well short of mathematical rigour. The intention here is to give an idea of how such a remarkable result comes about, the main point being to demonstrate that the preference assumptions are not as innocuous as they seem at first sight, certainly when combined with the structural assumptions.

1. It's pretty obvious that preferences which are represented by expected value are transitive, monotonic and additive, and the certainty equivalent can be the expected value. The tricky bit is to show the reverse, that expected value follows from these four preference assumptions. This is the subject of the next six steps.
2. First, it is straightforward to use transitivity to show that if you are indifferent between *A* and *B* and indifferent between *B* and *C* you must be indifferent between *A* and *C*.
3. Then you need to use (strict) monotonicity to show that the certainty equivalent represents your preferences. If you are indifferent between *A* and *B*, you are indifferent between CP(ce(*A*)) and CP(ce(*B*)) which means ce(*A*)=ce(*B*). Here CP(*a*) means the certain proposition with outcome *a* for all states of nature. Just to be clear, the certainty equivalent (ce) is a *number* which is why I am (pedantically, compared with most texts) introducing CP as a *proposition*.
4. Similarly, if you are indifferent between *A* and *B* then additivity says you are indifferent between *A*+*C* and *B*+*C*. If you are indifferent between *C* and *D* you are also indifferent between *B*+*C* and *B*+*D*. And using 2. you are indifferent between *A*+*C* and *B*+*D*.
5. Using this with *B* as the certainty equivalent of *A* and *D* as the certainty equivalent of *C* you have indifference between *A*+*C* and CP(ce(*A*)+ce(*C*)) which gives you the certainty equivalent of *A*+*C*: ce(*A*+*C*)=ce(*A*)+ce(*C*), using 3.
6. If *C*=*A* this shows that ce(2*A*) is 2ce(*A*) which, with a bit of mathematical fiddling around using rational numbers and continuity arguments, can be generalised to ce(*kA*) = *k*ce(*A*) for any real multiplier *k*. And in the specific case that *A* is the proposition under

which you get £1 if a specific state of nature, s, materialises, you can see that the certainty equivalent of getting £x if that state of nature materialises is $w(s)x$ where $w(s)$ is the certainty equivalent of A. This defines $w(s)$ for all states of nature, s.

7. Any given proposition, A, can be built up by successively adding each state of nature and the corresponding outcome, $x(s)$, that is, working left to right across the outcome matrix. Thus, its certainty equivalent can be built up by successively adding the certainty equivalent of the proposition that you get that outcome. As a result $ce(A)=\Sigma w(s)x(s)$ where the sum is over all states of nature. This is what we set out to prove, given that ce represents our preferences, with $w(s)$ as the decision weights.

You are invited to contemplate at which particular stage in this conjuring trick the magic was applied. My attempted answer is in the main text.

If the answer is £x then additivity can be used to show the answer is £x whatever the base proposition is. x is the ratio of the decision weights of the two states of nature. Put another way the additivity criterion can be used to compare propositions which are primarily about impact with those that are primarily about your belief that each state of nature will materialise. The resulting tradeoffs are linear and again the result is inevitable.

This slightly understates the role of the certainty equivalent which tells you a tradeoff between states of nature and impact exists. For example, if in the vendor example you are indifferent between (£100,0,0) and (0,0,£200), this is an indication that you think *Sunny* is more likely than *Rainy* by a factor of two. If the certainty equivalent is £(50,50,50) you are indifferent between the sum of the first two propositions and twice the certainty equivalent, that is, between (£(100,0,200) and £(100,100,100). Adding the proposition £(-100,0,100) to each of these tells you you are indifferent between (0,£100,0) and (0,0,£100) showing you think *Dull* and *Rainy* are equally likely. Additivity has been liberally used here, but you need the concepts of the certainty equivalent to get going.

However it's fair to day that, after the structural assumptions and the certainty equivalent, it is additivity which is primarily responsible for expected value as a decision criterion. And from the box we now know that the decision weight, or subjective probability, of each state of nature is the certainty equivalent of the proposition under which you get £1 if that state of nature materialises and 0 otherwise. This provides a crude operational method for eliciting subjective probabilities.

We shall come to preferences under which additivity does not hold presently but first it is enlightening to consider another set of preference assumptions which is logically equivalent to EV.

The structural assumptions are unchanged for the time being, but the preference assumptions are now: P1 – transitivity, P2 – no Dutch book and P3 – certainty equivalent. Monotonicity and additivity have gone.

P2 No Dutch book

Your preferences are such that there is no Dutch book. A Dutch book comprises two sets of *n* propositions such that for each number up to *n* the proposition in the first set is preferred to that in the second set, but the sum of outcomes in the second set exceeds the sum of outcomes in the first set for all states of nature.

The significance of the Dutch book is that it turns you into a certain loser. Given successive choices between each member of each set, you choose from the first set each time. Your opponent gets the members of the second set and ends up with more than you whatever the state of nature. Of course, you also need a structural assumption about your willingness to actually act on your preferences.

S5 Commitment

You are prepared to act on your preferences, that is, you will swap a less preferred proposition for a more preferred one. With a bit of economics thinking thrown in you can be turned into a money pump.

The proof of the alternative is given in the box on the next page.

You can see that the whole machinery of decision theory depends on your willingness to express your preferences over the whole range of possible hypothetical propositions, not just the options on offer. What's more your fear of a Dutch book among your preferences is really only provoked if you are willing to enter any gamble on terms which are

Proof of no Dutch book

Once again it's pretty obvious that using expected value will lead to no Dutch book. The tricky bit is to prove the reverse. Our approach is to show that the absence of a Dutch book implies your preferences are both monotonic and additive so the previous proof of EV applies. And specifically, we do this by showing that (a) any violation of monotonicity or (b) any violation of additivity without violating monotonicity will lead to a Dutch book.

For (a) monotonicity it's obvious with n=1 as whatever pair has A preferred to B in spite of B having an outcome which is no worse under all states of nature will constitute a Dutch book. As ever this needs a bit of tidying up for weak and strict preferences.

For (b) as monotonicity holds, we can use certainty equivalents in the knowledge that they represent our preferences (see proof of EV above). For any pair of propositions A and B we show that ce(A+B)=ce(A)+ce(B). If ce(A+B)<ce(A)+ce(B) we would have the following Dutch book with n=3.

Preferred	Not preferred
A	CP(ce(A)
B	CP(ce(B))
CP(ce(A+B))	A+B
A+B+CP(ce(A+B))	**A+B+CP(ce(A)+ce(B))**

The three (weak) preferences are in fact indifferences, but this does not detract from the argument. You construct a Dutch book the other way round if the inequality is reversed. It follows that if A if preferred to B then ce(A+C)=ce(A)+ce(C)≥ce(B)+ce(C)=ce(B+C), so A+C is preferred to B+C and additivity holds, as required.

aligned with your preferences, any number of times. in which case you would become a money making machine. It depends on the structural assumptions S4 and S5. These assumptions are highly unreal. You have to decide if this lack of reality means you don't want to pursue the EV route, or whether you think that, in spite of this unreality, the elegance of the mathematics means that EV is the right way for you to make decisions.

I'm sceptical. On the one hand, I do like the idea of subjective probability. Not only can it be argued that there is actually no such thing as an objective probability (see previous box on the topic), but in my experience individuals and teams representing organisations have little difficulty reaching a consensus about characterising the likelihood of different possible futures in terms of probabilities.[10] What people have difficulty with is using expected values rather than taking account of the whole range of possible outcomes.

On the flipside EV is just a scoring scheme of the sort I don't like. More constructively, it's an optimising scheme; it makes minor adjustments to bring matters to a theoretical level of perfection rather than introducing a material level of decisiveness. An insight into the dubious value of optimisation came to me when my financial advisor wanted to charge me a decent proportion of my pension pot to sell the stuff that had done well and buy more of the stuff that had done badly in the name of 'rebalancing' my portfolio, that is, bringing it back in line with some theoretical ideal of what is optimum. We shall have more on portfolios shortly and a lot more on optimisation later.

Finally it is hard to take EV too seriously when one of the cherished 'reasonable assumptions' is thrown away to go to the next stage of rational decision making, as we now see.

Expected utility

We made the assumption previously that all the outcomes of our decision problem could be monetised. This can happen because – as, arguably, in the case of the vendor – money is the only outcome that matters or because we are prepared to state a financial equivalent for all outcomes. If we adopt the philosophy of the 'pretty reasonable' assumptions we used to justify EV we can be forced into this anyway. By expanding the requirement to express our preferences for all propositions involving money to all propositions whatever the nature of the outcome, we can retain EV. Depending on your perspective this sleight of hand changes

---

[10] Indeed sometimes they stall at calling the numbers they dream up *subjective* probabilities at all!

nothing or everything. It changes nothing in the sense that you are just required to express your preferences; it changes everything in that you are required to monetise all the things that are important to you, including wellbeing, relationships, social standing and, potentially, certainty about the future. And we want to do this in a way which is consistent, a concept I'll define shortly.

But first we notice that one of our assumptions from EV is perhaps too strong. It is a commonplace observation that we will value our second million pounds less than our first. Consequently most people would prefer £1m to entering a lottery where they obtain 0 or £2m with equal probabilities. In fact they'd probably prefer £500k or less. This introduces the idea of *utility*, a number which represents the desirability to you of a given outcome. Utility is a subjective construct just like probability. And, guess what, with a slightly amended set of 'pretty reasonable' assumptions about your preferences I can show that they must be represented by expected utility, the so-called EU decision rule. So if you buy into these assumptions you will make decisions by defining your subjective probability over the states of nature and defining your subjective utility over the set of outcomes and choosing the option which maximises expected utility. I can help you determine both your probabilities and your utilities by suitable questions about your preferences, and giving you a prod if they don't satisfy the assumptions. What could be easier? Or more rational?

Of course you shouldn't answer that until I tell you what the assumptions are. Not surprisingly we drop the additivity assumption. As I said we are no longer in the situation where £1m has the same value whatever else is going on. More fundamentally we are now recognising that it no longer makes sense to add propositions: we cannot necessarily add one outcome to another prior to valuing it.

We replace additivity with tradeoff consistency. The technical definition of this is quite complicated and hard to understand, but what it is getting at is that our preferences between different outcomes are preserved whatever the context in terms of the propositions we are considering. So if we think getting £2m instead of £1m is as good as getting £500k instead of nothing in one set of preferences, this should be preserved across all sets. In a sense this just prefigures the existence of utility, or, more accurately, utility differences and is a mathematical statement to ensure its existence.

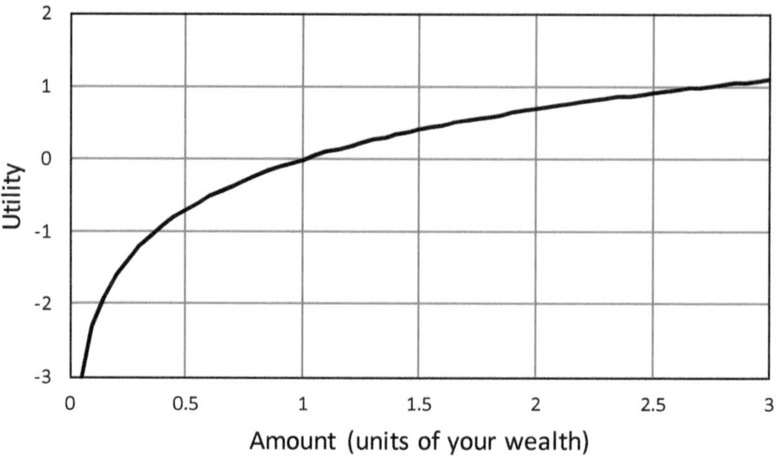

Figure 34 Risk averse utility function

We can also abandon the idea of a certainty equivalent and replace it with a continuity condition. This is a geometrical concept which in this context means that if you take a specific proposition, the set of propositions that are weakly preferred to it is well behaved with a well-defined boundary. There are no outliers floating around. This tackles the idea that small changes in outcomes lead to small changes in preference, as I have previously mentioned.

If you prefer £1m to the evens gamble on £2m the implication is that your utility function is concave (that is, concave down), see Figure 34, for example. This shows a classic logarithmic utility function which has specific value units which reflect infinite disutility for losing everything: the units are your current wealth. You can see the extra utility of doubling your wealth is 63% of that of tripling it (not 50%). We shall use this utility function several times in what follows.

Returning to the general case, concavity means that the utility of £1m is more than the average of the utility of 0 and the utility of £2m. This is known as being *risk averse*, though, as everyone points out, this is nothing to do with risk or probability, but is solely concerned with outcomes. This is a key characteristic of expected utility as a recipe for decision taking and one we will return to later: EU is just concerned with outcome rather than the nature of the uncertainty which leads to this outcome. This is somewhat counterintuitive but for the time being we will accept this situation and the associated definition of risk aversion, which is our first indication of an attitude to risk. However, broadly speaking, although subjective probabilities represent our beliefs about the future and subjective utilities represent our values or desires, we have not so far expressed our preferences concerning risk or uncertainty in any way. This is not part of the EU picture.

In fact the more important feature of what has happened here as we have adopted EU is the transition from monetised outcomes to more general ones. There are theories of multi-attribute utility which can specify the form of the utility function based on tradeoffs, but we shall not pursue this here. It is unlikely you will want to go beyond an additive utility function.

An example – portfolio theory

To illustrate expected utility we'll develop an example of a portfolio of shares as originally explored by Harry Markowitz. Figure 35 shows four securities plotted on a risk-return chart. Return is the expected fractional increase in value and risk is the standard deviation of this return. It is assumed you can measure each of these by looking at market statistics. The line on the top left of Figure 35 shows the risk-return profile of portfolios composed of just two of these securities, the highest return and lowest risk ones. Because they are assumed to be completely correlated with some market (and therefore with each other) they form a straight line between the two securities.

If the securities are completely uncorrelated with each other the portfolios lie on a partial ellipse-like shape, shown on the top right of the chart.

And with partial interdependence, the shape is still there, though less pronounced, as shown on the bottom left. Again I have assumed that correlation is something you can measure (the famous beta factor is a measure of the correlation with the market).

This is all easy to model on a piece of paper, but if you add a third security the mathematics becomes difficult and simulation is the easiest way to understand the patterns which emerge. All these charts actually show 2,000 specimen portfolios picked at random, and marked as blobs. The bottom right of Figure 35 shows the set of possible portfolios with the third share added in and you can now see a cloud with an extension towards the relevant point.

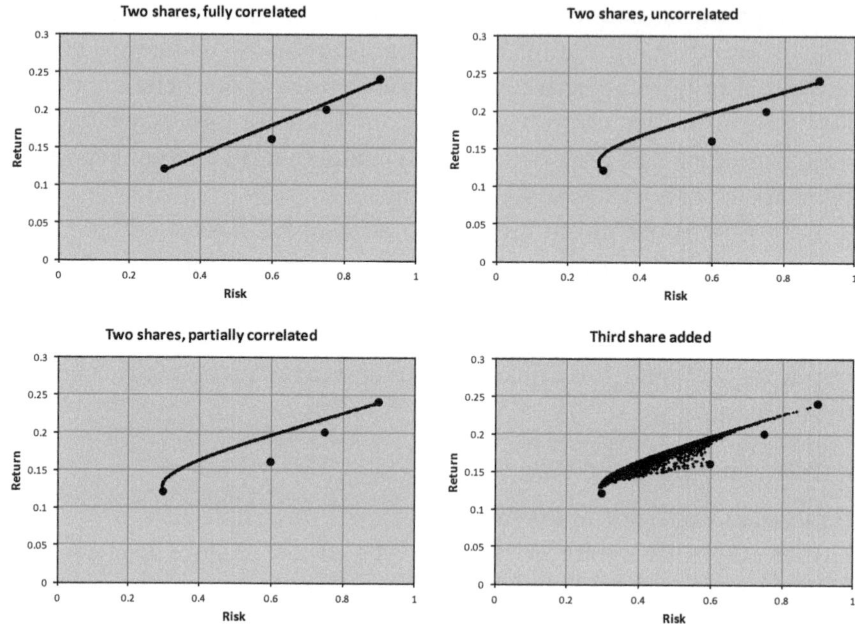

Figure 35 Risk vs return for portfolios of two or three shares

Adding the fourth security, which in this case is negatively correlated with the market, gives a more pronounced result, as shown in Figure 36. The shape is the so-called Markowitz bullet. It shows how you can use well-constructed portfolios to reduce the risk for a given return. In particular you can aim to reduce the risk in your portfolio by diversifying, especially where there are assets which are negatively correlated with each other. (Which as Brealey *et al* in their bible[11] of corporate finance say are as rare as pecan pie in Budapest, whatever frequency that implies.) The only portfolios it makes sense to put together are those on the upper border of the bullet, the so-called efficient frontier, since others are higher risk for the same return or lower return for the same risk.

To complete the picture you can add a risk free asset and carry the picture down to zero risk. This will lead you to the celebrated CAPM model of risk pricing. This is not, however, our purpose here.

---

[11] Fundamentals of Corporate Finance, Richard A Brealey, Stewart C Myers, Alan J Marcus, McGraw Hill International, 2007.

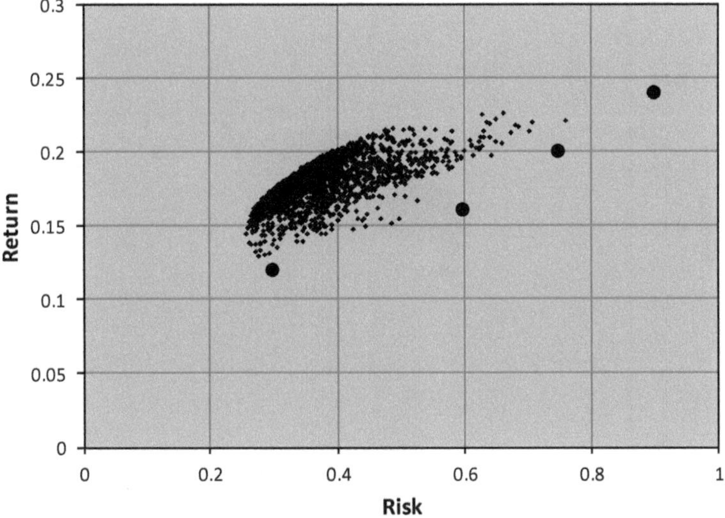

Figure 36 Four share portfolio

Figure 36 is the picture which has unleashed untold numbers of financial adviser consultations. You answer some silly questions, pay a fee to be told you are cautious, pay another fee to be told what the cautious portfolio is, on the efficient frontier of course, and pay another fee to maintain it there, that is by selling stuff which does well so you can buy more stuff which has done badly.

But, you should be asking, why bother anyway? If you are rational you just want to maximise expected value so why not just pick the highest return equity and buy that. Although I could reduce the risk quite a bit by accepting a smaller return, it would, as they say, just not be coherent.

One answer is of course that this does not allow for utility. If you have a risk averse utility curve, the log of your current wealth, for example as illustrated in Figure 34, you can do the calculation to maximise expected utility and get the chart in Figure 37. This shows a line of constant expected utility in white, specifically for the expected utility which is tangential to the efficient frontier. In other words, the utility maximising portfolio lies where this touches the efficient frontier, shown as a white blob. (Obviously this has actually been done by choosing the portfolio in the sample with maximum expected utility.)

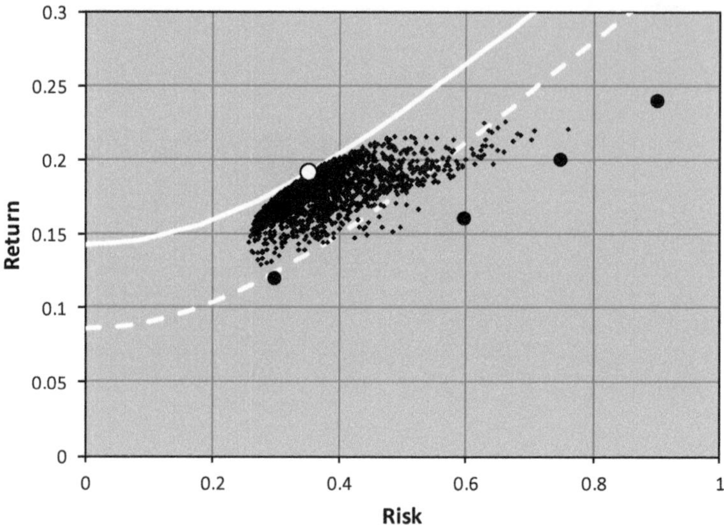

Figure 37 Curve of expected utility

I have not mentioned the scales of these charts up to now. In principle such charts can be drawn up for day-to-day fluctuations in asset prices right up to as many years as you think the return and risk numbers are valid for. In line with the rules of probability the return will increase linearly with time and the risk like the square root. To give the graphs some structure they are measured in terms of your total wealth as in Figure 34.[12] The optimal portfolio will, roughly, increase your wealth by 19% on average, but at a risk of around 35% of your wealth. Evidently the risks have to be substantial for the risk aversion to kick in.

It is interesting to think about the materiality of this optimisation. Evidently, if the risks are high there is a good chance that the returns will be substantially less than the desired, or expected, 19%. Figure 37 shows another line of equal expected utility, this time in dotted white. This line is actually the P43 utility of the optimal portfolio. It encompasses almost all the portfolios. So following the optimisation, there is a chance of more than 40% that the outturn will be worse that the *expected* outturn of any of the other portfolios.

---

[12] I have used lognormal distributions for the portfolios to make the calculations tractable.

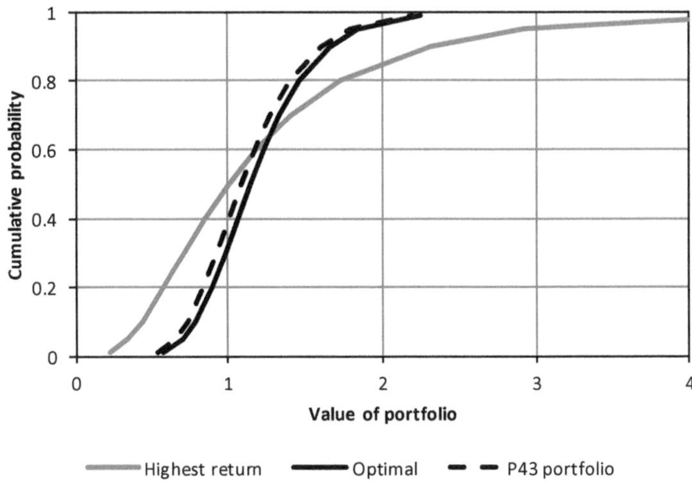

Figure 38 Demonstration of risk reduction

Or, putting it another way, Figure 38 provides a comparison between the S-curve of the optimal portfolio, the highest return asset and a P43 portfolio (one which has the same risk as the optimal portfolio but lower return).

This shows clearly how the risk has been reduced with relatively small impact on the return. However, I think it's clear you would never actually put your fortune into such a risky portfolio. I've constructed this example only to (a) show the effect of a risk averse utility function and to (b) make the point that risk aversion modelled like this does not seems to reflect our preferences. In practice the portfolios would be much less risky and the concave utility function would be neither here nor there. Of course, the financial advisors have some snake oil about your risk attitude to put you somewhere on the efficient frontier. It's not based on explicitly assessing your utility.

I've gone into this in such detail partly because it's interesting, partly because it's important (it won Markowitz a Nobel prize), partly because I want to get some probabilistic modelling into this book which is not just the usual 4-point, QSRA stuff, partly to demonstrate the effect of risk averse utility functions, but mainly to allow you to think through in some detail the benefits of optimisation techniques such as this. Because they operate near the top of a hill, as it were, there are plenty of other solutions which are nearly as good. You can hardly distinguish the S-curve of the P43 portfolio from that of the optimal one on Figure 38. It is the dotted line to the left of the optimal portfolio. We'll come back to 'good enough' solutions later.

A couple of paradoxes

At this stage we turn from the mathematical approach of using plausible assumptions to determine our decision behaviour to understanding how people actually take decisions in the face of uncertainty. Do they, either explicitly or tacitly, maximise expected utility?

When we have covered this descriptively, we will come back to the maths. But let's just finish with two paradoxes which have been put forward as showing that maximising expected utility does not align with some fairly plausible preferences.

The Allais paradox comprises a famous set of propositions that was presented to the pioneers of EU to convince them they had it wrong.

- Most people prefer £5m with probability 10% to £1m with probability 11%.
- However instead of an 89% chance of £1m, a 10% chance of £5m and a 1% chance of nothing they prefer a sure thing of £1m.

These preferences cannot be represented by expected utility as all that has happened is that an 89% chance of £1m has been added to each proposition and this has reversed the preference. It's worth doing the sum to check. These preferences violate tradeoff consistency, not just additivity; they cannot be explained by any utility function. However, they can be modelled by some of the techniques introduced later in this chapter.

Ellsberg's paradox is that we prefer to bet on drawing a white ball from an urn containing 50 black and 50 white balls rather than drawing from an urn with 100 black or white balls but with the split unknown. What rationale can support this preference?

We'll return to the mathematics of how these paradoxes can be resolved later, but now I want to come to a description of how real people actually form their preferences and take decisions.

HOW WE (INDIVIDUALS) ACTUALLY MAKE DECISIONS

What I've just described is pretty simple stuff – childishly simple scoring rules to make decisions supported by some rather obscure mathematics. The human mind is much more sophisticated and complex in its workings so it's no surprise to find that the way we think about and decide about things is not well described by these simple approaches. I'm going to describe two streams of work on this here.

How we think

Psychologists have designed many experimental tests to help them build models of how we think and decide. Some of this work is well described in Daniel Kahneman's lucid and accessible book.[13] This book should be required reading for all risk people and most readers will be familiar with the key points. So I'm just going to give a superficial overview here, apart from where it bears directly on decision making.

But first let's ask why we bother with this at all, especially when the theory is going to get more complex and the mathematics harder. There are two aspects to the study of decisions in the face of uncertainty. One is the descriptive – how people do it in practice – and the other is prescriptive (or normative) – how they should do it. Kahneman's work focusses on the descriptive and it's commonly accepted that his models should not be prescriptive: what we ought to do is maximise expected utility. And if you, as an individual decision maker, should do this, then how much stronger is that the case for organisations?

I am going to take a critical approach to this. At the very least we need to understand what horrors await us if we don't follow the prescription. What's more it's no surprise that there are good arguments that the prescription is too prescriptive and we should think more broadly. Setting these arguments out will enable us to take a comprehensive view when we return to the organisation and its risk attitude.

---

[13] Thinking, Fast and Slow, Penguin, 2012.

Coming back to Kahneman, it's hard to improve on the summary with which he opens his concluding chapter:

> *"I began this book by introducing two fictitious characters, spent some time discussing two species, and ended with two selves. The two characters were the intuitive System 1, which does the fast thinking, and the effortful and slower System 2, which does the slow thinking, monitors System 1, and maintains control as best it can within its limited resources. The two species were the fictitious Econs, who live in the land of theory, and the Humans, who act in the real world. The two selves are the experiencing self, which does the living, and the remembering self, which keeps score and makes the choices."*

The six paradigms are instantly recognisable, providing clear signposts of the direction Kahneman is taking. The banter between the Humans and the Econs is at the core of this book and I will return to that in some detail. The role of the personal or organisational memory in taking personal or organisational decisions is also an important matter to pursue. But let's start with Systems 1 and 2.

System 1 is a highly evolved data processing and decision-making system, wide-ranging and fast-acting. Not surprisingly though, it makes mistakes. The role of the slow and resource-constrained System 2 is to correct these mistakes, by identifying where the data has been mis-processed and doing better (for example by building payoff matrices and analysing outcomes).

Here are some of the mistakes that your System 1 makes:

- You may believe that *what you see is all there is* and neglect to take account of missing information.
- You may succumb to the *halo effect* where your initial knowledge or prejudices lead you to unsubstantiated conclusions.
- You may be *anchored* to your initial opinion even where contradictory evidence emerges; you display *confirmation bias.*
- You may be affected by *availability bias* where your understanding of a situation is modified by the last thing you thought about.
- You may perpetrate the *simulation heuristic* by thinking that what you can easily imagine is more likely than what is less easy to picture.
- You may use the *representativeness heuristic* and wrongly assess a situation as if it were a similar situation.

- Your judgement may be subject to *optimism bias*, an unreasonable belief that things will turn out well.
- For example, you may commit the *planning fallacy* where you compile the perfect plan (taking the *inside view*) and believe that is how things will turn out (ignoring the lessons of history from the *outside view*).
- You may try to solve a problem by *framing it too narrowly*.
- You may try to solve a problem by *substituting* it with an easier one which is apparently related.
- You may indulge in an emotional response and use *affect heuristics*.
- You may be unwilling to give up a cherished project and commit the *sunk cost fallacy*.
- You *identify patterns* which have in fact arisen randomly (or could most likely have).
- You may be generally poor at estimating probabilities (where they exist) as a result of *calibration error*.
- You may be systematically *overconfident* in your beliefs about uncertain propositions (where probabilities do not exist).
- You may forget that *sampling error* is relatively bigger in small samples.
- You may assume that outliers are typical and commit the *regression fallacy*.
- Your memories of past events are dominated by the extreme and final (peak-end) conditions and the time they last is subject to *duration neglect*.
- And finally, you may believe the stories you made up to explain previous System 1 mistakes, committing the *narrative fallacy*.

These are serious. Kahneman shows that experts using their judgement are almost always outperformed in their prognoses by simple data-based algorithms which you might have thought were far too crude.

In some ways to focus on these mistakes gives an unfair impression of the fallibility of System 1. Of course it has evolved to do a pretty good job most of the time, in most day-to-day situations. But one weakness is the lack of an effective warning bell to spur System 2 into action when that would be beneficial. Even Kahneman admits that despite his intimate – unparalleled, even – understanding of how System 1 can go awry:

> *"Except for some effects that I attribute mostly to age, my intuitive thinking is just as prone to overconfidence, extreme predictions, and the planning fallacy as it was before I made a study of these issues. I have*

> *improved only in my ability to recognize situations in which errors are likely."*

This suggests that System 1 can be trained to ring the bell,[14] but this training is not always effective and may fall down when most needed. What's more, System 2 is not immune to error. We have difficulty in framing problems well, we tend to commit *assumption neglect*[15] and – guess what? – we still tend to behave more like a Human than an Econ.

Which brings us to decisions. Kahneman finds our preferences and decisions are inconsistent with expected utility.

- We display risk seeking and risk averse preferences even where the stakes are small and utility should be linear.
- Specifically our risk attitude changes depending on whether we are considering gains or losses. That is, our utility is not a global property (a function of our wealth, for example), but is affected by a reference point (relative to which we may gain or lose). This *reference dependence* can be manipulated by problem framing.
- Most people are risk averse to gains but risk seeking where losses are concerned. It is this switch in risk attitude when all the options are bad (which leads us to prefer a 90% chance of losing £1,000 to a sure loss of £900) which is the most unexpected feature of Kahneman's work.
- But this behaviour is reversed where the probabilities are low: we take out insurance and enter lotteries.

Kahneman and his collaborators constructed a generalisation of expected utility to model these preferences. It is called *prospect theory* and I will describe it in some detail shortly when I resume the mathematical thread.

I need to conclude this section on the psychological aspects of risk with a discussion of whether the psychologists themselves believe this

---

[14] Of course Systems 1 and 2 don't really exist. My picture here is that System 1 is the real time system, operating continuously, which loads up System 2, complete with its spreadsheet, when required.

[15] My term, used several times in this book, to emphasise the point that we forget what we have assumed, we tend not to return to our assumptions, and once you have created a risk model, senior managers, simple souls that they are, tend to believe in it literally and with commitment.

work has anything to say about prescriptive decision support. Kahneman himself is apparently unequivocal. He considers the example of Sam who rejects the offer of entry into a rather favourable lottery – an evens shot at winning £200 or losing £100 – because the possible loss would be too painful. Sam is knowledgeable about probability, though, and is willing to accept the opportunity to enter the lottery 100 times as he realises he is almost certain to win.[16] Kahneman gives Sam a lecture to convince him his aversion to losses in bets of this type is unreasonable. The lecture revolves around repeated decisions to refuse this type of lottery and the resulting losses Sam will accumulate over his lifetime. Over time Sam will be a money creating machine and surely he doesn't want that.

Kahneman notes that the argument does not apply where the probabilities are small, the stakes are high, or the lotteries are not independent. Otherwise he thinks Sam is being unreasonable in rejecting the rational (expected utility) model.

The discussion about descriptive versus prescriptive revolves around what is regarded as rational. Kahneman seems willing to go along with an Econ definition of rationality as coherence or consistency. We have already met tradeoff consistency as the defining assumption of expected utility and yet more bizarre forms of consistency will underpin prospect theory. But Kahneman sees irrational as rather a rude word, certainly not the complement of rational defined this way, and is upset if his work is characterised as showing that we are irrational when we make decisions in the way he has elucidated. Nonetheless he seems to see it as unreasonable (whatever that means). We shall return to rationality and prescription later.

Meanwhile there is a bigger problem in Kahneman's lecture to Sam. It only works where the probabilities are known. There is no way in which you can apply the thought experiment of large numbers of repeated gambles to situations where you might formulate a decision rule based on subjective probabilities, which is most situations in the risk management world. Kahneman himself notes that "simple gambles (such as '40% chance to win $300') are to students of decision making what

---

[16] According to the Central Limit Theorem the probability distribution of his winnings is normal with mean £5,000 and standard deviation £1,500. The chance of losing is thus about 0.04%.

the fruit fly is to geneticists," cleverly evoking the feelings of irritation occasioned both by fruit flies in my kitchen and recurring invitations to determine preferences and values while reading decision texts. I think that the apparent ease with which the theories move us from random situations with known probabilities (decision making under risk, in their terminology) to subjective probabilities (decision making under uncertainty) leads us to greatly underestimate the differences between the two situations and the vastly increased difficulty of framing and quantifying the second case. In honour of Kahneman, let's call this *probability bias*.

Econs are almost entirely concerned with risk (continuing to use their terminology, which, you will have noticed, is not mine as deployed in this book) and the psychologists have pretty much followed this path. Wakker[17] treats risk as a special case of uncertainty, albeit one he devotes half his book to. What he neglects to say is that it is a trivial case. This is not surprising considering the fun that economists and mathematicians have had with it. But for you, the risk manager, the key issue is uncertainty. Situations where there are only known probabilities are rare and, in my opinion, uninteresting. What's more they may be rarer than you think. System reliability models have been constructed for many years using databases which store information about the reliability of components. But some authorities believe this is worthless as a way of characterising the behaviour of systems. Risk managers have to beware of probability bias and focus on the much greater challenge of decisions under uncertainty.

Bounded rationality

There is another way to think about how we make decisions known as bounded rationality. It is based on two propositions:

- optimisation is bad idea
- nature, and evolution in particular, has provided us with efficient and effective ways of making decisions, which we can call the adaptive toolbox.

These two ideas formed the basis of bounded rationality when Herbert Simon put forward the metaphor of a pair of scissors: one blade is our

---

[17] *Op cit.*

cognitive limitations and the other is the environment. We can cut it only by addressing both blades. Bounded rationality is also associated with Gert Gigerenzer, who has written on the statistical illiteracy of the medical profession and the difficulty people have in formulating and understanding conditional probabilities. An accessible account of both this and bounded rationality can be found in his popular book *Risk Savvy*[18] and a more detailed account of bounded rationality in a collection of papers[19] by people associated with this concept. Most of the following discussion is extract from this latter book.

What is key about bounded rationality is that its proponents are unambivalent about promoting its use for decision making. This contrasts with Kahneman's essentially descriptive stance and endorsement of EU in his debate with Sam.

Optimisation is a bad idea

Bounded rationalists argue that the whole process of maximising expected utility is one that goes well beyond our cognitive capabilities and is therefore not worth worrying about from the practical point of view. We have already seen that the theoretical basis of these ideas comprises a number of assumptions about our willingness to express our preferences across a range of real options and hypothetical propositions and to subject ourselves to being turned into money pumps if we are not willing to act at all times in alignment with these preferences. I have already argued that this is not compelling, particularly in situations which are not random and the probabilities are simply personal decision weights. I have described the maximisation of expected utility and will come later to the attempts made by Tversky, Kahneman and others to represent their findings as the optimisation of distorted probability and utility functions as if people took decisions this way. These can all be regarded as optimisation approaches and are all subject to the criticism of the lack of plausibility of the structural assumptions.

Bounded rationalists go beyond this by arguing it's just not practical, particularly when you take into account that you need to get the decision structure right; you need to identify all the events which comprise the

[18] Risk Savvy: How to make good decisions, Gerd Gigerenzer, Penguin, 2015.

[19] Bounded Rationality: the adaptive toolbox, Gerd Gigerenzer and Reinhard Selten (Eds), MIT Press, 2002.

future states of nature and all the propositions over which you will have preferences. You need to work out all the probabilities and utilities. What's more you need a stable situation with all contingencies identified and no provision for adaptation. Even if you try to limit the problem by not using all available information or not seeking more information you will run into meta-problems about deciding how to do it. If you don't get all this right you will be wasting your time trying to optimise. The bounded rationalists regard optimisation as a fiction.

Finally we can note that even if you can do all this, optimisation is something of a waste of time in the sense that typically there are lots of solutions which are nearly as good as optimal. There are plenty of places near the top of a rolling hill which are nearly as high as the summit. Expected utility functions do not generally have Matterhorn-like peaks. I've already mentioned this in the context of portfolio theory but we'll also discuss an example offered by Gigerenzer (slightly adapted).

The CEO of a bank is looking for a new soothsayer and you have applied. It turns out that there is an unexpected perk: you are expected to marry a rich and handsome City trader who will keep you in the appropriate style. To demonstrate your soothsaying skills you have to pick the richest of a hundred indistinguishably attractive traders. The rules are that you can ask as many of the traders as you wish how rich they are but you must immediately select or discard them. You can't go back. When you point out to the CEO that these traders are all Talebian lucky fools, subject at any minute to an irreversible collapse in their fortunes, the reply is unsympathetic. If you fail you can marry a black swan instead (a horrific fate, known as being thrown to the beasts in the original).

With so little to go on, you might at first put your chances of survival at 1%, but after a little thought you must be able to exploit the knowledge you can potentially gain about the traders' wealth. But how? What benchmarks do you have for the wealth of a City trader anyway? None, as it happens. One strategy is to ask a sample of traders what their wealth is and go through the rest picking the next one which has more than the maximum in the sample. Obviously this increases your chances and you do some sums to see what the optimal number of traders is for the initial sample. It turns out to be 37 and chances of surviving using this strategy are 37%, see Figure 39.

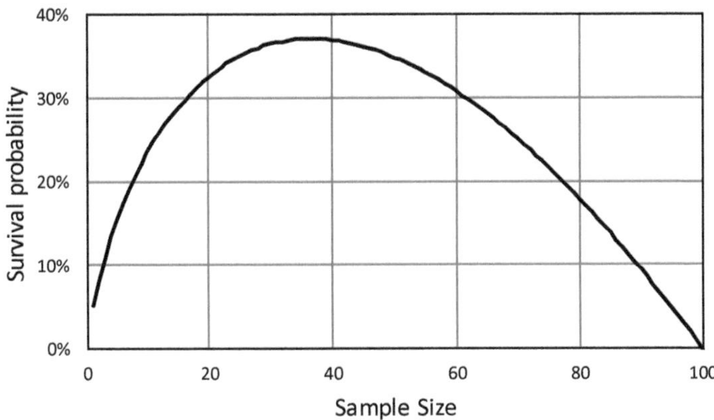

Figure 39 Soothsayer survival versus sample size

You might it find it surprising that you can increase your chances to that extent (and the black swan fate is still more likely than not) but it's a significant improvement on 1%. This is Gigerenzer's point: that simple prescriptions can be surprisingly effective.

But you can also see from the chart that around the optimum the survival chances are only weakly dependent on sample size. If you want to have a 30% chance of survival the minimum sample size is 17 and the maximum is 61. You don't get a great deal out of the calculation. You might intuitively think that looking at the first third and then trying to find something better would be a good approach. Many more and the intended partner will already be in the test sample; many fewer and you will not get much of an idea from the sample.

Note also that you do not need any prior information about the wealth of traders. You get that as you go along; importantly the method depends only on the ranks, not the absolute values.

Finally, I noted earlier in the chapter that Markowitz optimisation of portfolios brought little real advantage, except for financial advisors.

The adaptive toolbox

Most real decisions are made using simple heuristics, within the cognitive capabilities of the species making the decisions. Bounded rationality does not apply only to humans.

To that end we use simple search rules to find options, simple stopping rules and simple decision rules.

Gigerenzer asked groups of Americans and Germans to rank medium-sized US cities by population. It turned out that the Germans did better, because they just assumed places they had heard of were bigger than those they hadn't. Americans took all kinds of other stuff into account. This is an example of the *recognition heuristic* and also showed another of Gigerenzer's precepts, that *less (information) is more.*

More generally, this illustrates a *fast and frugal heuristic* which is both quick to implement and sparing in its use of information. It lies well within our cognitive abilities, in terms both of processing and data. Fast and frugal heuristics are one of the cornerstones of bounded rationality.

Of course recognition is of little use in situations where you know nothing. This illustrates another key point of bounded rationality, that the elements of the adaptive tool box are environmentally sensitive, that is, they only work in specific circumstances. Gigerenzer calls this *ecological rationality*. Part of the cognitive load is deciding what tool to use, finding the right tool for the job at hand. One of the images used to bring this home is that of a backwoods car mechanic and used parts dealer who has to keep vehicles going with less than perfect tools and stores of random parts. You will also notice from the previous chapter that this is an issue with adopting lean production techniques: infatuation with specific tools rather than the philosophy – the *management fad heuristic.*

This picture is supported by analysis of chess masters and how they structure their decisions using progressive deepening of the analysis for a relatively small number of the possible moves. The thinking is not so much probabilistic as opportunistic. This analysis suggests that rather than optimisation you decide on a course of action that is not clearly inferior to any other option, given a reasonable exploration of the situation. This approach can be seen in the heuristics described here. It is considered that good methods can arise from combinations of Tversky and Kahneman's availability, representativeness and simulation heuristics.

Another example of ecological rationality is where the decision is based on a single criterion, the most important. This is known as *take the best.* I was once involved in selecting risk database software for an organisation. An elaborate scoring scheme had been drawn up to aid the decision and much time and effort was expended on eliciting information about various bells and whistles the different software solutions offered.

But in the end there was a corporate standard for the underlying database system which only one of the candidates met. Decision made! You can forget about tradeoffs more often than you think.

It's pretty much always the case that elaborate scoring schemes for decisions are a waste of time, as I noted in an earlier chapter. They are generally fiddled to get the desired answer and exist only as back covering exercises to convince gullible people that a proper process has been followed. But we know now they are ecologically irrational!

Another cornerstone of the adaptive toolbox is *satisficing* as originally proposed by Simon. This means stopping your search when something is good enough. This is what the aspirant soothsayer did. You need a criterion for what is good enough and in this case the soothsayer took a sample and decided that anything better than what is in the sample would be good enough. As the soothsayer worked through the sample, the criterion for good enough increased as richer traders appeared and this illustrates a typically adaptive approach to setting stopping rules.

This opens up the question of how much more efficient the soothsayer could be by sacrificing some simplicity. If trader number 36 turned out to be much richer than 1-35 it might make sense to stop immediately and select him. How much richer? One obvious approach is to use a Bayesian method. You could make some assumptions about the underlying distribution of wealth, update them and recalculate every time to decide whether to stick with the current trader or twist the next. This approach would require some sort of assumption about the underlying distribution of wealth, normal, uniform or, most likely Pareto. You would also need some sort of stopping rule, presumably based on the probability that the current trader is the richest together with an element of clutching at straws as you advance further into the process. I'm guessing that the increase in efficiency over 37% would not be much, but the increase in the cognitive and computational loads would be enormous. What's more it would presumably vanish if your assumption about the underlying distribution was wrong.

This is reminiscent of the work of Martignon who shows[20] that fast and frugal heuristics represented as trees are effective ways to replicate the results of much more sophisticated Bayesian networks, to the extent

[20] For example in Chapter 9 of Gigerenzer and Selten, *op cit.*

that these can be solved by the probabilistic optimiser. This, in itself, is no mean feat, and requires several short cuts.

In summary this discussion has indicated how the adaptive toolbox can emerge from the three key premises of bounded rationality:

- psychological plausibility – use heuristics so that your brain is up to the job; bounded rationality is very concerned with cognitive capability in the sense both of its limits and accepting that it has evolved to be good at its job
- domain specificity – you can expect that heuristics will work only in specific situations or environments and may be composed of more fundamental building blocks, for example, choose the familiar
- ecological rationality – the study of the match between the heuristics and the physical and social characteristics of the environment, for example, choose the US city you've heard of if you have to divine which has the bigger population.

It is characteristic of these heuristics that you search for potential solutions as you go along, not as part of the overarching analysis and that they deal naturally with multi-objective preferences without the construction of utility functions. Because they are adapted to the environment, they can result in so-called psychological fallacies of the type studied by Tversky and Kahneman: they are not so fallacious in their original environment, but may be maladapted to new ones.

The best heuristics are simple because they are not 'overfitted'. This is by analogy with modelling data. If you do a simple regression you are more likely to get accurate predictions of new data points compared with making some very close mathematical fit which is likely to perform very badly on new data points, especially those that lie outside the domain of the existing information. I should note that the term adaptive toolbox reflects our philosophy of adaptive risk management, here in the sense that you need to choose new tools to adapt to a changing environment.

But we can note for future reference that established members of the adaptive toolbox are likely to perform worst when the environment changes most and it is then that the more established risk analysis approach of looking for possible futures and deciding how to deal with them is most useful.

Evolution, emotions and social effects

The bounded rationalists are unambiguous about the prescriptive nature of their ideas. Failure to optimise is not a failing, it's characteristic of all decision-making organisms, including superorganisms such as bee swarms deciding where to set up their hives.[21]

The rationale for this is that satisficing, and the other fast and frugal heuristics, have been honed in the course of evolution to be effective and efficient, fit for purpose. And a key feature of the results of evolution is organisms which live in societies so we can expect that the heuristics will be adapted to a social existence and build on it. What's more, humans, at least, experience emotions and it is unsurprising that not only is some of our decision making driven by emotions but some of the speed and frugality results from emotions as well.

Nature has taken hundreds of millions of years to do its job, the argument runs. Ignore the results at your peril.

Of course, we need to remember that evolution is a random process, not a system driven by objectives, even the survival objective. But it's plausible that genes that incline a being to choose a remote chance of survival and a high chance of a painful death rather than the certainly of famine and disease might preferentially survive. Those same genes today are seen by Kahneman as optimism bias, or risk-seeking behaviour when the options are unattractive. Clearly the survival of these genes is not a good reason of itself to enter a lottery with a 95% chance of losing £1,000 instead of suffering a certain loss of £900 (should that unlikely need arise).

The simplest of the social heuristics is imitation: doing what the others do or choosing what the others choose. This is a simple heuristic which is successful most of the time for directing organisms to do things that will keep them fed, but not poison them, keep them safe from predators and so on. Humans are not much different but there is a greater emphasis on vertical transmission (that is, from parents to children) and the use of language to make it all more explicit. As a result human behaviour is biased towards conformist norms.

It has been shown that in a conformist society, innovation is carried out by the lower ranked, unsuccessful members who are forced to do

[21] Using the waggle dance, see Gigerenzer and Selten, *op cit*, Chapter 14.

something different, to experiment. If the innovation proves successful the others imitate. If not, the innovators fade out of the picture.

Humans also benefit from emotional responses to hone their decision making. These can be background emotions, task-related emotions or anticipated emotions (for example, regret). Emotions help with learning the heuristics. One classic decision problem is mate selection, as we have already seen with the soothsayer and the traders. Leaving the CEO out of it now, the soothsayer will make a nuisance of herself flitting from trader to trader as a better endowed one comes into view. But if she falls in love with trader number 5 who is adequately rich, and he with her, a much more efficient solution is found.

In species where rank is important as a means of ensuring the survival of the fittest genes, the lower ranked males have to take risks to subvert the higher ranks and mate with the superior females. In humans this heuristic is supplemented with the emotions of pride and shame, so that for example, young men take great risks to avoid losing face in front of an audience, much more than could be inferred from any rational risk-benefit calculation. This can be linked back to self-esteem; those with the highest self-esteem are least prone to feeling shame as a result of public failure, and therefore less likely to take risks.

The essential elements of a wide range of human decision making and behavioural patterns are formed by simple imitation or social learning heuristics, which in turn give risk to adaptive (but environmentally specialised) complex sets of emotions, decision processes, rules, cues and procedures, and also combine to give adaptive group processes. So there is a question mark about how to make the learning of these tools as effective as possible and this is where culture comes in. Gigerenzer at al define culture as follows:

> *"Culture is information, stored in people's heads, that can be transmitted among individuals. This information can be thought of as ideas, values, beliefs, behavioural strategies, perceptual models, and organisational structures, …, which can be learned by other individuals though imitation, observation (plus inference), interaction, discussion and/or teaching. Culture is not institutions, technology or social structure but is inextricably related to the evolution and functioning of each."*

I have used this, pretty much verbatim, as our definition in Chapter 3.

Culture is not of itself defined as shared ideas, but some ideas come to be shared as a result of transmission mechanisms such as imitation of dominant members, or copying of most common behaviours. This becomes in turn a decision-making algorithm. An example is some tribesmen who use a religious belief about the behaviour of birds to randomise garden plot selection (instead of all selecting a bad plot for some common reason). This is a fast and frugal heuristic to adapt to a wide range of habitats.

Culture is key element in guiding our behaviour with regard to reciprocity, mate selection and food choice. Cultural evolutionary products limit choice sets and mental models, and social decision mechanisms solve adaptive problems that individuals could not (for example, Micronesian navigation involves a knowledge base which is distributed across many individuals).

It is a key feature of this argument that the heuristics tend to work well only in the environment in which they have evolved. As we noted, this is ecological rationality. Some heuristics are adapted better to different environments; others are very specialist and may quickly lead to a species dying out if the environment changes.

As an example, there is a desert ant[22] which, like bees, can detect the polarisation of solar light. They use this to find their way home, but unfortunately their perception of the polarisation changes quite frequently and they have to make adjustments to their direction of travel. This heuristic system gets them into the neighbourhood of home, but then they have to switch over to identifying landmarks. What the ant doesn't do is integrate his speed and direction of travel (as an economist presumably would). None of this would work if the direction of the sun changes during their excursion, but then if they went a long way they would be fried by the heat anyway. This is a highly adapted system which would fail the insect if it moved to a different environment.

Dealing with risk and games

Not surprisingly, bounded rationality has little to say explicitly about uncertainty and risk. Yet every satisficing decision comes with the risk that it is not good enough or that you do not find any solution which meets your criteria. Every application of a fast and frugal heuristic has the risk

[22] Gigerenzer and Selten, *op cit*, Chapter 5.

that it is too fast – you should have looked a bit more – or too frugal – you should have sought and used more information. Bounded rationality is suffused with risk, but does not make the mistake – if mistake it is – of trying to develop a complete description of what the future might hold and quantify the very many possibilities. Bounded rationality adapts to uncertainty, but without using the decision theoretic framework.

We have seen that evolution will tend to favour certain risk-taking behaviour, especially on the part of individuals with poor prospects. We have noted that this is not necessarily the best course to pursue in other situations. Bounded rationality does not explicitly take on board ideas of likelihood as a determinant of risk decisions but instead tends to look for other cues to feed into the heuristics. These might include concepts like not betting the farm, the use of liquidity ratios, percentage contingencies and safety margins, and affordability. We recognise these parameters from decision making approaches which do not depend on the detailed analysis of risk.

The need to take group risk decisions can lead to a social impact on risk taking. It has been shown that if the decisions are properly structured the quality of decision making is improved, for example through excess risk vetoing, a simple decision algorithm.

Furthermore, because of its evolutionary roots, bounded rationality does something that standard risk management cannot deal with and that is to adapt to environments which contain other rational (albeit only boundedly!) beings pursuing their own objectives. These beings know about us and take decisions in the light of what they think we will decide and do. And we, in our turn, …

These situations are the topic of the discipline known as game theory. This discipline evolved in parallel to classical decision theory, but it has proved much harder to find solutions to general problems which are analogous to the use of expected value. Many years ago my colleagues and I accepted a contract to apply the fault tree methods used for nuclear reactor safety (or rather modelling nuclear reactor accidents) to nuclear safeguards, that is, examining the risk of nuclear proliferation in an environment subject to an inspection regime designed to prevent it. The methods we developed became very complicated as they tried to deal with a rational enemy rather than random failures of electrical and mechanical components.

To develop this point (and at the risk boring many readers) I will take a little time to expand on the classic prisoner's dilemma game.

To provide a little context, my example is set in the hypothetical world of the British Labour Party undergoing one of its periodical swings to the left. You and your friend are junior shadow ministers and, having centrist tendencies ("Blairite scum"), have been discussing the possibilities of deposing the new leftist Great Leader. Unfortunately you have been insufficiently discreet and have been marched into the shadow chancellor's office and given a choice. You can confess your sins or maintain your defiance. You are also told your friend is with the party chief whip and is being given the same choice. If you both confess you will be given a warning about your future behaviour and continue to be regarded with suspicion. If you confess but your friend continues to be defiant, you will be deselected as an MP and lose your job while your friend will be seen as falsely accused and promoted to the shadow cabinet. And vice versa if she confesses and you hold out. If you are both defiant you will both be kicked out of your ministerial posts but continue as MPs. Naturally you are not allowed to communicate with your friend.

Your payoff matrix is shown in Figure 40 where now the 'states of nature' are your friend's decision. You notice that, whatever your friend does, you will be better off to remain defiant so it seems like a no-brainer. You maintain your defiance. Your friend has the exact same payoff matrix where your possible responses form her states of nature and she defied too. You both end up as back-bench MPs with a slippery pole to climb and growling Momentum adherents in your constituency.

Comparing notes over a drink with your friend afterwards, you then notice something slightly surprising. If you had both confessed you would both now still be shadow ministers. How did that happen when

Friend / You	**Confess**	**Defy**
Confess	Warning	Lose job
Defy	Promotion	Demotion

Figure 40 Payoff matrix for prisoner's dilemma

you both behaved so logically? (Slightly unrealistically I am assuming that the preferences of both of you are such that you would sooner be a junior minister than a back-bencher.) If you could have communicated and agreed on mutual cooperation (which is the standard jargon for the *C* in Confess) you would both have been better off providing you were willing to take the risk that your friend might defect (the standard jargon for the *D* in Defy) and get promoted, leaving you without a job.

A one-shot game of prisoners' dilemma is interesting but perhaps only as a curiosity, particularly if you cannot actually communicate. What is of more practical interest is repeated games where the long term, strategic advantages of cooperation can be set against the short term, tactical advantages of defection. If I take your credit card number but don't deliver the book, I am better off, but you are unlikely to buy anything else from me and nor will your friends whom you tell.

So a lot of bounded rationality research is about how you, or society, learn these winning, cooperative strategies which are the foundations of trade and healthy economies. There are many simulations of repeated and randomised prisoners' dilemma games where different strategies evolve. One is known as tit-for-tat where you defect in the next repetition if your opponent does in this one, but not otherwise. The way these models simulate actual sequences of games can be used to calibrate or adjust them. For example it turns out that a version of tit-for-tat which is more forgiving of defection better describes our behaviour. We may all occasionally defect by mistake. This in turns leads to psychological models which underpin the strategies. These models contain modules such as goodwill accounting, reputation, cheater detection, mindreading, friend or foe identification and punishment. Some of this thinking rationalises social institutions such as money, courts or trading rights which promote socially beneficial cooperation. The level to which these mental modules or institutions have developed vary between different societies.

Summary

This section has presented two contrasting approaches to how we make decisions under uncertainty. Both approaches present a world of heuristics, but the psychological approach sees this as a necessary evil to meet System 1 requirements for speed whilst bounded rationality embraces fast and frugal heuristics as the only practical way to decide what to do.

As a result, Kahneman and his colleagues live in a world of biases and fallacies and look for adjustments to expected utility in order to rationalise our revealed preferences. They see expected utility as the sole prescriptive tool for System 2. Gigerenzer's school think of an adaptive toolbox, honed by millennia of evolution to effectiveness, at least in the environment to which it applies.

Which is right? Or, put better, which provides a sounder approach to define the organisational risk attitude? Before we try to answer that I want to record a bit more of the mathematics of the psychological approach, but a few comments are in order.

- Both theories give us valuable insight into individuals, their beliefs, their attitude to risk and how this feeds into their behaviour. In other words these theories provide a framework for investigating the risk culture and planning initiatives to change it.
- While as individuals we may mainly work on System 1 and occasionally boot up System 2, this is not a very useful picture for the organisation which just wants good decisions.
- Similarly, we might by inclination be more Econ than Human (or even what you might call a Gigerenzer being), but again the organisation needs to decide how to approach things without falling into the trap of being one or the other.
- I find the bounded rationality critique of optimisation totally compelling. I emphasised earlier in this chapter that the structural assumptions of expected value and utility are contrived and impractical. Bounded rationality underlines this.
- On the other hand, more so than for an individual, it seems reasonable that an organisation should survey its risk environment and express its preferences in a reasonably comprehensive way. This is what the organisational risk attitude statement should address.
- I am all in favour of adaptation, but equally I am very wary of a toolkit which is the product of evolution. There is a clear and difficult meta-decision problem of what tool to select, if, indeed, any.
- Building on this, it is clear weakness of bounded rationality ideas that there is no mathematical theory we can deploy to describe it and, maybe, prescribe what we should do.

We'll pick up on these points when we come to the section on the organisational risk attitude, but first I want to enlarge on how we adapt expected utility to reflect the findings presented here on how people actually form their risk preferences and act on them.

THE MATHEMATICS OF HOW WE MAKE DECISIONS

This section picks up the mathematical thread from expected utility. It discusses how we can model the observed behaviour of individuals by extending the preference model we worked with there. It's quite technical and somewhat away from the mainstream of this book. But I do think it's important to have some familiarity with prospect theory and it's important to have this background before addressing the question of the organisational risk attitude. There are also some interesting links with the way we build risk models and present the results.

Probabilistic sensitivity

What the psychologists have found is that when faced with downside we both buy insurance (risk averse) and grab at risky lifelines (risk seeking); when faced with upside we enter lotteries (risk seeking) but eschew the chance of a big gain for the certainty of a moderate one (risk averse). These apparently unexceptional preferences give Econs a nervous breakdown. There are two reasons for this. Firstly the range of outcomes has a reference point against which we measure gains and losses with differing attitudes to reach. Secondly we appear to overvalue small probabilities.

The first objection is not fatal for expected utility, just inconvenient. We can envisage a utility function with a kink in it at the reference point. Above this point the function represent risk aversion and below it, risk seeking attitudes. The reference point might move around a bit, so that the utility function changes with time, but we know this is an issue we may have to tackle when we come to think about serial decision makers, such as organisations. A company's attitude to loss and gain may vary depending on the current circumstances.

The second objection also has an apparent resolution in that the decision weight you assign to each column of the payoff matrix could be increased for small probability states of nature. In the same way that utility is a distortion[23] of value, we could introduce decision weights that are a distortion of probability. At this point the risk manager might ask what the problem is anyway. She is generally concerned only with situations where there are no probabilities and you can make your decision weights – subjective probabilities – what you want anyway. This potentially runs into trouble in hybrid situations, where there are some (objective) probabilities, but there is a more subtle objection to this solution, as proposed, which is how do you define small probabilities anyway.

Decision theorists live in a world of discrete states of nature, each with its own, possibly subjective, probability. Risk managers, by contrast, live in a largely continuous world – the cost of a project, the remaining years of life of a patient – and they see quicker than the theorist that there is no such thing as a low probability state of nature: you can always partition it into two states (or events) to get smaller ones, or combine states to get higher probabilities.[24] To get around this you have to consider *cumulative* probability distributions – the S-curves that risk managers, or at least their risk analysts, generally work with – and look at the low probability extremes. This is the topic we address next as we seek to generalise the expected utility model – that is, weaken the set of assumptions which define the model – to accommodate the preferences which the psychologists have inferred from the choices that people make.

The simplest shot at expressing preferences among different outcomes for different states of nature was expected value, based on probabilities of the states and the (financial) value of the outcomes. We generalised the way we valued the outcomes by introducing utility. This is in any case a necessary step to deal with multi-attribute outcomes. Now we want to generalise the probability element of the preference function. This has always been a tempting way to think about preferences, mainly

---

[23] A more mathematical statement would be "non-linear function of," but you get the picture.

[24] This is a huge oversimplification which serves only to make the point about small probabilities in simple ways. Theorists go to some lengths to define *events* as subsets of the set of all states of nature which have defined outcome and use them as the building blocks of their models. I have tried to spare the reader the complexities of this. However it's worth noting that neglect of this simple point led the psychologists to get it wrong in their first attempt at prospect theory. It was based on small probability *events* but led to a violation of a fundamental principle of rational preferences (stochastic dominance, since you ask).

due to some obvious shortcomings of expected utility. As such, it is anathema to Econs, something we will need to discuss in detail, from both the prescriptive and descriptive viewpoints.

The simplest generalisation of expected utility which starts to distort probabilities is *risk-weighted expected utility* (REU). The way that expected utility is generalised is as follows:

$$\text{EU} = p_1u_1+p_2u_2+p_3u_3+ \;........\; +p_Nu_N$$

where the p_i are the probabilities of the states and the u_i are the utilities of the corresponding outcomes. It is assumed that the utilities are ordered so $u_1 < u_2 < u_3 < \;......\; < u_N$.

This can be rearranged as

$$\text{EU} = u_1+P_2(u_2-u_1)+P_3(u_3-u_2)+ \;......\; +P_N(u_N-u_{N-1})$$

where

$$P_i = P_{i-1}-p_{i-1} = p_i+p_{i+1}+p_{i+2}+ \;......\; +p_N$$

is the cumulative probability, that is the probability of an outcome better than or equal to u_i (and therefore sometimes called the good news probability).

This is now in a form to apply probabilistic sensitivity in the form of a weighting function $W(P)$:

$$\text{REU} = u_1+W(P_2)(u_2-u_1)+W(P_3)(u_3-u_2)+ \;......\; +W(P_N)(u_N-u_{N-1})$$

where $W(0) = 0$ and $W(1) = 1$.

This formulation reflects a view that you start with the worst case outcome, u_1, as a certainty and then consider the uncertainty associated with successive improvements, u_2-u_1, u_3-u_2, etc.

How does the weighting function, $W(P)$, reflect preferences? A subject of a pessimistic frame of mind – let's call her Lara – might discount the possibility of successive improvements, and the more the outcome is better than the worst case the greater this tendency might be. Thus she might set $W(P)$ to be less than P, and the smaller P is (that is the better the news, the way we have defined things here) the greater the extent of the discount. A weighting function which would have this effect is $W(P)=P^2$, as shown on Figure 41, marked *Pessimist*.

You can check that the value to Lara of an evens chance of £1,000 is only £250, so she would not be interested in such a proposition even if the entry price were only £300, say, much less than the £500 expected

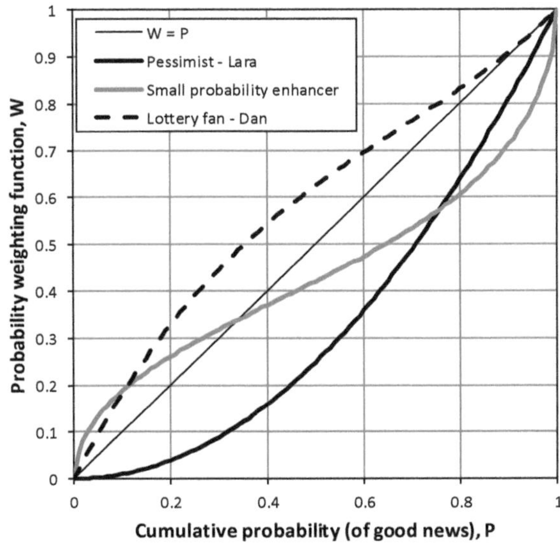

Figure 41 Probability weighting functions

value. And Lara would certainly buy insurance as the value of a loss of £10,000 with a probability of 1% is £199, compared with a premium around the expected value of £100. This weighting function is shown on the chart. It lies below the $W(P)=P$ line and this is why it represents pessimism. It underweights good outcomes which Lara believes are more unlikely than the probabilities suggest. Evidently we shall need to return to the question of whether this is 'rational', but the important point is that we have modelled so-called risk averse preferences without needing to introduce utility, but instead by defining decision weights based not only on probability, but also on the ranking of outcomes.

The formula for REU can also be rearranged as:

$$\text{REU} = \text{RDU} = (1-W(P_2))u_1+(W(P_2)-W(P_3))u_2+ \\ +(W(P_3)-W(P_4))u_3+ \;......\; +W(P_N)u_N \\ = q_1u_1+q_2u_2+q_3u_3+ \;.....\; +q_Nu_N$$

where

$$q_i = W(P_i)-W(P_{i+1}) = W(p_i+P_{i+1})-W(P_{i+1}).$$

RDU stands for rank-dependent utility, which could be regarded as an alternative name for the technique reflecting a slightly different line of development. You can see that this is now an expected utility approach with different probabilities, q_i replacing p_i. The risk manager might justifiably enquire what all the fuss is about. The probabilities are subjective decision weights anyway so you can use what you want. It's true that this view of preferences really makes sense only where there are objective probabilities available for distortion. But I do just need to underline one point. The RDU method is not just a transformation of probabilities. If it were, it could be accommodated by expected utility; you would just be adjusting the subjective probabilities. The way the probabilities are transformed depends on the rank of the corresponding outcome. So the decision weight of a particular state of nature varies depending on how the outcomes are ranked for a given option. This is the important point about these methods.

We shall come to the formulation of RDU when there are no objective probabilities later. For now it's instructive to consider how this works with continuous variables rather than discrete states of nature as the formulae are simpler.

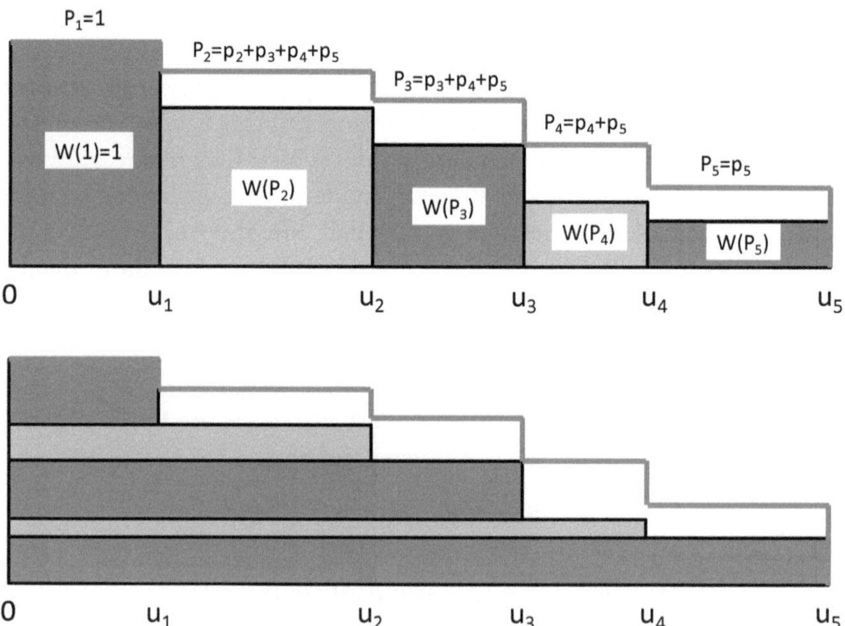

Figure 42 Illustration of REU (top) and RDU (bottom) formulations

Figure 42 shows a graphical representation of both the REU and RDU formulations. The grey line is the cumulative good news probability, *P*, and the areas of the boxes are (in the case of REU) the height, *W*(*P*), and the width, the utility increment. You can see the area of each box has been reduced (for Lara the pessimist). This is a distortion of the 'S-curve' by a factor *W*, and this feature is unchanged where we have continuous distributions and real S-curves. If we consider typical S-curves for cost or time, say, then bad is on the right and *P* increases from left to right with some variable, *x*, for the outcome. This is the opposite situation to that just discussed.[25]

This is illustrated for a typical cost-type S-curve in Figure 43 which shows that for Lara, with $W(P)=P^2$, the effect of the distortion is that uncertainty is reduced but the perceived S-curve (dashed) is centred at a higher level. I think this chart throws light on the nature of REU, but also shows it in a rather mundane light. Is probabilistic sensitivity just a distorted S-curve?

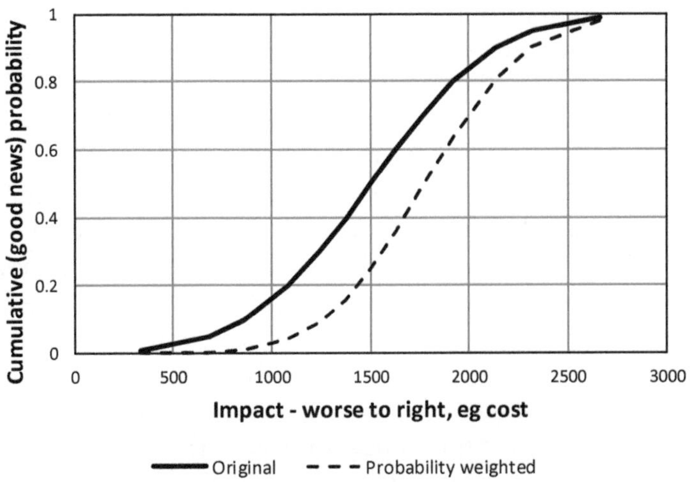

Figure 43 Risk-weighted S-curve

[25] It's important to get this right as the cumulatives can get very confusing. For example, as defined here, the good news probabilities are highest for the worst outcomes (because for these there is a greater probability of better ones).

Suppose now that you are not so much a pessimist as someone who thinks that small probabilities are underrated. In that case your preferences might be represented by the line marked 'small probability enhancer' in Figure 41. The higher slope at either end will ensure that you give greater weight to the extremes of distributions. Not only will you buy insurance – driven by the right hand end – but you will also enter lotteries, because you will overrate your chances of success. With this curve the value of a lottery with a prize of £10,000 and a 1% chance of winning is £226.[26]

We started this section with a typical Kahneman subject who enters lotteries, but buys insurance, has little interest (relatively) in quadrupling his wealth but clings to lifelines. In contrast with the previous subject, it's probably fair to say we buy insurance because we cannot afford large downsides: the disutility of penury is very large and we are sensitive to outcome. But we enter lotteries because we are optimistic: we know the probability of winning is very small but buy the ticket anyway - we are sensitive to probability. So it makes sense to represent our next subject – let's call him Dan – with a risk averse utility function but an optimistic probability weighting. In fact we assume Dan, the lottery fan, is optimistic where the win probabilities are small as also marked on Figure 41.[27]

We can then plot when Dan changes his mind about buying insurance, entering lotteries and so on, as in Figure 44. What this shows is where Dan chooses either to accept the certainty equivalent (that is, a certain amount equal to the expected value) or take the gamble. The gamble is accepted between the two curved lines and rejected outside, as indicated by the comments. With his risk averse utility function Dan would never take a risk and the lines would shrink to the vertical $x=1$ line; it is his optimistic take on probability which inflates the curves.

The axis is relative wealth. For gains we look at propositions where there is a win probability of doubling Dan's wealth, say, and compare whether Dan will enter the lottery or accept the certain equivalent in terms of the expected value. (This means all outcomes are upsides; the analysis would be complicated by thinking about a lottery entry price as

[26] For the record the weighting function shown is $W(P) = P(1.3(1-P)(1-2P)+1)$.

[27] Again for the record the utility of wealth w is $u(w) = \ln(w)$ and the probability weighting function is $W(P) = P(2-2P+P^2) = P((1-P)^2+1)$.

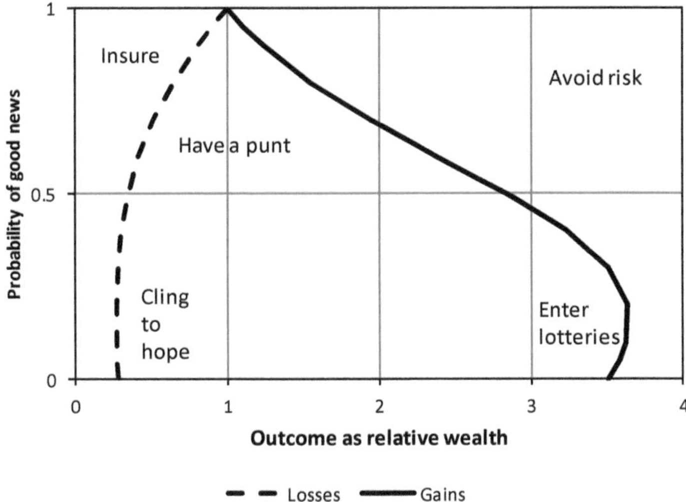

Figure 44 When the risk averse probability optimist takes a gamble

a downside.) Likewise, for downsides, Dan is offered propositions where there is a probability of losing a fraction of his wealth and chooses between this or losing with certainty the expected value (the insurance premium).

The chart indicates that Dan shows traditional risk-averse behaviour at top left and top right, driven by the utility function. He buys insurance and avoids fairly-priced upside propositions. He prefers to double his wealth with certainty to an evens chance of tripling it (that is, get double the gain). But there is a wedge of optimism intruding on this risk-averse behaviour. Dan is willing to have a punt on any fairly priced proposition with small or moderate stakes and is keen to enter lotteries with large prizes but small probabilities of winning (up to a point). What's more, in situations with quite painful downsides, he also prefers taking the risk to paying the insurance premium. For example, you can see that Dan will risk an evens chance of losing half his wealth in preference to giving up a quarter of it.

Dan has preferences which lead in some way at least to the behaviours exhibited by Kahneman's subjects. However we need to generalise the preference model yet again to get to the model Kahneman actually espouses.

Loss aversion

Perhaps the most significant feature of the research described in Kahneman's book, at least as regards how we make decisions when faced with uncertainty, is loss aversion. We hate losing £100 much more than we value winning £100. Typically people will require a prize of £200 to enter an evens lottery where the losing stake is £100.

This preference can be modelled by a kink in your utility at zero. Above zero – gains – the utility increases in the normal way. Below zero – losses – the utility decreases much more rapidly.

That's straightforward. What's interesting is to think about what zero means. Conventional Econ theory proposes a utility which is a function of the goods at your disposal framed in absolute terms, your wealth, if you will. Loss aversion requires that you define a specific reference, the reference wealth, against which you can experience gains and losses. Typically the reference point is the status quo, your current wealth, but it doesn't have to be. If your expectations have built up so as to expect an inheritance of £10,000 from your grandmother, you may see the lucky cats' home as a personal loss, with all the disappointment and resentment that may entail.

The reference point where loss aversion kicks in changes. It changes as our personal circumstances change, and it also changes depending on how we frame the propositions at our disposal. In one experiment the subjects were asked to contemplate a hypothetical lethal disease. Their preferences between different treatments depended on whether the reference was 'everybody survives' with superimposed risks of some people dying or 'everyone dies' with superimposed opportunities of some surviving. The propositions were identical in terms of absolute outcome.

Indeed there is evidence that our attitude will vary depending on whether a reduction in wealth is presented as a cost or a loss. Some of us will happily enter a lottery with a ticket price but will refuse to do so if this price is presented as a loss if we are unsuccessful in the lottery. Again the two propositions are identical; the only change is that a cost becomes a loss.

There are other aspects of this. The endowment effect means that we are generally unwilling to sell our goods at a small profit. We may get a bottle of fine wine for £30 but be unwilling to sell if for £60. The choice of fine wine as the example here is no accident. Some goods are 'kept for use' rather than (like money) 'kept for exchange'. There is inherent value in their possession and their loss is felt much more deeply than their gain. It seems there is an important practical purpose in this: the endowment effect stops us spending all our time making trades or upgrading husbands – well most of us anyway. We met this already in the discussion of bounded rationality.

This reminds us that the primary function of the utility concept is to help us deal with multiple types of goods. The loss aversion kink may well differ depending on what we are contemplating putting at risk.

None of this is particularly surprising. What we are seeing is System 1 heuristics, laden with emotional instincts and a relative perspective, tempting us away from properly invoking System 2. That's not necessarily bad as we find it hard to incorporate the emotional content of loss and gain, instant gratification versus long term happiness and so on into our absolute utility function and our probability weights. So it's also unsurprising that putting a theory around this is difficult. Wakker[28] laments that:

> *"[Reference dependence] is of a different nature than the concepts we have defined so far. It depends on aspects of framing and entails, I think, a bigger deviation from rationality than probability weighting. It is so volatile that it is hard to model theoretically [references supplied], and much of the handling of reference dependence takes place in the modelling stage preceding the quantitative analyses presented in this book. Hence, up till now, hardly any theory has been developed for reference dependence. Nevertheless this deviation is of major empirical importance. I think that more than half the risk aversion empirically observed has nothing to do with utility curvature or with probability weighting. Instead it is generated by loss aversion, the main empirical phenomenon regarding reference dependence."*

Remember the key feature is not that there is a reference point, but that the reference point changes. It changes not just to reflect your current wealth, the *status quo*, but also in ways that are quite capricious – how the propositions are phrased and the nature of the goods at risk. Wakker is saying we just have to put a kink into the utility function, please don't ask why it's where it is.

---

[28] *Op cit*, page 234 (start of chapter 8).

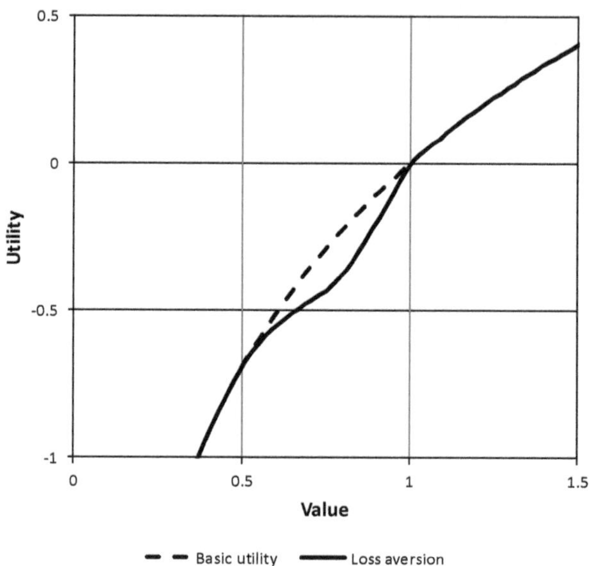

Figure 45 Loss averse utility function

One way to think about this is to consider an underlying absolute utility function which is risk averse, the classical logarithmic utility, say. This is then subjected to a local perturbation to reflect loss aversion, as illustrated in Figure 45. The main feature of this chart is the change in slope at 1 which is considered to be your current wealth, so for small wagers you will need a prize of £200 where there is an evens chance of a loss of £100.

An appealing feature of this chart is that in order to get back to the global utility function there is a region of risk seeking for losses – the convex section of the curve – in line with Kahneman's observations. You can demonstrate this using the plot corresponding to Figure 44 – the dotted line has a similar, but slightly different shape with this utility function. However, this is probably looking rather too far into the entrails of these artificial preference functions.

The loss aversion distortion reflects our System 1 decision heuristics and can move around as the status quo demands, or the framing suggests to the subject. This leads to the predictable inconsistencies and paradoxes which the theorists observe for situations with small or moderate stakes are involved. We expect (or at least we hope) that System 2 will be invoked for important, life-changing decisions, with large stakes, and that it will keep the underlying global utility function in mind, altered as necessary to embody our true, considered preferences.

Prospect theory

Building on this, *prospect theory* is the term Twersky and Kahneman used to describe their all-embracing model of people's preferences. 'Prospects' is the term used in decision theory for what I have called propositions. I've avoided the term as it did not seem very meaningful to most people, and also because prospect theory is really only Twersky and Kahneman's theory of prospects and you could quite justifiably have your own, different one. Talking about propositions instead, enables us to reserve the term 'prospect theory' for Twersky and Kahneman.

Prospect theory has two features:

1. it has a reference point relative to which gains and losses can be defined, and loss aversion is experienced
2. different RDU probability weights are used for gains and losses.

With regard to point 1, prospect theory is determinedly local and relative, and makes no attempt to integrate with global, absolute, concerns like the model above. It is a theory of low and moderate stakes decisions. Point 2 appears to be largely driven by the fact that it is possible to have different probability weighting functions once you have created a distinction between gain and loss. Note too, that prospect theory is formulated as RDU rather than REU, as it needs to be if it is to distinguish conveniently between loss and gain. However, the probability weighting functions are $W(P)$ as in the REU formulation, so the utility weights are differences in W.

For continuous random variables we have an effective cumulative probability of $Q(x)=W(P(x))$, as we showed earlier, see Figure 43 for example, so the effective probability density $q(x)=p(x)\mathrm{d}W(x)/\mathrm{d}P$. This is what is used to weight the utility values.

Figure 46 shows an example model of preferences proposed by Twersky and Kahneman for both utility and the two probability weighting functions. The subject here, let's call him Amos, has the typical

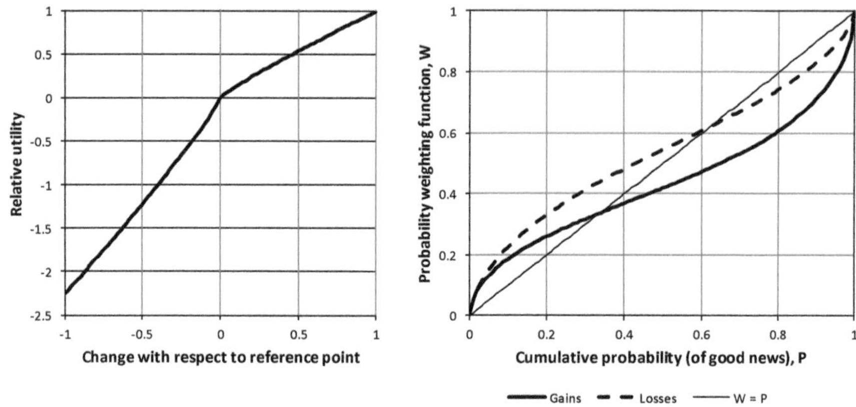

Figure 46 A typical prospect theory preference model

preferences of Twersky and Kahneman subjects. Amos is loss averse and a small probability enhancer for both loss and gain.

For the record the model (as reported by Wakker[29]) is:

$$u(x) = x^a \text{ if } x>0 - \text{gains}$$
$$= -b(-x)^a \text{ for } x<0 - \text{losses}$$
$$W(P) = P^c/(P^c+(1-P)^c)^{1/c} \text{ for gains}$$
$$= 1-(1-P)^d/(P^d+(1-P)^d)^{1/d} \text{ for losses}$$

where a=0.88, quite close to linear, b=2.25, creating the loss aversion kink, c=0.61 and d=0.69.

Amos's utility curves, in spite of being power laws, are quite close to linear (since a is close to 1). The risk aversion and risk seeking behaviour is not pronounced. Nor is it obvious that with this power law format the gradient of the utility is infinite (on both sides) at zero, which is undesirable. Amos exhibits clear loss aversion, however, with factor 2.25, that is, the utility of avoiding a £100 loss is 2.25 times the utility of a £100 win.

For the probability weighting functions, I have adopted the convention of using the good news probabilities for consistency. Often the probability weighting for losses is expressed in terms of the bad news

[29] *Op cit* page 256, taken from Twersky, A, and Kahneman, D, 1992, Advances in Prospect Theory: Cumulative Representation of Uncertainty, Journal of Risk and Uncertainty, 5, 297-323.

probability, cumulated in the opposite direction. It shows that, for good news probabilities less than about 35%, Amos is optimistic, driving lottery entry. Conversely for bad news probabilities of the same order he is pessimistic and he is likely to buy insurance.

Because Amos's utility is scale-invariant his preferences depend only on probability. His indifference chart is less interesting than Dan's. He enters lotteries rather than accepting a fair value for certain if the probability of winning is less than 24% and he buys insurance similarly. Of course if he regards the price of the lottery ticket as a loss he will only enter lotteries with probabilities he is very optimistic about: in fact the probability has to be less than 3%, but no doubt this is going outside the realm for which the preference data is valid; this is a mathematical curiosity only.

Rank-dependent utility and ambiguity aversion

In introducing probabilistic sensitivity I mentioned two formulations, one focussing on differences in utility, REU, and one on differences in the weighting functions, RDU. The weighting functions are functions of cumulative probability and we have kept probabilities in mind throughout the subsequent discussion. The probabilities might be either real or subjective, but our development of REU and RDU depended on their existence.

This raises the idea that perhaps we can develop a model of preferences under uncertainty which depends on the rank of the outcome but does not necessarily involve the intermediate construct of probabilities. Needless to say the answer is yes, and all we need is a function defined for all subsets of the set of states of nature.

To see what this means, let's think about Lara, the pessimist, who is now in charge of the street vending business we introduced this chapter with. The states of nature are the weather tomorrow: *Sunny*, *Dull* or *Rainy* and she thinks they're all equiprobable. If she sells ice-creams then that's the ranked order and, with her P^2 weighting she assigns weights of 1/9 to *Sunny* and 4/9 to {*Sunny* or *Dull*}. The decision weight of *Dull* is therefore the difference, 1/3, and the decision weight of *Rainy* is 5/9. If she sells umbrellas, the ranking changes and the decision weight of *Rainy* is now 1/9 and so on. The decision weights are the differences *after ranking* between the values of a weighting function, w, where *w*(*Sunny*) = *w*(*Dull*) = *w*(*Rainy*) =1/9 and *w*(any two of the three) = 4/9. *w*, as defined here, can be interpreted in terms of weighted probabilities, but the concept is more general than this.

w is not a probability because it is not additive: *w*(*Sunny*) + *w*(*Dull*) is not equal to *w*(*Sunny* or *Dull*); the fact that it is less reflects Lara's pessimism.

A model where preferences are represented by a weighting function, *w*, defined on all subsets of the set of states of nature and in which the decision weight allocated to an outcome within a proposition is the difference between the weight of the states which have that outcome or better and the weight of the states which have a strictly better outcome under that proposition is the generalised version of rank-dependent utility (RDU). Our specific case of probability weighted expected utility is technically known as RDU with probabilistic sophistication!

Lara's *w* function above was derived from probabilities but a general *w* model doesn't have to be. Indeed, the principal advantage of this model is that it can address ambiguity. Consider Ellsberg's paradox, that we prefer to bet on drawing a white ball from an urn containing 50 black and 50 white balls rather than drawing from an urn with 100 black or white balls but with the split unknown. We can deal with this by assigning higher weights to events where uncertainty about the first urn is eliminated (leaving residual uncertainty concerning the second urn) than to the opposite situation. For example Wakker[30] provides an example complete quantification in which $w(W_1)=w(B_1)=0.45$ and $w(W_2)=w(B_2)$ $=0.35$. Essentially you would need the prize to be £2.22 to prefer the gamble with the first urn to a certain £1 and £2.86 for the second urn. None of this can be represented by subjective probabilities, even if weighted.

What Ellsberg's paradox demonstrates is ambiguity aversion: our preferences are conditioned by the source of the uncertainty. This is a potentially interesting line of approach given the importance of ambiguity in many risk management applications. However, it is also rather intractable due to the many degrees of freedom available for selecting the weights and the conceptual difficulty of defining non-probabilistic functions on the sample space. Wakker[31] puts some ideas forward, mainly

---

30 *Op cit*, page 286.

31 *Op cit*, Chapter 11.

involving distorted or multiple probability functions but I shall not discuss this highly technical area further.

While this has nothing to do with this topic, you do have to be careful about ambiguity and how much there is. I was once involved with a railway upgrade project. For most of the existence of the railways the philosophy of avoiding collisions has been to split the track up into blocks and design a signalling system which ensures no train enters a block until you are sure the previous train has left it. One easy way to do that is to wait until the train has entered the block after that, meaning the back of the train has left the block in question. This *fixed block* signalling method is palpably suboptimal; now we have software and radio systems and so on we can design a *moving block* signalling system where trains essentially carry a protected zone around with them. Unsurprisingly, given the high level of system reliability required, the development of moving block systems has not been trouble-free. As a result, there would have been quite a lot of ambiguity about the system design. So the project director decreed an important risk control measure: no moving blocks! That seemed like a good idea until the we looked into the detail of the fixed block system we bought, which had its own innovative and hitherto unproved features. I have no idea if the moving block would have been easier to prove and install, but the moral of the story is that you need to watch out for unanticipated ambiguity.

Summary

This section has taken a journey through some generalisations of the expected utility formalisms which are intended to model the way people actually make decisions:

- we began by noting that to express sensitivity to probability in the same way as utility expresses sensitivity to value we needed a rank-dependent formalism and derived risk-weighted expected utility, REU, based on utility differences
- we noted a different perspective on this based on utility called rank-dependent utility, RDU
- next we noted the asymmetry of the preferences of many subjects to gains and losses and discussed the issues this raises

- we combined these two concepts, probabilistic sensitivity and reference dependence, using both a utility function with distinctly different behaviour for gains and losses and a model of the RDU type which is different for gains and losses – this is prospect theory
- and finally we demonstrated a more general form of RDU which goes beyond probabilities and can model ambiguity aversion.

These steps were taken largely in the context of objective probabilities which, in the risk manager's world of subjective probabilities or decision weights, raises questions of meaning. However, it seems plausible that if a subject can determine her preferences from a pessimistic view of objective probabilities, it may also be helpful for her to go through a two-stage process, first determining subjective probabilities of events and then from preferences based on sensitivity to this. As a result, different probabilities or weights may be allocated to events depending on the rank of the outturn under the different actions considered. Alternatively, a very sophisticated observer may model a subject's preferences with a decision weighting function that cannot be described as a probability.

The work has shown that classic risk averse behaviour can be modelled other than by concave utility functions. This is because all these methods explore the space of propositions sufficiently to reveal the tradeoff between likelihood and impact. The rationalisations of probabilistic sensitivity are intrinsically more appealing than those of utility, except to Econ extremists which brings us to the question of whether any of the models explored here should form the basis for rational decision making for individuals or organisations, bearing in mind that they have largely been developed to be descriptive, not prescriptive.

STAYING RATIONAL

I've described a series of models for decisions in the face of uncertainty of increasing generality. The full generality is required to predict how most real people take decisions. However, until now, I've avoided reaching any conclusions on whether these models are actually recommended for use. Should we take decisions like real people? Or should we restrict ourselves to behaving like Econs?

This leads us into a debate about what is rational, what is reasonable, what is coherent, what is consistent, what is sensible and so on. I don't find this very edifying as there are no independent and accepted definitions of these terms. You might think consistency is easy to understand and an essential requirement for decision making. You should set out your approach and stick to it. But consider this. You go to your local restaurant tonight and eat steak, and go again tomorrow and choose chicken. You are certainly being inconsistent and at a stretch you are irrational and incoherent too. Maybe the conclusion is that you will not eat with Econs. Or maybe that you need to add in the utility of variety (or the disutility of the routine).

Or maybe (to avert the effects of boredom, perhaps) you and a friend decide to pass the time by betting on coin tosses. You pull a coin out of your pocket and decide your subjective probability of heads is 20% so you happily agree to bet that the number of heads in 100 throws is less than 35. Congratulations: you are rational and coherent, but it is dubious whether you are being very sensible.

The best way to approach this is to think about the implications of accepting particular solutions. Each decision model implies a set of preferences between propositions and you can scan these preferences to see if there are any you don't like. The mathematicians have done this work for you. They have put together a set of preference conditions (or assumptions) for each decision model which has the property that the model implies the preference conditions and the preference conditions imply the model. This was demonstrated for expected value earlier, and I noted the assumptions for expected utility. So if you like the preference conditions, you use the model. These preference conditions are also known as behavioural foundations: they set the rules for your behaviour in reaching decisions, or, more accurately, expressing preferences.

Since the models are increasingly general as you move from expected monetary value to expected utility to risk-weighted expected utility to prospect theory the preference conditions become successively weaker. At each stage you are giving something up. You just need to decide if it makes sense to give it up.

Sounds simple, but there's a catch. And the catch is that the preference conditions are incomprehensible to normal people. For example, to move from expected utility to risk-weighted expected utility you give up full tradeoff consistency and just accept rank-tradeoff consistency according to Wakker.[32] What are the implications of this? No, me neither.

What we could do is go through the operational implications of weakening these conditions at each stage. This would provide more insights to help us understand each model. However we can shorten a long story fairly easily. First, we can note that it is necessary to define a utility function to address multi-attribute decisions: we need to find a common scale for disparate outcomes. In other words expected (monetary) value cannot do it for us. Secondly no-one, including Kahneman, argues that prospect theory should be a recommended approach to decision making. It is a descriptive theory which helps us predict what preferences people have, not what they should have. I noted that one distinctive feature of prospect theory is a moving frame of reference. Consistent decisions within the moving frame create anomalies, inconsistences and paradoxes when pinned down to a fixed frame. Once you have pinned the frame of reference down you can accommodate loss aversion through a suitable utility function (though this might not be sensible). One exception to this is the use of different probability weighting functions for gains and losses, but this seems to me to be of minor significance. Prospect theory only allows for this mainly because it can.

So the major debate is whether to move from expected utility to the more general risk-weighted expected utility. Buchak has devoted a book[33] to exactly this point, making the case for the rationality of the more general theory, at least in the form where the subject is a pessimist (subject Lara above). What's more, Buchak argues strongly that going beyond REU is irrational. We'll come to Buchak's arguments shortly, but it's instructive first to discuss briefly what we give up when we abandon expected value in favour of expected utility.

This leaves open the question of whether there is any value in pursuing the idea of a non-probabilistic weighting function as in the w-formulation of RDU. I have spent quite a bit of time in my career looking at non-probabilistic expressions of uncertainty. The search is inspired by the observation that lack of evidence for a conjecture is not the same as evidence that the conjecture is not true, Type 1 and Type 2 error in hypothesis testing if you like. Bayesian, probabilistic degrees of belief

---

[32] *Op cit* pages 112 and 297.

[33] Risk and Rationality, L Buchak, Oxford University Press, 2013.

about the conjecture do not allow for this. If your subjective probability that it is true is p, your degree of belief that it is false is 1-p. However, I am not going to pursue this here, and I am certainly not going to suggest basing your preferences on non-probabilistic functions on the set of all subsets of the sample space. It is dubious that the FD will be comfortable with that, even if it does express her aversion to ambiguity.

What we give up with expected utility

Expected utility is such a well-established approach to rational decision making that it is something of a surprise to realise that we have to give up a cherished 'behavioural foundation'. At the start of this chapter I concocted an argument for using expected value as a way of making decisions based on a vaguely plausible scoring scheme. The surprise is that you can replace this argument with a rigorous mathematical theorem which uses conditions that are not just plausible, but actually quite compelling, as I also outlined. So it's interesting to investigate what compelling condition we give up for expected utility.

It turned out that the main condition we conceded was additivity, or more flamboyantly, 'no arbitrage' also called 'no Dutch book'. Additivity means that if we prefer one proposition to another, adding a third to each does not affect our preference. A Dutch book is simply a set of preferences which, when systematically combined, produce the reverse preference.

So if we have a risk-averse utility function we might prefer £450k to a lottery ticket which pays £1m on heads. The same applies to one which pays on tails. Adding these suggests we prefer £900k to £1m on heads or tails which is perverse. If we were forced to trade in the tickets we would suffer a sure loss. Of course we are not forced to do this and we needed structural assumption S5, that we will always act in accordance with our preferences, to make us. The example reminds us that expected value is relevant where markets are trading and prices will adjust to eliminate arbitrage opportunities. For one-off decisions the 'no Dutch book' requirement need not apply; this also illustrates the lack of realism which is present in the formulation which requires every conceivable proposition to be considered in the preference structure.

What's more, a realistic analysis of the options facing someone in possession of both the winning and losing lottery ticket should start from a baseline of certainty in winning the prize. He should only sell the first ticket for an amount exceeding £550k. It is the second which is worth only £450k. You cannot consider propositions in isolation of your other risk exposures. This is evidently a key point in thinking about risk decisions.

What we give up with risk-weighted expected utility

Now let's turn to the rationalisation of probabilistic sensitivity as discussed extensively by Buchak.

She begins with introspection of a subject's motives. Probabilities are about beliefs and utilities are about desires. Probabilistic sensitivity is not about either of these, however, but how the subject wishes to structure her objectives. Specifically, she might be more focussed on the downsides of a proposition than the upsides. This is independent of how she values these downsides and upsides. She is keen to secure a minimum position and in the extreme she will be a mini-maximiser. Conversely, another subject might be upside focused and weight the highest ranked outcomes higher. In the extreme this subject would be a maxi-maximiser. Again, we see a clearly defined attitude to risk.

So far we have called these stances pessimistic and optimistic respectively in line with common practice. Not surprisingly Buchak does not like these terms and uses the alternatives *risk-avoiding* and *risk-inclined.*

It's worth saying here that terms of this sort have developed for historical reasons and that they are now quite confusing. Different shapes of utility function have been termed *risk seeking* and *risk averse.* Since they refer to desires they say nothing about risk. They reflect a growing appetite for goods and a diminishing one and for that reason would be better termed *greedy* and *saturating*. Similarly the way people structure the attainment of their objectives could be termed *downside-focussed* and *upside-focussed.* The term *risk aversion* could then be reserved for a preference for certainty (at the expected value) over uncertainty. It could be the result of either *saturation* or *downside-focus* as we have seen in the examples. *Risk seeking* could arise from *greed* or *upside-focus.* I think that's all much clearer.

Buchak does not spend much time on the small probability enhancer (which we might now re-christen *extremes-focussed*). She provides him with a rationale[34] but gives the impression she does not regard this stance as rational.

Buchak discusses at some length three possible arguments that risk-weighted expected utility is not rational:

- preferences will change when propositions are decomposed
- preferences will lead to Dutch books
- preferences applied to repeated bets will lead to almost sure losses when compared to utility maximisers.

For the first point Buchak turns, for example, to the Allais paradox presented earlier. These are preferences which cannot be represented by expected utility but which can be modelled by probability weighting.

Recall that most people prefer (L1) a 10% probability of winning £5m to (L2) an 11% chance of winning £1m yet prefer (L4) a certainty of winning £1m to (L3) a 1% chance of winning nothing plus a 89% chance of winning £1m and a 10% chance of winning £5m although the difference between the two sets of propositions in each case is that 89% of the chance of winning nothing is transferred to winning £1m. This violates tradeoff consistency, a basic preference assumption of

Outcome		**0**	**£1m**	**£5m**
Utility		u_0	u_1	u_5
Difference	(for REU)	u_0	u_1-u_0	u_5-u_1
L1	*p*	0.9	0	0.1
	P	1	0.1	0.1
L2	*p*	0.89	0.11	0
	P	1	0.11	0
L3	*p*	0.01	0.89	0.1
	P	1	0.99	0.1
L4	*p*	0	1	0
	P	1	1	0

Figure 47 Worksheet for Allais

[34] *Op cit*, page 67.

expected utility. Other behavioural foundations with the same effect are known as the sure thing principle or independence.

Doing the sum according to the worksheet in Figure 47 you'll find:

$$W(0.11)/W(0.1) < (u_5-u_0)/(u_1-u_0) <$$
$$< (1-W(0.99)+W(0.1))/W(0.1)$$

where the first inequality comes from L1 being preferred to L2 and the second from L4 being preferred to L3. With no probabilistic sensitivity, $W(P)=P$, and hence expected utility, this becomes

$$1.1 < (u_5-u_0)/(u_1-u_0) < 1.1$$

which is not possible for any utility assignment, but with Lara's risk avoiding weighting, $W(P)=P^2$, we need

$$1.21 < (u_5-u_0)/(u_1-u_0) < 2.99$$

which clearly is possible, though we also need risk aversion built into the utility. This is because the ratio cannot be as high as 5, which is what would be needed with linear utility. With logarithmic utility based on your current wealth, your current wealth would have to be less than £1.75m to replicate these common preferences. Which is reasonable, I guess, though I do not know if this has been tested.

As ever, it is instructive to look at this in pictures. Look first at the top diagram in Figure 48. This shows close ups, at top and bottom, but to scale as the vertical axis shows, of the relevant 'S-curves' (which are stepped) in a similar way to Figure 42. We can see that the preference for L1 over L2 is equivalent to being unwilling to swap rectangle A for B1. This appears reasonable. The preference for L4 over L3, however, indicates that the subject will swap A for B2, even though B2 is the same size as B1. This is the fundamental Allais property and because B1 and B2 both span the same value range, changing the utility scale does not help. When viewed with pessimistic probability sensitivity though (again as illustrated in Figure 42), and shown in middle chart, the preference for B2 over A can be seen as much more reasonable – A has shrunk to a tenth of its former size whilst B2 has doubled. Finally, the preference for B2 over A becomes even clearer with a risk averse utility distortion as shown on the bottom chart of Figure 48.

However, these preferences can be unstable over time. Consider the decision trees shown in Figure 49 in which we introduce a new lottery L0 in which there is a probability of 10/11 of winning £5m.

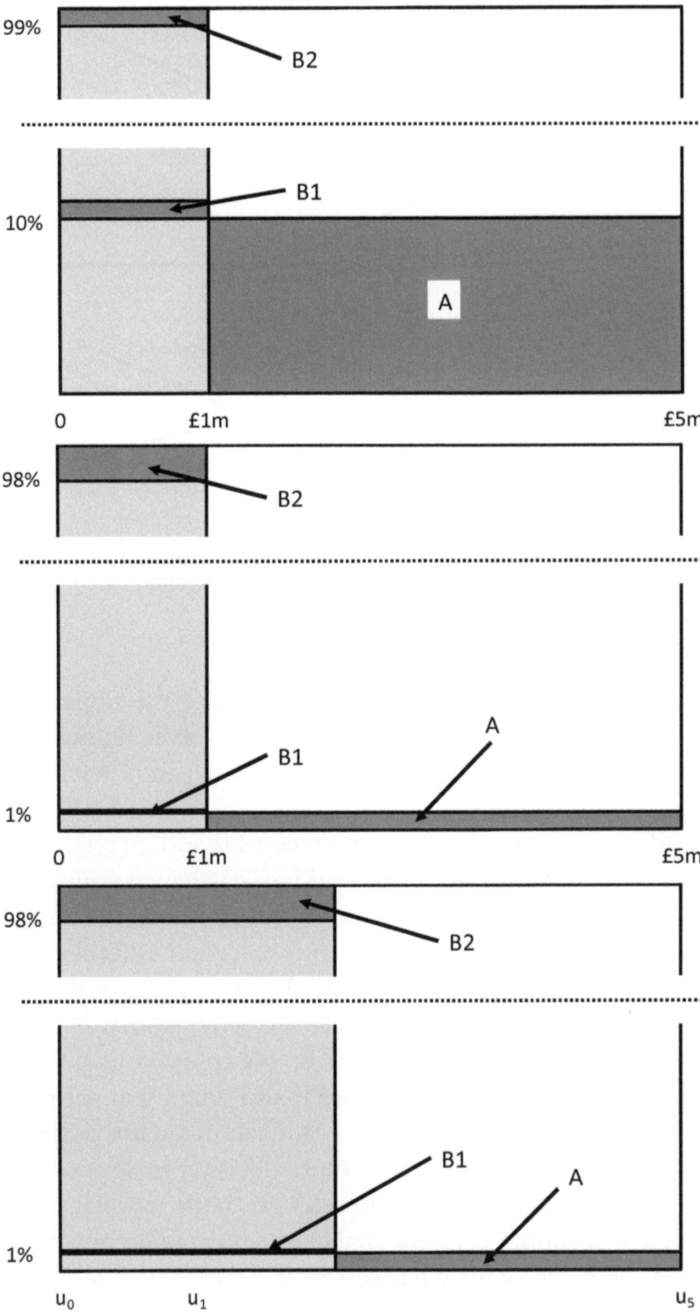

Figure 48 Allais in pictures

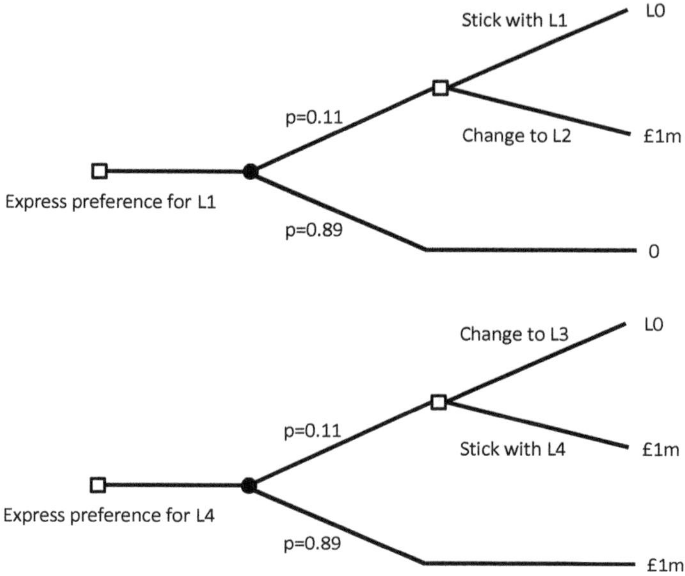

Figure 49 Allais decision tree

The upper decision tree represents L1 if you take the upper branch on the second decision and L2 if you choose the lower branch. Similarly, the lower tree represents L3 with the upper branch and L4 with the lower one.

Depending on your preference between L0 and a certain £1m, one or other of these decision trees will lead you to change your mind about one or other of the Allais preferences once you know the output of the first chance node. This node can be interpreted as whether or not you have won a chance to change your mind. In fact, you will almost certainly prefer L0 to £1m (do the sum to see why) so that if you are presented with the second tree and invited to express your preference for L4 over L3 you will change your mind if and when you get the chance.

It's not clear what to make of this. Buchak maintains that the stances either of sticking to the plan (the resolute decision maker) or of looking ahead (the sophisticated decision maker) are both rational. I'm not so sure. I think you should severely challenge your preferences if you *know* you will not be happy with what you have decided at some later point.

This discussion bears on what is already a slightly difficult point about probability weighting: it is independent of the scale of the uncertainty.

The probability weighter attends to the main source of uncertainty, after which the next most significant source springs up hydra-like demanding to be dealt with. The fact that the spread in outcome associated with it is much less than the initial spread is not relevant when we define probability weights solely in terms of the cumulative probabilities of good and bad news, independently of how good and bad the news is. This is also what is driving the apparent anomaly in the Allais propositions.

With regard to Dutch books the probability weighting subject is actually in a better position than the utility maximiser. As long as the point is accepted that bets are bought and sold in the light of your current exposure to uncertainty you can avoid a Dutch book. It is this point which is the downfall of Econ thinking. The whole theoretical framework of decisions under risk is based on determining preferences between pairs of propositions as we have seen. These preferences are considered as independent of any propositions you have already accepted: this is clearly a defect in the framework which is addressed by some of the more exotic models, but rather by the back door given the firmly established nature of the structural basis.

Finally Buchak argues that if you know a bet is going to be offered repeatedly you adjust your preferences accordingly. The result is that you move towards being a utility maximiser as a result of the law of large numbers. This is wholly unconvincing. Life does not generally offer a series of identical bets. But you can be sure it will offer a series of uncertain propositions, and that you will certainly lose out if you systematically fail to maximise utility. This is reflected in Kahneman's appeal to Sam on his hypothetical deathbed. On this basis I think it is irrational to use probability weighting where probabilities exist. What's interesting is where they don't, which, of course, is almost always for the risk manager.

SUMMARY

The discussion so far in this chapter has been a long and bumpy journey. I have gone into these matters at such length because I think it is important for those involved in organisational risk management to have a basic understanding of what is known about decisions under uncertainty. Specifically:

- it is important to know about basic expected value and expected utility, not least to put some of the wackier practices that get suggested into perspective
- it is important to understand how we can deal with an aversion to uncertainty, for example by probability weighting
- it is important to understand how people in organisations think and make decisions, so we will not be surprised if this is out of line with want we want and we can try to modify these behaviours if it is.

This explains the coverage of topics. I say it has been a bumpy journey as many parts of this account are quite difficult and uninspiring, but they are interspersed with sparks of interest and usefulness.

- A low point for me is the tedious framing of the problem with you, the agent, being required to express your preferences across all pairs of conceivable propositions.
- A high point is being able to show that, with an apparently unexceptionable set of assumptions about these preferences, we have to maximise expected subjective utility using a set of subjective probabilities. Who could have imagined that just another silly scoring scheme would have such an impressive justification?
- But a low point is the difficulty and abstruseness of this proof. You are bound to be suspicious if something is not fairly obvious.
- A high point is the realisation that one formulation of probabilistic sensitivity (REU) uses cumulative probabilities which we are very familiar with in organisational risk analysis.
- A low point is the realisation that Buchak's argument for the rationality of this is unconvincing, at least where probabilities exist. And for us users of S-curves, it's just a shift of the bad news probabilities downwards in a way that is arbitrary and not obviously useful or insightful.
- A definite high point is Kahneman's account of the psychology of how we think. System 1 and System 2, Econs and Humans are all too recognisable, and provide compelling and memorable explanations of how people actually behave. We now know we have to look for biases and heuristics, framing effects and loss aversion.
- A possible low point is the banality of the utility and probability weighting functions which arise from the prospect theory models. More generally, especially as you try out the numerical examples, you

realise you are dealing with optimisations which provide rather small benefits as you approach the smooth maximum. But a real low point is the complexity and confusion of the theoretical work. It seems to be a remote and arcane industry, inaccessible to those of us who cannot read the academic journals, obsessed with micro-weakening of the obscure assumptions in theorems before dignifying them as 'behavioural foundations'. You may find it hard to decide if your behaviour exhibits 'sign-tradeoff consistency' or not.

- A high point is the alternative view of life put forward by the bounded rationalists. Maybe we can develop a toolbox of fast and frugal heuristics to make decisions which are good enough.
- But a low point is the realisation that this toolbox is patchy, it is not clear what the appropriate tool is, or if there is even a tool available to suit out current position. We need to beware of doing things which helped our genes to survive in our evolutionary past but will not work for us now.
- An emergent high point is the realisation that fully general rank-dependent utility, RDU, can start to tackle ambiguity. This is tempered by the knowledge that this a rather advanced and undeveloped concept, quite hard to grasp if you are used to probability measures, and that in any case your quantification of Ellsberg's paradox implies you prefer the unknown urn once the probability of success with the known urn drops to some level, 30% say. Where does this come from?
- Another interesting point, which may be worth pursuing, is the emergence of fast and frugal decision trees from Bayesian modelling which may reflect an important link between theory and bounded rationalist. Sadly we cannot follow this up here.

This sense of muted disappointment with the achievements of decision theory is echoed by Nassim Nicholas Taleb in his trilogy on risk[35] (in a less muted way, of course). Taleb is contemptuous of the Econ Noble prize winners (with the honourable exception of non-Econ Kahneman, of course) and their emphasis on optimisation and doing what is mathematically doable.

---

[35] Fooled by Randomness, Texere, 2001; The Black Swan, Penguin, revised edition, 2010; Antifragile, Allen Lane, 2012. All by Nassim Nicholas Taleb, all UK editions.

Taleb's prescription is to avoid large downsides and to give yourself options as we discussed at some length in Chapter 3. The point about large downsides is that they are more severe and more likely than you think, and one day they will wipe you out, expected utility notwithstanding. This is evidenced by the prevalence of black swans and the probabilities of extreme market events, which are higher than conventional theory predicts (see for example the elegant fractal-style modelling by Mandelbrot[36]).

Creating options and exploiting the opportunities they offer is less controversial. In contrast with the fiddling around of optimisation, they can offer real utility benefits. A simple example is provided by Leach,[37] who discussed the introduction of new technology (laser welding) in a manufacturing company. He first demonstrates the benefits of piloting the technology before full implementation. As Leach recognises, this is a rather mundane conclusion, but he then goes on to illustrate how piloting the technology can add hundreds of millions of dollars of (expected) value, *even if you think it is unlikely to work*. The decision tree in Figure 50 shows why. Don't just pursue stuff you think will be successful, but don't bet the farm on it either.

There's plenty of food for thought here as we move to thinking about the risk attitude of organisations in the next section. I'll construct the menu shortly. But let's finish this section by taking the fight to the Econs on their own ground.

Harry Markowitz's portfolio theory with its bullet diagram showing the efficient frontier for risk and reward graces many textbooks of economics. And the idea it encapsulates informs the financial advice given to many seeking to invest their hard-earned wealth to provide for their future needs. How come, if all you care about is expected value ('reward')? The answer of course, is that with a risk-averse utility function you will trade off some reward for reduced risk as we showed earlier. And the more of your wealth is at stake, the more reward you will trade off. A complicating factor is that the trade-off is affected by the amount

---

[36] The (Mis)behaviour of Markets: A Fractal View of Risk Ruin and Reward, Benoit B Mandelbrot and Richard L Hudson, Profile Books, 2008.

[37] Why Can't You Just Give Me The Number? Patrick Leach, Probabilistic Publishing, 2006, page 134.

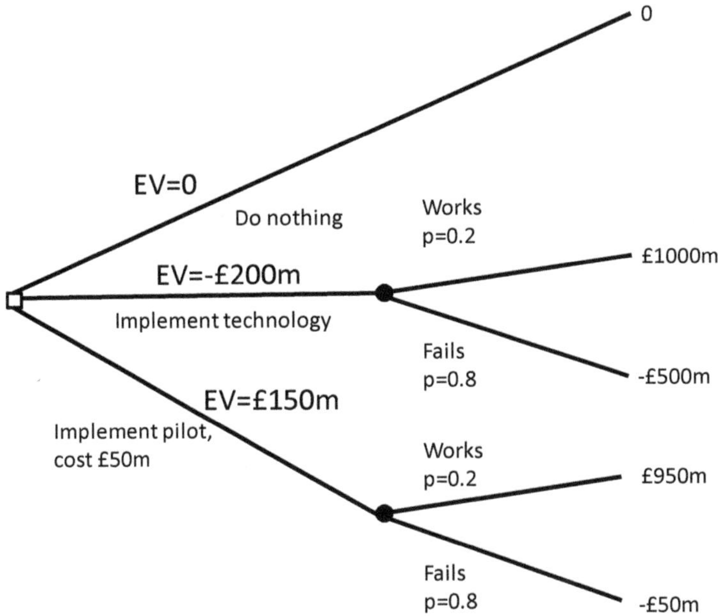

Figure 50 Decision tree for piloting technology

of time you hold the portfolio. That is why financial advisers point you at allegedly low risk portfolios as you approach retirement.

With all of this in place you can identify your optimal portfolio. In the example calculation this was considerably lower risk, although the risk was still substantial. But to make this interesting I had to postulate both a very risk averse utility function and a big gamble with all your current wealth. This is exacerbated in the case of shareholdings by the observation that the risk of these is greater than allowed for in the theory: as Mandelbrot shows, the chance of a significant loss is more power law than the very fast tail of a normal distribution. This is due to long term correlations which can be cleverly modelled[38] by combinations of random processes. Think hard before you invest in shares, and even harder before creating an optimal portfolio.

In any case does the optimal portfolio really reflect your attitude to risk? We know from the research that this does not represent most

---

[38] See, for example, Multifractal Volatility: Theory, Forecasting and Pricing, Laurent E Calvet and Adlai J Fisher, Academic Press, 2008.

people's attitude adequately and, what's more, I do not think it fully represents organisational attitudes either. If so, we need to look either at REU and the other optimising generalisations of EU, or take to well-chosen heuristics.

HOW SHOULD ORGANISATIONS MAKE RISK DECISIONS?

Apart from the quite interesting insights it provides, this chapter has primarily been directed at answering the question of what attitude to risk an organisation should have. I think we should assume that the organisation wants to be rational in some sense.

It's worth starting with a reiteration of what Kahneman[39] has to say about organisations. He begins by noting how hard it is for System 2 to ride shotgun on System 1. We are not good at noticing our own mistakes and there is no automatic alarm bell to sound when System 1 makes it worst errors. However we are much better at spotting where others are going wrong, and maybe even identifying the error as one of Kahneman's biases or fallacies.

> *"Organizations are better than individuals when it comes to avoiding errors because they naturally think more slowly and have the power to impose orderly procedures. Organizations can implement and enforce the application of useful checklists, as well as more elaborate exercises such as reference class forecasting and the premortem."*

In some ways this is contrary to the idea of natural risk management, a practice which I see as a manifestation of System 1. The implication is that the people in the organisation have to cooperate to improve the quality of (organisational) System 1 decisions, exploiting the alarm bells which are available when working in teams. According to Kahneman we also have to take steps to continuously improve the quality of decisions, using the tools that he and others have bequeathed to us. So the first part of our organisational risk attitude has to be to nurture the quality of our System 1. This is the task of risk culture improvement, and in

---

[39] *Op cit*, last couple of pages.

assessing the quality of our conversations about risk we need to bear the strictures of Kahneman, Gigerenzer[40] and others in mind.

What about System 2? What formal guidance can we provide on formal decision making about risk?

If we take Buchak's position that REU is the most general rational approach to decision making we can see that there should be three clear elements to any organisational risk attitude statement:

- **Desirability of outcomes** The organisation should publish its multi-attribute utility function for all types of impact within its risk profile.
- **Beliefs** An instruction to develop a set of probabilities – objective where possible and subjective where necessary – for each relevant aspect of its risk profile. The mathematics of probability can then be used to construct its risk models. These beliefs relate to which of a comprehensive set of states of nature, over which the organisation has no influence or control, will actually materialise. The organisation may want to be directive as to what certain probabilities should be, for example future inflation in relevant sectors.
- **Attitude to uncertainty** I use this term in preference to Buchak's attitude to risk both because I am reserving that for the larger statement covering all three of these bullet points, and because Buchak's W-function attitude to risk strictly applies only where there are objective probabilities, whereas there is scope to expand the concept to the subjective probabilities developed as part of organisational risk analyses.[41] For example, we might systematically slide the S-curve from a risk model up towards the worst case, thus reducing its spread.

In practice no organisation does these things.

The reasons are partly pragmatic, for example being unwilling to articulate the details of tradeoffs such as that between safety and cost, and openness to criticism for such a defined set of tools. As we have also seen, the decisions made with such a prescription will be visibly in conflict with the decisions people naturally make – not that that should really

[40] As set out in Risk Savvy (*op cit*) and other works as well as bounded rationality.

[41] However I am ignoring any scope to develop Wakker's non-probabilistic *w*-functions to subsets of the sample space as impractical, interesting though it is as a potential way of dealing with ambiguity.

be an issue. However I think we can see that the main reason ought to be that which is inherent in the main critique of the bounded rationalists: that the optimisation inherent in this three-stage approach is a chimera.

In these circumstances we must accept that an organisation's risk attitude is more likely to be a set of pragmatic tools rather than a coherent mathematical algorithm. We have learned about the important of a flexible and adaptive toolbox both from our discussion of lean production and construction, and from bounded rationality. We have also noted that System 1, the natural risk decision maker, operates on a number of heuristics, which may be helpful, and biases, which are probably not.

The tools might include:

- replacing the tradeoff for some risks (such as safety) with compliance, either with external regulations or internal norms
- complete avoidance of high negative consequence outcomes – no betting the farm
- using the outside view as well as the inside view to inform your risk models and risk decisions
- arbitrary pricing rules such as P80 – or even a 10% contingency
- reducing the chance of making a loss, or failing to recover corporate overheads, to an arbitrary (subjective) probability, 5% say
- investment guidelines with a risk-weighted cost of capital
- and even using concepts such as risk appetite to limit the risk undertaken in the absence of a corresponding benefit, or to allow risk decision making to be delegated efficiently.

In deploying these tools it will be important to maintain much of the theoretical paraphernalia:

- use probabilities, subjective as necessary
- develop risk models
- give yourself options and opportunities which may be exploited later
- don't commit to things before you have to
- think about the opportunities of cooperation and the risks of defection
- ensure you cover all the risks in the system you inhabit, not just those that are local to you
- and if all else fails, remember you take risk because it is outweighed by the rewards and maximise expected utility.

But most importantly, the lessons from both lean production and bounded rationality are that you must not be seduced by the tools or a specific tool in particular. The idea of a toolbox is a good one, but you must remember there is still a meta decision problem of which one to choose – or whether you need a new one. I collated the ideas for the toolbox you might want to deploy in Chapter 5.

The theme of this book is that doing risk management will improve your future. What the good futures look like and the bad ones is something rather relative. As a final exploration of what a winning attitude to risk might be, let's come back to the contractor who is bidding for work. We've mentioned this contactor several times in the course of the book and now is the time to look at the relevant risks and the resulting attitude.

As Econs we'll construct a model. The model is very simple and could be elaborated in any number of ways to be more realistic.

You, the contractor, want a turnover of £1bn per year (roughly) and want to get a contribution of £100m, £50m to cover overheads and £50m profit. Jobs have a value of £500m (roughly) and opportunities of this size arise once a month so you need to win one in six. You can bid for all with a probability of winning of 1/6 or bid for one in three with a 50% probability of winning.

The £500m size is the baseline cost. On top of this there is risk, represented by an exponential distribution with a given mean. This distribution is chosen as it is typical of projects with their key risk of overrunning. The P50 is 69% of the mean for this type of distribution which is what you might expect. Ideally you would price at mean plus £50m so as to give you the £25m overhead contribution and £25m profit. It's assumed the revenues arrive over 3 years for each job, so than on average you have six on the go.

It's straightforward to build a random walk model with these characteristics which covers 20 years, and, because we want to look at the chance of bankruptcy, we'll assume there's an initial cash buffer to cover working capital and losses. This is assumed to be 2 years of overhead, £100m.

Let's look at four pricing scenarios; they are summarised in Figure 51. One is where the jobs have a mean risk of £25m and are priced in line with your objectives at £575m. One has a mean risk of £50m and is priced at £600m, so again this has proper pricing. The third scenario also has a mean risk of £50m, but this is mistaken for a risk of £25m and priced at £575m and finally, the same situation, but priced at £560m. You can see that the third scenario is actually the breakeven one, just recovering your overheads on average, whilst the final one might be regarded either as the third with a £15m hit on profits to win the job, or else a breakeven price with the actual risk assessed at P50 – there is a £15m difference between P50 and mean, as noted above.

For the low risk case you are bidding at a level which reduces the probability of no overhead contribution to 5%, which might be normal practice. This rises to 30% for the competitive bid, which has a 50% probability of not making a profit (since the price is £25m over the P50 of £35m). I've dropped the £500m baseline from the table and subsequently.

	Low risk	High risk	Under estimated risk	Competitive
Mean risk (£m over baseline)	25	50	50	50
Price (£m over baseline)	75	100	75	60
Cost for no profit (£m)	50	75	50	35
Probability of no profit	14%	22%	37%	50%
Cost for no OH contribution (£m)	75	100	75	60
Probability of no OH contribution	5%	14%	22%	30%
5 year bankruptcy probability	10%	18%	47%	77%
10 year bankruptcy probability	11%	21%	61%	93%
20 year bankruptcy probability	11%	21%	73%	99%

Figure 51 Pricing scenarios

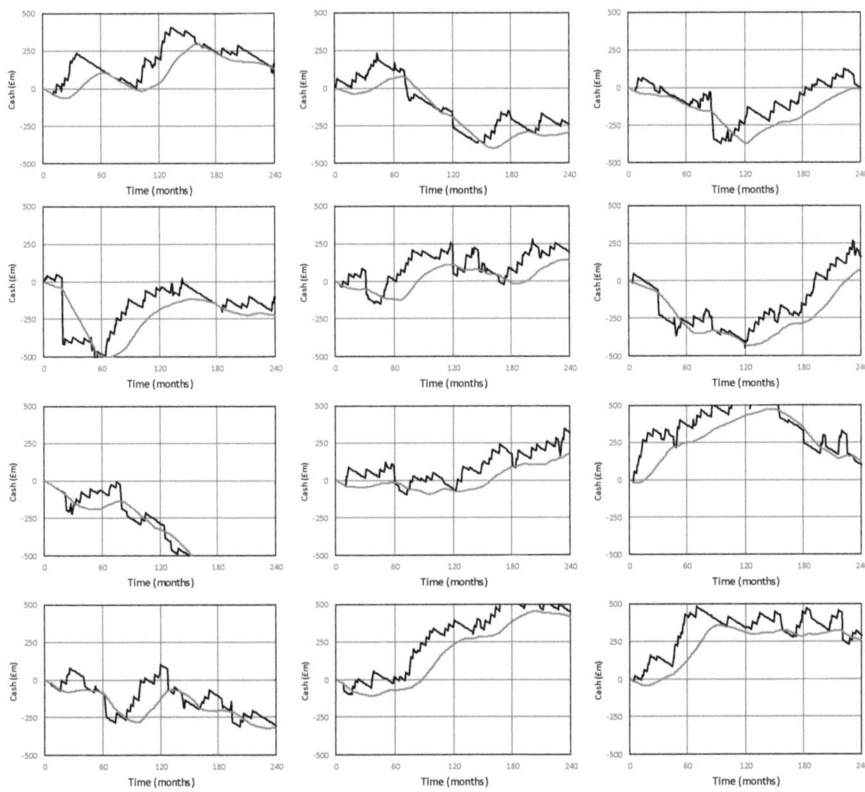

Figure 52 Typical random walks in a construction business (breakeven case)

Figure 52 shows some typical random walks for the breakeven scenario. It's always useful to look at the actual simulations to assess their realism and to get a feel for what the randomness actually looks like. What's shown is both the profit (or loss) as it arises on winning the job (not that any construction company would ever state that, of course) and also the cashflow which is spread out over the three years, shown by the grey lines. The difference shows the smoothing and working capital requirements.

The S-curves of profit (as it arises) are shown in Figure 53 for the 5, 10 and 20 year horizons, this time for the profitable high risk case. Being the sum of many random variables, they are, of course, normal and show

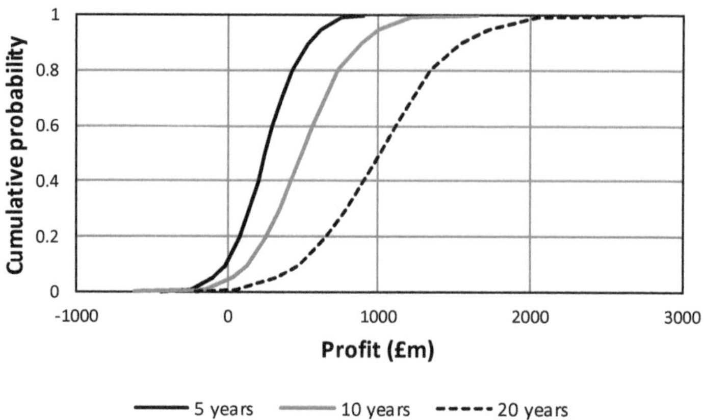

Figure 53 S-curves of profit (high risk case)

the profit growing at £50m per year at the mean/P50.[42] Even with this profitable bidding scenario, there is a decent probability of a loss. What's more, I noted earlier that Mandelbrot's multifractal modelling of markets[43] shows that the very fast cut-off on the low probability tails of normal is unrealistic, something constantly reiterated by Taleb in his work. The chances of adverse downsides are probably much higher than indicated here due to correlating factors over time.

The bankruptcy probabilities are included in the table in Figure 51. Even with the relatively safe pricing scenario (low risk jobs, fully priced) you still have 10% probability of going bankrupt and this rises to a certainty with the 'competitive' bidding strategy. Even the profitable situation in Figure 53 has a bankruptcy probability of around 20%.

The critical issue here is the relationship between price and the probability of winning. You need to remember the following points.

- You are probably overconfident in the baseline. Cost engineers and planners have their own assumptions which invariably get neglected, or they may forget something. One of your competitors may well think the baseline is less than you do; if he thinks it is £475m you are unlikely to win.

[42] Which are the same over many jobs thanks to the Central Limit Theorem, in spite of being significantly different for a single one.
[43] *Op cit.* Chapter 11.

- You are probably overconfident in your ability to manage risk (the third scenario), so you make a loss.
- One of your competitors is more overconfident than you are in his ability to manage risk, so you don't get the job.
- One of your competitors may be more confident than you are of successfully pursuing claims or profitable variations.
- One of your competitors may be more desperate than you are, or have lower overheads or lower profit expectations.
- If you get lucky, you can be more relaxed about pricing; if you have been unlucky, you get desperate and end up with loss-making jobs. This results in vicious or virtuous circles, amplifying your performance to date. I have not modelled this feature.

These are difficult issues to navigate between. On any given job it's hard to think you have a better than 1 in 3 chance of winning (in spite of brave statements about buying jobs). So you need to bid maybe six a year to hit turnover.

To summarise, our contractor needs to (a) price low enough to win work and (b) price high enough to make a profit. Both the risks implicit in this are difficult to quantify, in the first case because of the competitive situation and in the second because of uncertainty about what the costs will be. Both risks are also moderated by a client with uncertain behaviour and their own desires, beliefs and attitudes. And given that the contractor has to do it consistently and continually it is not hard to imagine that he will almost certainly go bankrupt eventually, either from lack of work or taking an increasing burden of unprofitable work.

You will have to develop some sort of view of the relationship between pricing and the probability of winning and from that you can deploy your attitude to risk. In doing this I don't think maximising utility will play much of an explicit role. You probably just want to maximise your survival probability. And inevitably the focus will be on the 1-year survival probability rather than the 20-year version. The prospects and the attitude to risk are not appealing.

There are two ways to escape from this bind it seems to me, short of restructuring the industry. One is increase one's size and financial strength so you are better able to survive the inherent volatility of bidding for and delivering projects. The other is to be genuinely disruptive, finding ways of doing things that cost less (for example, use fewer, but better, people) and deliver more.

None of this is helped by unrealistic views of uncertainty. Boards seem to think they just have to knock a bit off to be sure of winning. They are extraordinarily overconfident of their cost projections, even when using new technology. Being realistic about the risks and uncertainties, and the presence of lurking black swans, is the best tool of all to make better decisions.

These observations also lead us to a rather gloomy view of the future of most organisations, not just construction companies, and the conclusion is that they should come to terms with their own mortality. The risk landscape for most of you is very challenging and is likely to threaten your existence every year with some small probability. In my experience people, whether they express it or not (and they generally don't), don't take business risks with a lower probability of 5% into account. I think this is pretty much a general rule of organisational behaviour. You could turn this into an expected lifetime of 20 years (by conveniently turning 5% into 5% per year). If you can hone your risk attitude to improve on this, you might just have a better future than some of your competitors.

Chapter 8

Final thoughts

The future of risk management – maybe

As well as being a textbook on organisational risk management, this book has explored a number of ideas which I think may help improve things.

The first of these is that we should forget about risk management processes. Instead, all management processes should acknowledge the existence of risk and uncertainty. In doing so they should also acknowledge that the future is more uncertain than we generally like to think.

Secondly, we need to build more on a natural approach to risk management. History shows we are quite good at survival and we have done so without voluminous – wide as well as long – risk registers and cumbersome QSRAs. This means placing a renewed focus on the risk culture, how the knowledge, beliefs and values of the people who make up the organisations come together to determine behaviour – decisions and actions – taken within it.

In spite of these two points we need to recognise the importance of formal process for most organisations and this emerges as two layers wrapping natural risk management, the management layer and the governance layer. These layers must not hinder the need for swift and adaptive decision making and action. The paradigms which involve formulating a plan and plodding through it are broken. They need to be replaced with a recognition that plans should be reviewed and changed frequently in the light of circumstances.

We also noted that, in spite of a long and glorious history, the theory of decision making under risk is quite disappointing. It is based on unappealing assumptions and most people do not make decisions that way; it is not natural and it is not practical. As a result, the way organisations express their attitude to risk has developed to be piecemeal and sometimes perverse – risk appetite anyone? – and it is hard to argue that that is not the way it should be. Nonetheless we do learn from these theories that comprehensive exploration of possible futures and using probabilities to inform decisions are a good idea, though not necessarily the whole story.

In fact all these threads lead us to see risk management not as a grand theory of everything, but as a series of tools. These tools include risk analysis techniques, ideas for adapting management processes to deal better with risk and uncertainty, fast and frugal decision-making heuristics and apparently arbitrary levels of contingency. The art of risk management is knowing what tools to deploy when and understanding their limitations.

These ideas have been in my mind for a decade or more and the fact that I enlarge on them in this book indicates that I think they are worthwhile. For all this time I have thought that improving risk management needs two things: a focus on risk culture, as I have just mentioned, and smarter ways to build risk models. I think the first of these is now much more widely recognised and is something of a solved problem as I hope Chapter 3 makes clear. But I am intensely disappointed with progress on the second.

The risk world is still dominated by giant risk registers from which it is impossible to gain any compelling understanding of the impact of uncertainty and how it might impact different aspects of the organisation. I have been asked countless times by senior managers for copies of the risk register for a project or a business who are seemingly under the impression that, by looking at a table of maybe concise, maybe verbose descriptions, coloured traffic light schemes, and greater or lesser quantities of made-up numbers, they can see a light shed on the darkness of future uncertainty. They can't, though it's very helpful to drive up contingencies in an apparently justified, scientific even, basis. As I finish this book, I have just returned from a seminar in which a railway project was described which had struggled with some of the worst software imaginable for risk databases and QSRAs.

So I think this is where we need to look next. We need to define some kind of fundamental particle of uncertainty – the *riskon*, perhaps, but definitely not the *risk* – that we can use to develop a risk model in a way that is reasonably formulaic and that we can interrogate to gain real risk insights. Chapman and Ward's encomium[1] to identify all the sources of uncertainty, but analyse only the most important is really helpful here. My personal approach is just to explore the landscape and follow this up with reflection until some deadline causes the panic execution of what I think is the best model. It works most of the time but there must be a better way to improve the future.

[1] How to Manage Project Opportunity and Risk, Chris Chapman and Stephen Ward, Wiley, 2011. (Advertised as the third edition of Project Risk Management, Wiley,1997 and 2003.)

Index

D

E

F

G

H

I

J

K

L

M

N

O

P

S

T

U

V

W

About the author

Andy Garlick is in the forefront of risk management professionals. For 35 years he has provided advice to clients on many different aspects of risk, and has helped to build risk-based consulting businesses. For the last 14 years he has been a freelance risk consultant who continues to promote new and different ways of dealing with risk and uncertainty.

A mathematician by discipline, Andy originally worked on modelling fluid flows, particularly the modelling of interstellar gases, star formation and explosions. During a long period with the United Kingdom Atomic Energy Authority he started working on the analysis of the safety risk posed by nuclear reactors and other installations. Randomised methods, also called Monte Carlo, became one of his particular interests.

With the privatisation of the UKAEA as AEA Technology, Andy moved into management roles. He became particularly interested in the adaptation of the risk-based approach for other types of plant and, beyond this, to commercial applications in business. His aim was to make the techniques more relevant and more accessible. His final role with AEA Technology was to help found the management consulting practice, Risk Solutions, which is now a successful independent firm.

As a director of Manex (UK) Limited, Andy's main project was the London Underground public private partnership. Andy then set up his own consulting firm, The Risk Agenda, which has carried out numerous assignments in the transport and construction sectors. More recently he temporarily moved out of his consulting comfort zone and spent 15 months as an actual risk manager, working for CVB on the East section of the Thames Tideway Tunnel.

In 2007 Andy published his book[1] on risk analysis which is now used as a textbook on many courses. This reflected the purpose of The Risk Agenda to improve the way organisations deal with an uncertain future:

- by contributing to the advancement of good practice
- by helping organisations adapt this good practice
- by working with them on their specific risk challenges.

Better Futures has been in development ever since and reflects Andy's experience and thinking on these matters.

Andy is a member of the Society for Risk Analysis and a Fellow of the Institute of Risk Management. For many years he helped organise the North-West branch of the IRM and its special interest group on PPP/PFI.

You can find more about Andy and The Risk Agenda by visiting the website riskagenda.com. This site contains material on risk analysis and risk management, and provides tools and other materials for free download. Andy also runs a blogging site on cloudsofvagueness.com, named for Ken Arrow's famous quotation which so accurately reflects the challenge the risk manager faces. Finally, he has set up the ratitles.com site for sales and feedback on this book and others.

As well as consulting services, The Risk Agenda offers courses and lectures based on this book, *Estimating Risk* and other topics which can be customised for different organisations and audiences. If you would like to learn more, you can email Andy at andy.garlick@riskagenda.com.

[1] Estimating Risk: A Management Approach, Andy Garlick, Gower, 2007.

www.ingramcontent.com/pod-product-compliance
Ingram Content Group UK Ltd.
Pitfield, Milton Keynes, MK11 3LW, UK
UKHW041830200726
13854UKWH00002BA/975

9 781999 664503